Making Race Matter

Making Race Matter

Bodies, Space and Identity

Edited by

Claire Alexander
and
Caroline Knowles

First published in 2005 by   **1004785845**
PALGRAVE MACMILLAN
Houndmills, Basingstoke, Hampshire RG21 6XS and
175 Fifth Avenue, New York, N.Y. 10010
Companies and representatives throughout the world.

PALGRAVE MACMILLAN is the global academic imprint of the Palgrave
Macmillan division of St. Martin's Press, LLC and of Palgrave Macmillan Ltd.
Macmillan® is a registered trademark in the United States, United Kingdom
and other countries. Palgrave is a registered trademark in the European
Union and other countries.

ISBN-13: 978–1–4039–0413–3 hardback
ISBN-10: 1–4039–0413–8 hardback
ISBN-13: 978–1–4039–0414–0 paperback
ISBN-10: 1–4039–0414–6 paperback

This book is printed on paper suitable for recycling and made from fully
managed and sustained forest sources.

A catalogue record for this book is available from the British Library.

A catalog record for this book is available from the Library of Congress.

10 9 8 7 6 5 4 3 2 1
14 13 12 11 10 09 08 07 06 05

Printed in China

Contents

List of Figures

Notes on Contributors

Dr Claire Alexander is Lecturer in Sociology at the London School of Economics. Her research interests are in the area of race, ethnicity, masculinity and youth identities. Her main publications include *The Art of Being Black* (Oxford University Press 1996) and *The Asian Gang* (Berg 2000) and she is co-editor (with Brian Alleyne) of 'Beyond Difference', *Ethnic and Racial Studies* (July 2002 issue).

Suki Ali is Lecturer in the Department of Sociology at the London School of Economics. Her research interests focus on issues of identification and multiplicity, drawing upon feminist, postcolonial and cultural theory. Her recent publications include *Mixed-race, Post-race: Gender, New Ethnicities and Cultural Practices* (Berg 2003).

Les Back teaches Sociology at Goldsmiths College. His recent books include *The Auditory Cultures Reader* (co-edited with Michael Bull, Berg 2003); *Out of Whiteness: Color, Politics and Culture* (with Vron Ware, University of Chicago Press 2002) and *The Changing Face of Football: Racism, Identity and Multiculture in the English Game* (with T. Crabbe and J. Solomos, Berg 2001). The chapter in the present collection emerged as part of a research project entitled *'Finding a Way Home': Young People, Urban Space and Racial Danger* (with Michael Keith and Phil Cohen).

Parminder Bhachu is Professor of Sociology at Clark University in Massachusetts, USA. She is a thrice migrant, being a product of East Africa, London and now the US. She is former Henry R. Luce Professor of Cultural Identities and Global Processes and also a Director of Women Studies. She works on emergent cultural forms and identities in border zones innovated on the margins by multiply moved global citizens. She is the author of *Dangerous Designs: Asian Women Fashion the Diaspora Economies* (Routledge 2004); *Twice Migrants* (Tavistock 1985), and co-editor (with Sallie Westwood) of *Enterprising Women* (Routledge 1988) and (with I. Light) *Immigration and Entrepreneurship* (Transaction Press 1993).

Hazel V. Carby is Charles C. and Dorathea S. Dilley Professor of African American Studies and Professor of American Studies at Yale University where she has taught since 1989. Her books include *Reconstructing Womanhood* (Oxford University Press 1987), *Race Men* (Harvard University Press 1998), and *Cultures in Babylon* (Verso 1999). Recent essays include: 'A Strange and Bitter Crop: the Spectacle of Torture', *Open Democracy*, www.opendemocracy.net/debates/article-8-112-2149.jsp and 'The New Auction Block: Blackness and the Marketplace', in Lewis Gordon (ed.) *Companion to African American Literature*, (Blackwell forthcoming). She is currently working on a new book, *Child of Empire: Racializing Subjects in Post WWII Britain*.

David Theo Goldberg is Director of the University of California Humanities Research Institute and Professor of African American Studies and Criminology, Law and Society, and a Fellow of the Critical Theory Institute at the University of California, Irvine. He is the author, inter alia, of *The Racial State* (Blackwell 2002); *Racial Subjects: Writing on Race in America* (Routledge 1997) and *Racist Culture: Philosophy and the Politics of Meaning* (Blackwell 1993). He is also the editor or co-editor of *Anatomy of Racism* (University of Minnesota Press 1990); *Multiculturalism: a Critical Reader* (Blackwell 1995); *Race Critical Theories* (with Philomena Essed, Blackwell 2001); *Relocating Postcolonialism* (with Ato Quayson, Blackwell 2002); *A Companion to Racial and Ethnic Studies* (with John Solomos, Blackwell 2002); *Between Law and Culture* (with Michael Musheno and Lisa Bower, University of Minnesota Press 2002), and *A Companion to Gender Studies* (with Philomena Essed and Audrey Kobayashi, Blackwell 2004). *tRACEs: Race, Deconstruction and Critical Theory* (with Kim Furumoto and Dragan Kujundzic) is forthcoming from Duke University Press 2005. He is currently at work on a book, *The Death of Race* (Blackwell 2005/6).

Caroline Knowles is a Reader in Sociology at Goldsmiths College. Her research interests include issues of race, ethnicity, migration and post-colonial landscape. Her recent books include *Race and Social Analysis* (Sage 2003) and *Bedlam on the Streets* (Routledge 2000) and she is joint editor (with Paul Sweetman) of *Picturing the Social Landscape* (Routledge 2004).

Denise Noble's doctoral research in the Department of Sociology at Goldsmiths College, University of London presents a genealogy of African diaspora womanhood and African-Caribbean women's discourses and practices of freedom. She teaches Sociology, Media and Cultural Studies. She also an occasional freelance Diversity trainer and consultant reflecting her earlier career in social work education and training. She is author of 'Ragga music: dis/respecting Black women and dis/reputable sexualities' in Barnor Hesse (ed.) *Unsettled Multiculturalisms* (Zed 2000).

Constantinos N. Phellas holds a doctoral degree in Sociology from the University of Essex, UK. His primary area of research, publications and conference presentations focus upon the intersection of gender, culture, and issues of sexuality in ethnic minority communities and also on public health, health education and promotion. He is author of *The Construction of Cultural and Sexual Identities: Greek-Cypriot Men in Britain* (Ashgate 2002).

Kate Reed is a Lecturer in Sociology at the University of Sheffield. Her research interests are in the areas of health, illness and medicine, social theory, race and ethnicity, and gender. She is the author of *Worlds of Health* (Praeger 2003), and *Beyond Social Theory* (Sage 2005).

Brett St Louis is currently Assistant Professor in Ethnic Studies at the University of California, San Diego and is about to move to the Sociology department at Goldsmiths College, University of London. His research interests include the function of sport within processes of racialization. This work has been recently published as articles in *Body and Society* and *Leisure Studies*.

Ossie Stuart has, as an academic, combined his research and writing about 'race' and ethnicity with that on disability. For him, the latter is not about a condition, but a question of rights. After a decade-long academic career that took him to the universities of Oxford, York and Surrey, Ossie has, since 2001, been a diversity consultant. He now provides organisations such as the Metropolitan Police Authority, Great London Authority and numerous universities with advice about their 'race' and disability policies.

Miri Song is Senior Lecturer in Sociology at the University of Kent. Her research interests include ethnic identity, immigrant adaptation, racisms, and family economy. She is the author of *Choosing Ethnic Identity* (Polity 2003).

Acknowledgements

The editors would like to thank all the contributors to this volume for their chapters and for their patience during the editorial process. We would also like to thank Catherine Gray, Emily Salz and Sheree Keep at Palgrave Macmillan for their continued support of the project through its development and transformations, and the two anonymous reviewers for their detailed comments. We are also grateful to a number of friends and colleagues for their understanding and kindnesses over the past two years. In particular, we would send love and thanks to Wendy Bottero, Kevin Farnsworth, Jane Franklin, Raminder Kaur, Liza Schuster, John Solomos, Finn Stepputat and Pauline Leonard.

Foreword

HAZEL V. CARBY

In the Autumn of 2003 a prominent British historian, with all the requisite degrees earned from Oxbridge and the Ivy League, was extremely distressed by a lecture of mine, a lecture which argued that British subjects were racialized in very particular ways in the years immediately following World War II. With a slight tremor in his voice, a tremor which betrayed the existence of strong emotions simmering beneath a surface of intellectual detachment, this historian forcefully declared that 'race' was a concept that was absolutely irrelevant to understanding British history, for 'we British' were never motivated to act upon beliefs about race. On the contrary, he concluded, 'history demonstrates that the British just don't like strangers.' Claire Alexander and Caroline Knowles have assembled an impressive collection of essays which expose and counter precisely this type of historical amnesia and denial. They show just how much race does matter, how race is constantly being made *to* matter and made *into* matter, given a material reality, an identity, an embodiment. Racialization, this book argues, is a constant process of becoming: it is matter which adheres to all aspects of everyday life.

The publication of *Making Race Matter* is an important intervention in this particular moment, a moment when so many intellectuals are responding to what they perceive as a crisis of nationhood and national identity. The call to defend Britain and Britishness is characterized not only by expressions of fear for the fragmentation of a national identity but by a deep melancholy for the loss of empire. Meanings and interpretations of time, space, place and bodies are fiercely contested and rhetorical claims are being made over the shape and sites of memory, over subjecthood and subjectivity. In particular, many notable historians are wielding their pens against the past and future implications of a multicultural Britain: they write to reestablish exclusive and authentic national roots, to reclaim 'their' heritage and disentangle it from that of the multicultural hordes whose presence threatens British national identity and whose voices speak heresy to the greatness of its imperial past. History has become the domain for the establishment of British 'difference' and singularity.

Claire Alexander and Caroline Knowles argue that 'our understandings of what "race" means' have been transformed since W. E. B. Du Bois declared that 'the problem of the 20th century is the problem of the color line,' evoking the time when ' "race" was traced on the skin or in the blood and could be mapped onto geographical space'. The essays they have selected to include in this volume provide rich analytic evidence of this transformation and demonstrate how ' "race" and racial attitudes' are not only 'changing and complex', but are 'a product of culture rather than nature'. But reading them can also help us critique recent work that evokes culture with the intention of demonstrating the existence of absolute differences between peoples. In many of these accounts evocations of affiliation and allegiance based on blood and spatial belonging remain.

Simon Schama's *Landscape and Memory* (1995) is a good example of a regressive return to the use of the body, to the 'bone of my bone and flesh of my flesh' analogies that Du Bois (1903/1969) inherited from nineteenth-century racial discourse. Schama, in his introduction to *Landscape and Memory*, places his authorial self as emerging in intimate relation to a very particular space, time and place:

> ... the low, gull-swept estuary, the marriage bed of salt and fresh water, stretching as far as I could see from my northern Essex bank, toward a thin black horizon on the other side ... Kent, the sinister enemy who always seemed to beat us in the County Cricket Championship ... When the tide went out, exposing an expanse of rusty mud, I could walk for what seemed miles from the shore, testing the depth of the ooze, paddling my feet among the scuttling crabs and the winkles, and staring intensely at the exact point where, I imagined, the river met the sea. (1995: 3–4)

The place where the river meets the sea is claimed by Schama as the source of national and imperial greatness and pride, evoking as he does later in the passage, the navy that gathered there on so many occasions; it provides Schama with an occasion to reflect upon Joseph Conrad's use of the estuary as a site from which to tell the story of empire.

Landscape and Memory also returns to nineteenth-century ideas of race, identity and land through the words of Henry David Thoreau which frame the book:

> It is vain to dream of a wildness
> distant from ourselves. There is non such.
> It is the bog in our brains and bowels, the
> primitive vigor of Nature in us, that inspires
> that dream
> Henry David Thoreau, *Journal*, 30 August
> 1856, quoted in Schama (1995: 3)

Thoreau's bog becomes Schama's estuary and the ooze is moulded and sculpted into the primeval matter of a national identity through space and place, a landscape of apparently shared cultural memory, English county cricket matches. Schama aims to create an autochthonous relation between his youth, his self emerging as historian, and the soil of the land from which he sprang: the mud which oozes up between the young boy's toes forms the location from which the adult historian gains the authority to speak. His premise is that '... inherited landscape myths and memories share two common characteristics: their surprising endurance through the centuries and their power to shape institutions that we still live with. National identity, to take just the most obvious example, would lose much of its ferocious enchantment without the mystique of a particular landscape tradition: its topography mapped, elaborated, and enriched as a homeland' (1995: 15).

This authentic homeland has its authentic English bards who have sung praises and its authentic English heroes whose blood has fed and invigorates its soil. But Schama rebels against what he feels is the negation of this past and its values. He recovers the Rudyard Kipling of his youth, a celebrant of empire, that Schama discovers many years later he isn't 'supposed to like'. The tone of injury in which this 'discovery' is expressed is elaborated in the introduction to the book into a regret for a loss of a heritage Schama is now 'supposed to deny'. *Landscape and Memory* works to retrieve and cement the relation between national identity, blood, soil and English heroes. The most vivid of these occasions is a description of the beheading of Walter Raleigh whose blood, 'running over the block ... formed little ponds and streams between the cobbles, before draining finally into the moist, Thames-side earth'. This blood circulates in the earth preserving a nationhood that Schama can access between his toes four centuries later (1995: 312).

Linda Colley, in *Britons: Forging the Nation 1707–1837*, wonders whether Britishness will survive. In Colley's terms Britons emerge at a very particular time and place in history: '... between the Act of Union joining Scotland to England and Wales in 1707 and the formal beginning of the Victorian Age in 1837 ... it was during this period that a sense of British national identity was forged, and that the manner in which it was forged has shaped the quality of this particular sense of nationhood and belonging ever since, both in terms of its remarkable strengths and resilience, and in terms of its considerable and increasingly evident weaknesses' (1992: 9).

What a startlingly static understanding of history this is! Like Schama, Colley refuses the possibility that Britishness is a complex and contradictory formation, constantly shaped and reshaped through and by a multicultural and multi-ethnic array of affiliations and allegiances. In

Britons ethnic and cultural diversity is present only as the English, Welsh and Scots who forge their Britishness out of the confrontation with the absolute difference of the country's enemies and its colonized others. National identity, Colley argues, is initially forged by war, '[a]nd, increasingly as the wars went on, they defined themselves in contrast to the colonial peoples they conquered, peoples who were manifestly alien in terms of culture, religion and color'(1992: 5).

In stark contrast to Colley's thesis, contributors to *Making Race Matter* present the formation of subjecthood and citizenship in all its multiplicity and complexity and show us how historically constructed and contested racialized identities are embedded in relations of power in a whole range of localities: from the UK, in which African, Asian, Caribbean, European and North American histories converge and coalesce in particular cities and neighborhoods, to the routes of diasporic and global relations.

Niall Ferguson, in *Empire: How Britain Made the Modern World* (Allen Lane 2003), an unapologetic defence of the 'good' that Britain's imperial ventures brought to peoples across the world, claims a national identity which is global in its reach. I realized, when reading the book that Niall Ferguson and I are not only both children of empire but distinctly different products of the 1948 British Nationality Act. I was born in Britain, the daughter of a Jamaican father who had served in the RAF and a Welsh mother who worked in the Air Ministry. After the war British politicians realized that it was the United States of America and the Soviet Union that had emerged as the preeminent powers on the global stage. It was emigration from Britain that established its international presence and the ties of those emigrants to Britain that maintained it. The aim of the British Nationality Act was to secure Britain at the centre of empire, in the face of American and Soviet hegemony, as a great power among great powers and it tried to accomplish this by 'balancing several different, competing communities of Britishness within a single empire' (Paul 1997: 9). These competing and contradictory articulations and definitions of Britishness embodied in the Nationality Act can be found inscribed in and through both my and Niall Ferguson's lives and work.

The British Nationality Act created a type of global citizenship, extending British subjecthood to all members of the empire. In practice, however, a multiplicity of definitions of Britishness emerged. Emigrants from Britain that secured its imperial presence were regarded as 'British stock'.

Although all 'British stock' were British subjects, the political elites of the United Kingdom and the 'old' dominions did not consider all British subjects to be British stock. Rather, policy makers conceived of separate spheres of nationality: residents of the empire with a white skin and

European cultural descent were British stock; residents of the empire with a skin of color and African or Asian heritage were British subjects only. 'British stock' described 'a familial community defined by blood and culture' (Paul 1997: 26). It was a restrictive term that contradicted the universal language of the Act.

Within the notion of imperial subjecthood were incompatible ideas of belonging which constituted a minefield that I as a young black girl would have to negotiate. I grew as the contradictions between and among conflicting communities of Britishness increased, culminating in the passing of the Commonwealth Immigrants Act of 1962 which eradicated any remnant of equality of subjecthood, policed the borders of the nation against black migrants and heralded my adolescence. Throughout the fifties government reports and working parties debated ways to limit the migration of black British subjects while not threatening the stability or unity of the Commonwealth upon which Britain's 'greatness' depended. The racial hostility toward black citizens on the national stage had its counterpart in my local universe. I was born a few months before the Nationality Act was passed, but because all domestic Britons were considered to be of pure European descent my being was consistently referenced through the paradigm of immigrant. While totally unaware of the machinations of Anthony Eden's and Harold Macmillan's cabinet-level discussions of the 'immigrant problem' I was aware of the fact that my belonging was daily in question.

In *Empire* Niall Ferguson, who spent his childhood years in Kenya has no doubts about his right to 'belong' and speak with the authority of 'British stock'. For him, to reassert the 'good' of empire is synonymous with the recovery of a national identity which has a simultaneous global existence through kith and kin:

> Thanks to the British Empire, I have relatives scattered all over the world – in Alberta, Ontario, Philadelphia and Perth, Australia. Because of Empire my paternal grandfather John spent his early twenties selling hardware and hooch to Indians in Ecuador ... my other grandfather ... spent more than three years as an RAF officer fighting the Japanese in India and Burma ... Thanks to the Empire, my Uncle Ian Ferguson's first job after he qualified as an architect was with the Calcutta firm of McIntosh Burn ... Ian had started his working life in the Royal Navy; he spent the rest of his life abroad, first in Africa, then in the Gulf states ... His brother – my father ... defied the advice of friends and relatives by taking his wife and two infant children to Kenya ... Thus, thanks to the British Empire, my earliest childhood memories are of colonial Africa ... We had our bungalow, our maid, our smattering of Swahili – and our sense of unshakeable security. It

was a magical time, which indelibly impressed on my consciousness
the sight of the hunting cheetah, the sound of Kikuyu women singing,
the smell of the first rains and the taste of ripe mango. (2003: xiii–xiv)

Here is an extraordinary, unquestioned sense of entitlement to walk
the globe, to settle at will and to have your domestic needs taken care of
by a Kenyan maid; this is the embodiment of racial privilege and racial
power. The romance of memory fills the senses of the white British subject, eyes, ears, nose and tongue transmit empire as a sensuous lingering
pleasure, the loss of which is occasion for deep regret. Niall Ferguson's
allegiance to this 'magical time' is what Schama calls a 'ferocious
enchantment' with 'the mystique of a particular landscape tradition'. In
this landscape the subject is master over all he surveys, all that surrounds
and services his needs is absorbed into the production and maintenance
of the white male British subject.

As Claire Alexander and Caroline Knowles state, unequivocally, 'race
still matters … it is an ongoing *issue* for academic concern and for study,
and … it carries consequence.' In the British academy, perhaps, race has
never mattered more and because of that we have never needed this
book more than now.

New Haven, Connecticut
July 2004

Introduction

CLAIRE ALEXANDER & CAROLINE KNOWLES

> The problem of the twentieth century is the problem of the color line – the relation of the darker to the lighter races of men in Africa and Asia, in America and the islands of the sea.
>
> W. E. B. Du Bois 1903

> The capacity to live with difference is, in my view, the coming question of the 21st century.
>
> Stuart Hall 1991

In 1903, W. E. B. Du Bois famously foretold, 'the problem of the 20th century is the problem of the color line' (1995: 41). Just over a century later Du Bois' words still hold a powerful resonance, although the terrain has shifted. However wars, decolonisation and migration have transformed the global landscape, race remains a definitive marker of identity, difference, inequality and violence – race still matters. This is not to argue, of course, that nothing has changed in the past 100 years – the ways in which race matters, the forms through which race is lived and given meaning, the people whose lives are shaped through racial categories, where and with whom they live, how race is reinscribed or resisted, have undergone radical transformation. Certainly, our understanding of what race means has moved on from the stark divides of Du Bois' time – when race was traced on the skin or in the blood and could be mapped onto geographical space – to a recognition of race as socially constructed, as being *made* in the process of history, culture and social relationships. This shift has enabled an understanding of race and racial identities as changing and complex, as a product of culture rather than nature, produced and sustained through power and subject to resistance, reappropriation and subversion. This change in focus can be clearly seen in the opening quote from Stuart Hall, which both echoes and transforms Du Bois' prophecy. Hall's concern is not with race or the 'color line', but with the ways in which race has acquired meaning as a source of social classification and become embedded in systems of power. His focus also has shifted in space – from the encounters with 'Others' in the colonies to those within the metropolitan spaces of the West itself. The concern with 'difference' signals also the way in which race forms

1

part of a complex system of classification and hierarchy which is inseparable from other axes of identity such as gender, ethnicity, class, sexuality, age, religion and so on, which cut across and within each other, unsettling the certainties of all. Learning to 'live with difference' remains an unfinished and uncertain project.

In this post-Millennial world of 'difference', does race still matter? In what ways is race *made* to matter, by whom and for whom? How have traditional forms of raced identity been reinvented and reinvigorated? How is race *made* by individuals, communities, cultures, nations? What resources have formed the *matter* through which race is asserted or resisted? The current volume explores some of these concerns, treading a path between recognition of the continued salience of race as a category – both of inequality and violence, and of collective identity and political resistance – and an engagement with its changing contours. This ambiguous journey is captured in the title of the volume, *Making Race Matter*, which incorporates a number of, not necessarily compatible, possible interpretations. First, we acknowledge the constructedness of race as a social category – that 'race' is *made*, and that this making can be either an external ascription or an internal claiming of collective identity. Race is understood then as a category of power, but one that can be both imposed and (re)claimed. Second, this recognises that race is made and remade by people at the level of the everyday – race is *performed* in mundane encounters between individuals as well as at the interface between people and structures. Third, race is created by, inscribed on, and performed through, *matter*, by which we mean material substance. This volume explores the ways in which race is created through two forms of 'matter' – the body and space. Bodies, for example, are the physical matter through which race is signalled (as in Du Bois' blood and skin notions of race), the material base on which power is inscribed, and the substance through which individuals can lay claim to their own sense of embodied identity and resistance. Similarly, space is a physical environment that materially inscribes racialised meanings, exclusions and dangers; that is claimed and transformed through its use and reimagination. Fourth, we want to argue that race still matters (West 1994), that it is an ongoing *issue* for academic concern and for study, and that it carries consequence. We want to hold on to the continued materiality of race and racism as a source of social division, exclusion and marginality, and also explore some of the ways in which race is used to resist these divisions and exclusions.

At the heart of the ways in which race matters lies the issue of identity. One of the clearest shifts in the century between Du Bois' and Hall's pronouncements is the changing understanding of identity. This moves from a view of racial identity as relatively stable, uncontested and antagonistic towards a view of identity as 'difference' in its complex, fractured and unfinished forms. Recognition of the multiplicity, complexity and ambivalence of constructed identities has challenged the convenient black/white binary categorisations and oppositions of 'old' versions of racial difference, and insisted on the interrelationship and mutually constitutive nature of these categories. Developing the critical insights of black feminist scholarship (Carby 1982; hooks 1982; Mirza 1997), this conceptual shift has underpinned new ways of thinking about raced identities. It can be traced in the growing significance of postcolonial studies (Goldberg & Quayson 2002) and gender/masculinity studies (Segal 1990; Mercer 1994), challenging and reworking traditional academic disciplines and divisions. It has also opened new avenues in which the focus has turned towards dominant, previously invisible, systems of meaning and identity formations like Whiteness (Cohen 1996, 1997; Dyer 1997), and the role of performance and subjectivity in living through 'minority' identifications.

These developments are, however, not without their losses and silences. The focus on difference and the celebration of marginality that has accompanied the fragmentation of identity has made the structures that maintain racial violence, exclusion and inequality less visible (Sharma, Hutnyk & Sharma 1996). At the same time, the discussion of racism has disappeared from the political agenda. These conceptual developments have sacrificed a politics of practical engagement for a politics of representation, creating the impression that what mattered was what we thought about things and not what we did about them. Culture and cultural identity have become increasingly textualised and abstract, divorced from the empirical exploration of lived identities and seemingly oblivious to the continued materiality of everyday racism. However, we would argue that it is both possible and necessary to engage with the *politics* of identity and difference, and to do so in a way that transcends the purely theoretical.

This collection identifies with the need to engage with notions of identity and difference in ways that locate theoretical issues in the grounded contexts of everyday life. It is arranged into two core themes. Part I contains chapters that deal substantially with space and diaspora, Part II contains those that foreground the body and subjectivity. All of the contributions grapple with the performance and the nuances of raced identity in empirical contexts. They develop, in various ways, versions of identities constructed at the interface of cultural meanings, structure and experience. As Hazel Carby argues in the Foreword to this collection, the understanding of the intersection of race with space and the body has become all the more urgent in the current climate, which has seen the resurgence of fear for the loss of a national identity and the reclamation of a Britishness characterised by a revisioned history of Empire. This reclamation has attempted to resituate national belonging in an evocation of blood and soil – written across the body and the land-scape – in exclusionary discourses and practices which erase both a more complex history and contemporary black struggles for recognition and acceptance.

In the sections that follow we trace the conceptual landscape of the critical ideas that appear in this collection – space and diaspora, and the body and subjectivity. Obviously what follows can only provide a sketch of the emergence and transformations of these terms in relation to race and ethnicity, but the aim has been to identify key arguments and theorists, and to locate the subsequent chapters against this backdrop.

Making race: space and diaspora

In the Chicago School's classic concentric circles detailing layers of ethnic occupation and flight from the city centre, Park, Burgess and McKenzie (1967) mapped race and ethnic occupation onto urban space in the early years of the last century, making what was to be an enduring connection between race, space and migration. To these early-twentieth-century eyes a certain level of human mobility sustained the dynamic of modernity. Too little mobility produced premodern forms associated with the entrenched mentality of a peasantry but too much produced its own forms of urban social pathology in crime, delinquency, murder and home-lessness. The human capital of the American market system and the lives composing the fabric of the city-in-constant-flux was provided by waves of European migration. The 'pulse of the community' and the fabric of city life itself were conceptualised in terms of race and ethnicity (and class). It is via this route that urban environment became the place of race in America and in Britain, drawing links between the city, social pathology and race. It was not just the nation-building-through-migration development of America that conceptualised people in racial and ethnic terms, these properties were central to notions of human subjectivity and rights (Goldberg 1993). People and places were always conceptualised in racial terms and the traces of this deep historical connection remain in contemporary writing.

Three articulations of race and space have a salience in this volume: patterns of urban segregation, territory and nation. Drawing on the work of Lefebvre (1996) all three themes conceptualise space as displaying broader social (racialised) morphology and as shaped by the social relationships and social activities of people in the conduct of their everyday lives. Space is not a 'thing' but the outcome of past and present activities and social relationships: the social contexts of earlier networks coexist with new ones so that space always contains multiple temporalities, just as it sustains multiple and contradictory uses, meanings, associations with different kinds of people. Space both reveals social priorities – whose lives and activities matter most – and provides for alternate voices, uses and versions of what matters. Space simultaneously sustains the existing racial order and offers the prospect of its subversion and reordering.

Mapping race: ethnicity, migration and urban space

Following on from the work of the Chicago School, the articulation of race and space in racialised patterns of urban life in Britain were seen as the outcome of multiple forms of racialised social distribution – in jobs, wages, education and so on – and became an object of social research in the mid 1960s, following the early waves of substantial 'New Commonwealth' migration to postwar Britain. Rex and Moore's (1967) study of Sparkbrook, Birmingham and Rex's (1980) mapping of types of housing tenure onto race were interpreted as evidence of racialisation at the level of social structure. However, this ascendance of structure over (human) agency, in which minorities were aggregated as 'black' objects of systematic white racializing practices, was challenged by those writers who warned that this discounted local/global minority networks and the significance of entrepreneurial activity serviced by the proximity of ethnic concentration in certain areas (Dahya 1974). As attention turned from housing to neighbourhood so the visual marking of the landscape by 'ethnic' – not racial – difference became a significant theme in the literature. Ethnicity became 'architecturally encoded' (Farrar 1997: 113) to form a 'spatialised, politicised aesthetic' (Soja 1989: 22) through the fabrication of space, utilizing buildings and shop-fronts just as it was written on the bodies, clothes (see the chapter by Bhachu) and mobile habitus of ethnic occupation. This is the thinking behind the studies of Chinatowns and Little Italys. Smith (1993) differentiated *actual* patterns of racial and ethnic occupation from the *idea* of racial and ethnic occupation; and Cohen's work on East London (1996) showed that people imagine and navigate racialised space in their own way. The relationship between race and space in matters of urban occupation had become more specific, more biographical and more empirically grounded.

Les Back's chapter in this volume takes these arguments beyond the imagination and representation of urban space. Exploring the racial landscape of Deptford and the Isle of Dogs through personal maps of safety and danger negotiated in routine activities of white, black and Asian teenagers, Back shows that young people forge and walk alternate routes and maps of belonging which show conflicting interpretations of place as young people reshape the racist fear and stigma attached to their area by government policy and policing practice. These maps are not imaginary, they have material consequences for the gendered bodies that navigate their threats and violations.

Marking race: space, territory and identity

Territorial notions of space – our second articulation of race and space – are also significant in this volume. Racialised and ethnicised neighbourhoods are converted into territory by conflict and patrol. Patrol involves a particular kind of purposive walking which tests where you can walk, and exercise authority, and with what consequences. Armies and police forces patrol, and patrolling is also a colonial tactic (see the chapter by Knowles), a point which is not lost on those who live in spaces that are turned into territory. So do other, less formally constituted, groups of young men seeking to expand their influence or simply defend their own and others' bodies and neighbourhoods. The pattern of urban conflict in Britain is by now familiar, which is not to say that it lacks specific triggers, circumstances and configurations of raced, gendered and ethnicised bodies. Areas of ethnic residence, deeply inscribed by a tapestry of racialised social inequalities, have been repeatedly drawn into police/community conflict, in a dynamic of overenforcement and insufficient protection, and turned into 'territories'. The literature of the seventies and eighties details the summary invasion by police of 'black' areas, meeting places and homes (Kettle and Hodges 1982). SWAMP 81 – the saturation policing of Brixton in this period, which was condemned by the Scarman Report – turned neighbourhoods into territories containing contested racialised notions of place, local residents and civil rights; creating a 'geography of defences securing different privacies' (Feuchtwang 1992: 104). The battle lines once drawn in Toxteth, St Pauls, Notting Hill, and Tottenham have more recently been played out in Bradford, Burnley, Oldham and Stoke (see Alexander, this volume).

(Un)Making the nation: race and diaspora

Essentialised associations between (the space of) nation states and their (racially and ethnically conceived) populations, which involve simplified versions of belonging and unequal entitlement, underscore recent political debates about immigration and asylum seekers in Britain and form our third articulation of race and space. The setting of lineage in landscape (Soja 1989: 21, see Carby, this volume) is disrupted by the social practices of diasporas, who force the recognition that all nation states are now multiracial. Cohen (1996, 1998) argues that nativist associations between race and *local* place replicate and perform ideologies produced at the level of the nation-state, so that the grounding of white 'little Englander' nationalism is in fact about what is local and tangible. At the same time, Cohen argues that this version of white Englishness is readily unravelled as the rites of passage involved in crossing the sea transforms foreign invaders into potential kith and kin (Cohen 1998: 12). White Englishness is an open unstable category that readily absorbs others. Places – whether neighbourhoods or nation states – have no primordial or predictable connection with race or gender (Massey 1994). Like space, race acquires meaning and substance in action in particular contexts as the contributors to this volume show. Chapters by Reed, Bhachu, Knowles and Song contest primordialist associations between race and place-as-nation, exploring anti-asylum-seeker debates (Reed), the local and global spatial practices of white British lifestyle migrants in Hong Kong (Knowles), Asian diasporas in the US (Song) and the UK fashion industry (Bhachu).

The term 'diaspora' is used in the literature to think about particular kinds of migrant journeys, lives and political contexts. It developed from efforts to distinguish types of global migration, usually conflated in labour market models, which assume that people are mobile labour power in search of rational economic advantage (Samuel 1988; Kay and Miles 1992; Richmond 1992; Ongley 1995); a view which dominates the study of migration. By the 1980s, however, it was clear that the old geographies of migration – from rich to poor and black to white countries – no longer held, if indeed they ever really did fully describe the axes of migration. Efforts at untangling the geographies of labour migration (Sassen 1990; Zlotnik 1999) led to more complex models linking migration with direct foreign investment by wealthier countries (Sassen 1990) and to micro-studies (Chamberlain 1994; Zinn 1994) which paid more detailed attention to biographies and circumstances of migration. If the geographies of migration had become more complex, this insight did not impact on globalization studies (Featherstone, Lash and Robertson 1995) where powerful images of the club-class migrant erased less significant and more uncomfortable images of women domestic workers servicing the lifestyle of the wealthy (Brah, Hickman and Mac an Ghaill 1999). Massey (1999) and Hesse (1999) thus stressed the importance of understanding who went where and in what circumstances. There was a growing acknowledgement that this had a great deal to do with race, although the racial geometry of migration was, and is, not particularly apparent. More evidently racialised were the defensible (nation-state) spaces policed by immigration control which contradicted the dominant image of globalisation as 'flows' directed by the gradients of market forces (Massey 1999).

It was in this context of unpacking homogenised categories of migrants and circumstances through micro-studies that diasporas found a conceptual space. 'Diaspora' was often conflated with notions of transnationality – Bhachu (1996) uses both terms to discuss thrice-migrant South Asian women who have moved from India to East Africa to Britain to America – with both being used to explore the complex travelling lives and circumstances of migrants revealed in empirical research. Clifford (1994) astutely observes that diasporas are a blend of roots and routes: adjacent maps of connection and disconnection. Safran (Clifford 1994: 305) uses 'diaspora' to refer to those who have a history of dispersal; to whom myths and memories of homeland are important; who suffer alienation in their place of new belonging; who sustain the desire for eventual return to a homeland; and who have a collective identity which is defined by this relationship. Jews are the archetypal diaspora whose claims to a homeland are mediated by both anti-semitism and the contested rights of Palestinians. The other archetypal diaspora is the African diaspora of Gilroy's (1993) *Black Atlantic* in which a 'counter history of modernity is crucially defined by the still open wound of slavery and racial subordination' (Clifford 1994: 320; Mercer 1994 makes a similar claim).

'Diaspora' is more than a reference to a form of migration: it involves a politics of oppression and counter-assertion. It points to a practical set of living and travelling arrangements that expose the racial order of the world in which we live. It is part of a more general theoretical claim about the nature of human life and community as mobile. It disrupts modernist racialised associations between peoples and nation states as roots, tackling the idea of fixed origins (Brah 1996). It serves (Hesse 1999) as a beacon of hope and liberation, offering forms of hybridity and mixedness which defy essentialist accounts of racial identity, origins and belonging. Diaspora disrupts the racist politics that formed it. It insists that people can live anywhere, making new homes away from home: that there is no primordial connection between race and place. Contributors to this volume take many of these arguments further through their engagement with empirical contexts. Parminder Bhachu argues that diasporic British Asian women, with their ability to deal with dissonance and disequilibrium, have been able to stitch, design and market Punjabi suits in synch with new capitalist economies, making themselves successful fashion entrepreneurs in global markets. Bhachu presents diasporic women as literally fabricating their own and others' lives and identities through designing and making 'fusion' clothes. It is, argues Bhachu, precisely their position of ethnic and racial disadvantage in Britain that gives these women the edge over elite, static and nationally based Indian and Pakistani designers with a desire to 'make it in the West'. Commercial space is the terrain of racial and cultural battles and multiple migrations transfer the templates used for living into commercial success.

Miri Song's chapter also acknowledges the significance of racialisation and place and explores the importance of temporal depth in conceptualising Asian American diasporas. Focussing on some of the tensions that arise over the meaning of Asianness in the US, Song argues that ethnic and national distinctions are cross-cut by relationships between the newly arrived and fourth and fifth generations long settled in the US. She warns that: 'the term Asian American holds no automatic resonance for many of the people officially included in this category' and urges us to pay attention to the complexities of belonging and status in any given place. Place, class, sex, race and nationality interconnect in complex ways with boundary keeping, exclusion, multiple forms of differentiation and arguments about authenticity. We are duly warned to question ethnic ties and the benefits we assume accrue from them.

By contrast, Caroline Knowles chronicles the treatment of British lifestyle migrants in Hong Kong operating at opposite ends of the spectrum of advantage and disadvantage from the asylum seekers discussed by Kate Reed. These two categories clearly display some of the social contours of global migration, although not in ways that have a straight-forward relationship to race and ethnicity. Many of Reed's asylum seekers – particularly those from the former Yugoslavia – share racial if not ethnic categorisation with Knowles' British lifestyle migrants in Hong Kong. Reed's account of asylum seekers shows how they encounter narratives of nativism, in the calculation of belonging and entitlement, issues which are often neglected in research into the affairs of asylum seekers and refugees. These are migrants whose mobility is not part of the celebratory discourse of globalization, but part of a discourse of defence and entitlement. Reed argues that this particular group of migrants needs to be more centrally placed within the frameworks of academic study of race and ethnicity in which they currently occupy only a marginal position. Knowles' investigation of the spatial practices of British lifestyle migrants in Hong Kong unpicks some of the social processes involved in local and global space making and she uses this as a point of access to the social processes involved in white British race making. Knowles argues that whiteness is made in the racialised power geometries of global migration and in the terms of new settlement. In examining the details of everyday life and space making in two migrant biographies she traces the contemporary significance of empire in making white Britishness and the sense of entitlement embedded in it.

Embodying race and gender: the body and subjectivity

As with the concepts of space and diaspora, the focus on the intersection of race and the body is a comparatively new area of research in racial and ethnic studies. This is not to argue that conceptions of the body have not been central to the formation of racial ideologies and racist practices – clearly, racial difference (like gendered difference) is to a large extent historically predicated on the belief in distinct and observable physical features. However, the body has not traditionally been considered an appropriate object of analysis for social science (Shilling 1997), and it is only comparatively recently that scholars have started to look critically at the embodied formation of race. In the wake of Fanon's *Black Skin, White Mask* (1967/1986) and Said's *Orientalism* (1978) the past two decades have seen important critical and theoretical work around the body and race, which has served to undermine notions of natural or biological difference. This has recognised the role of history and power in the construction of embodied identities and opened the space for contestation of these identities. However, despite this important work, there has been very little empirical exploration of the ways in which racial categorisations impact upon the body as a *material object* and of the complex and often painfully contradictory ways in which identities are *actually* lived out at the level of embodied experience. The chapters on 'bodies and subjectivity' in Part II offer empirical explorations of, and reflections on, some of the theoretical understandings of race and the body.

The natural body: race, difference and racial science

It is important not to underestimate the primary role of physically observable difference in the construction of racial categories and meanings. Race, both historically and in contemporary commonsense, is grounded in the body – the body stands as a marker and guarantee of natural biological differences and effects (Fanon 1967/1986). Racial difference is held to be 'real' firstly because it is visible, and carries with it observable physical or biological characteristics – skin colour, hair texture, facial features. As Hall has argued further (1992, 1997), external bodily differences have been historically imbued with notions of absolute moral and cultural difference from the earliest encounters of European travellers with exoticised 'Others'. External differences become the bodily manifestation of internal characteristics, attitudes and beliefs, which are seen as fixed and immutable, and which are inseparable from notions of (white) superiority and (black) inferiority.

With the growth of natural and physical sciences in the 19th century, the notion of race as a symbolic and cultural marker transformed into a clear equation between race and biology. The racial body – external and internal – became a site for experimentation, measurement, dissection and display, which aimed at 'proving' the absolute differences between the races, around issues of intelligence, morality and sexual deviance (Gilman 1985). Sander Gilman has argued that black bodies were seen as inferior and as pathological, particularly when race intersected with gendered categorisations (McClintock 1995). That this period also saw the extension of imperialism, and the hardening of racial attitudes in the colonies and at home is not accidental. Indeed, the classification of racialised bodies mapped onto evolutionary theories in ways that legitimated colonial domination of inferior, uncivilised or childlike races within the discourses of progress and development (McClintock 1995; Shilling 1997).

Although racial/racist science lost credibility after the excesses of Nazi experimentation in World War Two, and the biological existence of race was disavowed (Solomos & Back 1996), the issue of the biological or physical dimensions of racial difference remains a vexed one. The periodic resurgence of controversies around race and IQ or more recently about the 'taboo' of racial advantage in sport (St Louis, this volume) are reminders that biological notions of race still carry some (mainly negative) weight, particularly in the popular imagination. With the centrality of debates around 'new genetics', moreover, issues of the biological/ genetic nature of race or racial/ethnic populations have again become a subject for discussion, though this is largely presented through the more acceptable discourse of 'ethnicity and health' (Shilling 1997). While some scholars have argued that the decoding of the human genome offers space for the final deconstruction of race, through its insistence on infinite diversity within races and shared, universal characteristics across races (Gilroy 2000), the danger remains in the ways in which 'race as biology' reenters through the back door (see Ali and Noble, this volume).

The constructed body: race, culture and difference

The biologisation of race, as with gender, has been a source of sustained critique within the academy, particularly since the 1960s. Feminist scholars, in particular, have challenged the notion that 'biology is destiny' (de Beauvoir 1953), and have sought instead to focus on inequality as socially, culturally and historically constructed. Race is understood as a system of social meanings and cultural classifications, which is created and sustained through relationships of power and hierarchy, but which changes over time and which can be contested and subverted. The emphasis in these analyses has been to place the body as a discursive site or symbol, as a blank slate onto which raced meanings are projected or inscribed. These approaches are crucial in challenging the 'naturalness' of the raced body and the related inevitability of hierarchy, but, as Shilling (1997) has argued, they have achieved this through rendering the body invisible as a material, emotional and physical entity. This has led to the analysis of the body as a textual object rather than as a living thing, as something which is passive and acted upon, rather than possessing or performing any autonomous sense of being or feeling – without subjectivity.

In the study of race, perhaps even more so than in gender studies, the body has occupied an uncomfortable and ambiguous position; at once a discursive construct with no foundation in biological or physical reality, and a material/physical presence which is acted upon, discriminated against, subjected to racist practice and violence, and which resists these practices. The dilemma facing researchers and writers is how to acknowledge the lived effects of racial categorisation, or racialisation, without reifying race as a biological reality. This has largely been resolved by a bifurcated approach to 'the body': on the one hand, important and fascinating work has been undertaken to place discourses about 'racial bodies' within an historical context (Said 1978; Gilman 1985; Goldberg 1993; McClintock 1995) and as part of historical and contemporary processes of representation (hooks 1992; Mercer 1994; Hall 1997). On the other, a vast quantity of (largely empirical) work has focused on the materialisation of race in specific sites – employment, housing, education, the criminal justice system, racial violence, politics and so on.

The corporeality of the racialised body has remained, however, something of an enigma, and comparatively little work has been done on either the embodied nature of racial discourse or on the embodied subjectivity of racialised individuals or groups. Where they appear, racialised bodies are seen as objects/subjects of control (Stoler 1995; Young 1995; Appadurai 1996), constructed and regulated through colonial and raced micro-discourses of power. This dimension is crucial in contemporary racial landscapes as a number of chapters in this volume make clear (Alexander), particularly as racialised bodies are positioned and move/migrate through space (Back, Reed, Knowles). The gendered nature of control should also be recognised, through the history of the exoticisation/eroticisation of raced female bodies (Gilman 1985; McClintock 1995; Bhattacharyya 2002; Nagel 2003) (see also Noble and Ali, this volume), the control of black women's sexuality (Davis 1981; Carby 1982; Amos & Parmar 1997) and the use of sexual violence as an instrument of racial domination (Davis 1981; Nagel 2003).

Assumptions of racialised (hyper)sexuality and sexual desire also lie at the heart of processes of stereotyping and the construction and representation of racial difference (Hall 1997). In this volume, Ossie Stuart argues that black masculinity has been inseparable from notions of hypersexuality grounded in the fetishisation of the black male body. Stuart explores how these images are displaced through the embodied experience of disability. Brett St Louis, by contrast, explores the reification of the black male (able) body through sport, and argues that the continued metonymic relationship between blackness and the body constrains the choices available to black men in contemporary (US) society.

The body and subjectivity

The discussions outlined above have focused primarily on the externality of the body, and the ways in which societal processes and discourses have sought to understand, appropriate and control racial difference. However, the boundaries of the body – particularly the skin – also form the site at which external constructions meet and intersect with internal processes of identity formation. As Shilling has argued (1997), insufficient account has been taken of the ways in which the body also serves as a sensory and emotional entity, encapsulating individual experiences and thoughts and desires. In addition, the focus on externality and historical construction has tended to overlook the ways in which the body works as a site of resistance and agency. The body is not only physical and material, it is also a focus of *subjectivity* – of how racialised and gendered individuals make sense of their being in the world (Knowles 2003). David Goldberg has thus written of subjectivity as 'the intersection of social discourses in the body' (1993: 60).

Subjectivity can be understood as having two dimensions which are always in tension: the external and historical constraints inherent in Foucault's notion of 'subjectification', in which the micro-physics of power serve to construct the body/individual in particular ways (1979); and the internal ways in which the individual seeks to create him/herself as a subject. bell hooks has written of 'radical black subjectivity' as 'That space within oneself where resistance is possible ... [where] one invents new, alternative habits of being and resists from that marginal space of difference inwardly defined' (1990: 15). Of course, the ability of the individual to create even a semi-autonomous sense of self varies according to the relations of power, whether around gender, race, class, body, age and so on. However, recognition of the role of individual subjectivity is crucial to an understanding of the ways in which race is 'made', resisted and performed in the 'rituals of everyday existence' (Knowles 2003).

The chapters on 'the body and subjectivity' in Part II of this volume are each centrally concerned with this interface between constraint and agency – between subjectification and subjectivity. Each author recognises the constitutive role of external construction and control in the formation of racial identities and of the intersection of these constructions with alternative dimensions of identity – ethnicity, gender, sexuality and disability. At the same time, each chapter is concerned with the unfinished nature of the external reach for subjectification and explores the ambiguous spaces of racialised subjectivity. Brett St Louis and Denise Noble, for example, both explore the complex and ambivalent consequences of the continued biologisation of race as part of an internal claiming of autonomous subjectivity. In a complex and thought provoking chapter, St Louis explores the ways in which the notion of the 'natural' primacy of the black body in sport has been claimed as a source of empowerment for black athletes, but also serves to reinscribe notions of inferior black intelligence. He argues this not only constrains the career choices available to black athletes within and outside the arena of sport, but also denies the role of the intellect in sporting activity. At the same time, the rejection of black physicality and the championing of intellect by the black middle class in the name of racial politics buys into the racialised mind/body dualism and hierarchy rather than challenges it. St Louis argues for an opening up of a critical space around the interpretation of physicality, which places the black athlete as a 'possibility', around which meanings are contested and ambiguous in effect.

In a similar vein, Denise Noble's powerful chapter explores the way in which racial biology forms a site for contestation and reappropriation in some forms of black identity politics. Noble discusses the way in which the symbol of melanin is used in Afrocentric life-coaching courses by black women as a marker of distinction and as a form of racial empowerment. Her chapter explores the way in which the black female body is reclaimed and revalued through such therapies, which advocate a highly biologised notion of race, focused on 'the womb' as the centre of identity. While critiquing the biologist assumptions of these courses, Noble nevertheless insists on the emotional and psychological investment in the notion of race by racialised subjects, particularly in societies still structured by racial disadvantage, discrimination, violence and terror, and on the role of memory and narrative in providing alternative spaces for subjectivity.

Suki Ali's chapter also examines the role of memory work and narrative in the negotiation of racialised identities in her personal and evocative exploration of 'mixedness'. Charting a journey through her own life and the lives of her family, Ali maps the shifting experience of claiming a 'mixed-race' identity in the space between the dominant imperatives of monoracial identities, the ambivalences of 'mixedness' and the search for subjectivity. Exploring the intersection of subjectivity with dominant notions of 'the exotic' and 'the erotic', Ali shows how biography and memory are used to re-vision embodied histories and to both manage and contest the discursive uncertainties of racialised bodies.

Ossie Stuart's scorching chapter also charts a personal narrative of embodied subjectivity through an exploration of the meanings and performances of black masculinity and sexuality, refracted through the lens of disability. Where St Louis' chapter explores the constraints and ambivalences of black masculinities embodied in the figure of the black sportsman, Stuart argues that the desexualisation of the disabled body, combined with the insistence on black masculine identities as hyper-sexual and hyperphysical, leads to a double erasure of his identity – he is neither fully male nor black. Stuart's chapter, through a combination of personal testimony and a reflective engagement with theorisations of dis-ability (including his own ground-breaking earlier work), traces a difficult, alternately painful and humorous, journey towards self-acceptance within this framework of embodied otherness.

Constantinos Phellas' chapter similarly explores the complex intersection of race, ethnicity and sexuality. His work critiques the ways in which dominant constructions of (homo)sexuality are premised on a homogeneous white identity, which obscures issues of ethnic and racial difference. He argues that for Greek-Cypriot gay men, there are alternative ways of constructing sexuality, through culturally specific notions of activity and passivity, which contest dominant constructions of gay identity, and that both reveal the unquestioned contours of hegemonic whiteness and the importance of difference subsumed within this cate-gory. His work explores the cross-cutting allegiances of family, religion and community, and the often painful impact that these emotional and psychological bonds have on ethnic minority sexual subjectivities.

Claire Alexander explores the intersections of race, ethnicity and masculinity with interpretations and performance of violence in the con-text of the reimagining of Asian-Muslim youth in Britain. Challenging judicial, political and popular interpretations of violence as the irrational, abnormal, practices of uncivilised, racialised bodies, Alexander draws on her empirical research with young Asian men in London to reveal the 'private', backstage, elements of racialised urban violence. She shows that the contours of violence are performed across fluid friendship groups, culturally inflected notions of family and masculinity, and community as territory and forms of sociality, and argues that violence needs to be understood 'in context' and as part of the ordinary and the everyday.

Conclusion

As David Goldberg argues in his 'Afterwards' to this collection, race still matters fundamentally to the ways in which we live (and die) in the 21st century. It operates (along with ethnicity) on the surface and in the deep structures of the world we live in as the contributors to this volume so ably demonstrate. It composes the very fabric of our corporeality, our comportment and our subjectivity; it is part of who we are and how we operate in the world, part of the substance of our bodies and minds. It is both inside and outside of us forming the fabric of the social and political landscapes on which we operate. Race is simultaneously mundane and lethal, a source of violence, hatred of self and others and, occasionally, unexpected forms of sociality that extend our humanity, our ways of being in the world in new ways. Because it forms the matter from which we and the world are socially and existentially formed, so race still matters today in ways that are difficult to overstate. It shapes the global order in which we live and the political regimes organising our lives, it features the calculations involved in the balancing of tolerance and terror and the connections drawn between places by bodies crossing borders in a search for less terrible lives. Race shapes us and our times in ways that are clearly marked by the past. How the racial contours of our post-colonial present are made through the regimes of our past is something we still struggle with; the relationship between the past and the present is never settled (see Hazel Carby's Foreword). In the words (and sometimes pictures) that follow, the chapters composing this collection speak about the production of race in particular and material terms in which our treks through daily life, our tangible embodied struggles for more than existence are subtly revealed and questioned in ways that are open to their reimagination.

SPACE AND DIASPORA

Chapter 1

'Home From Home': Youth, Belonging and Place

LES BACK

How do people – particularly the young – make cities a home? How are the spaces of the city marked by colour-coded exclusions and what are the risks involved in crossing its boundaries? In her beautiful memoir, 'From Deepest Kilburn', Gail Lewis described the London neighbourhoods where she was raised as a 'patchwork of no-go and go areas' (Lewis 1985: 219). While racists loomed and sometimes attacked, she portrayed the ordinary ways a young black woman navigated inhospitable streets and made them secure. 'I negotiated this chequerboard of on-off bounds easily and didn't really experience it as hardship. The only thing to avoid was the gangs and individuals who were at great pains to keep "their territory" free from "blacks"' (ibid.: 220). In short, she learned to draw a coded map of the area in order to both make sense of it and to move through its hospitable and inhospitable places.

Racism is by nature a spatial and territorial form of power. It aims to secure and claim native/white territory but it also projects associations on to space that in turn invests racial associations and attributes in places. Beneath the sign of places names like 'Brixton' or 'Handsworth' or 'Southall' are racial coded landscapes created as exotic or dangerous by turns that act like a kind of A–Z of racist geography (Keith 1993, 2003). In this sense racism draws a map, it creates places in the process of narrating them. This shading of place isn't simple or one-way; as Gail Lewis' account illustrates, alternative stories are told and in the process new maps of belonging, safety and risk are drawn. Neighbourhoods are thus made and remade as stories are told about them. Franco Moretti points out 'without a certain kind of space, a certain kind of story is simply impossible' (Moretti 1998: 100). These stories have consequences as they open up the social landscape and make potential action and behaviour possible. The aim of this chapter is to interpret this process in contemporary London and listen in particular to the way young people represent and inhabit the spaces of the city.

19

At the end of Italo Calvino's book *Invisible Cities* his protagonist says:

> The inferno of the living is not something that will be; if there is one, it is what is already here, the inferno where we live today, that we form by being together. There are two ways to escape suffering it. The first is easy for many: accept the inferno and become such a part of it that you can no longer see it. The second is risky and demands constant vigilance and apprehension: seek and learn to recognize who and what, in the midst of the inferno, are not inferno, then make them endure, give them space. (Calvino 1997: 165)

The inferno here might be analogous to the city of containers, of segments, of the chequerboard of hatreds and violence – a damaged home. The tactics that young people use that are described in what follows point to moments when refuge and belonging are given space. These openings cannot be reduced to a political manifesto, or some didactic call from the streets. Rather, they point to quiet transformations and fleeting moments in which living with and through difference are realised. Or, put another way, to make bearable what might be otherwise unbearable. Hanif Kureishi, commenting on his childhood experiences, said recently 'for me London became a kind of inferno of pleasure and madness' (MacCabe and Kureishi 2003: 40).

What follows is drawn from the *Finding a Way Home Project* which began in 1996 and focused on two parts of London – Deptford and the Isle of Dogs – and examined how young people navigate the spaces of the city, how they make a cosmopolitan and multiracist city their home. Anne Phoenix has pointed out that the reality of Britain today is that there has been a proliferation of transcultural openings or transgressions alongside, and sometimes inside, contexts haunted by multiply inflected racisms. Reflecting on the fiftieth anniversary of the arrival of the *Empire Windrush* – the ship that brought colonial citizen migrants to Britain from the Caribbean – she argued that 'the contradictions and complexities of multicultures and multiracisms are a notable legacy of the Windrush' (Phoenix 1998: 96).

The fact that London is a multicultural and cosmopolitan city is now beyond question but this brings no guarantees. What remains is the question of how we try and understand the ways in which people live in and through the paradoxes and incommensurabilities of racism. There are moments of critical opening to be found if we look and listen for them. The question remains: how might this be achieved and how can we recognise this process when we see it and hear it?

From exegesis to dialogue: the
Finding a Way Home Project

George Marcus has argued that in the wake of the criticism of ethnographic authority (Clifford and Marcus 1986), it is necessary to abandon the way of narrating culture from the vantage point of an omniscient 'eye' towards an account of culture from the positioned or situated 'I' of the ethnographer. In short he argues for 'redesigning the observer' (Marcus 1994: 46). He also argues for the importance of abandoning or at least unsettling the 'know it all' authority of realist accounts and moving from high minded exegesis (this is really how the world is!) toward dialogue. In a sense, this is precisely what we did in the *Finding a Way Home Project* as we offered young people a variety of techniques or technologies to observe (photograph, video or map) their own lives and narrate them (audio diaries, and conventional interviews). This experiment in dialogic representation was conducted over the course of a whole school year.

The Project began in 1996 and was a collaborative piece of work that included Phil Cohen, Michael Keith, Tamina Maula, Tim Lucas, Sarah Newlands and Lande Pratt. It was an attempt to redesign the relationship between the observer and the observed. We gave young people cameras, audio diaries and video cameras to grind their own lens to look and speak about the world through which they moved. While many of the materials generated in what follows are produced collectively (and I'd like to thank my colleagues for letting me use them here) the interpretations and shortcomings of what follows are my sole responsibility. In the writing and analysis of this work there is both a commitment to hold – however unevenly – to the spirit of dialogue while at the same time offering critical insights and reflections on what was offered in the representations made by the young people themselves.

The research has focused on young people between the ages of 13 and 14. The ethnographic work with young people is best described in two phases. Firstly, ethnography was conducted in the school setting operationalising a multimedia methodology and involved working with two classes of young people in a school in Deptford, South London, and Isle of Dogs, East London, respectively (see Figures 1.1 and 1.2). We chose these areas because while they are very close to each other and separated only by the River Thames they have very different histories of multicultural formation and popular racism. South of the river Deptford is part of former London dockland. It has ancient connections with imperial trade and expansion: it was where the East India Company was formed. It was also a place where popular racism reared its head.

Figure 1.1 *London and surrounding areas*

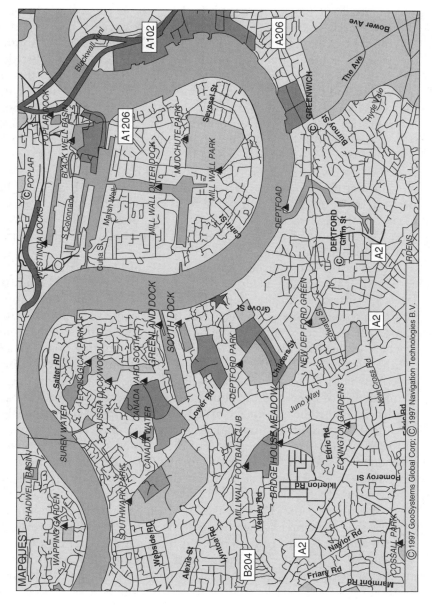

Figure 1.2 *Deptford and the Isle of Dogs*

In 1948 the National Union of Seamen agitated to stop black people working on British ships. Colonial citizen migrants established themselves in the area in the forties and fifties and experienced harassment and violent attacks from local racists. In 1977 the extreme right staged a famous march in this part of London. A few years later in 1981, 13 young black people died in a house fire in New Cross in the south of the area. To some degree as a result of the mobilisations against these events there is a strong sense that the racists have been run out of this part of London and that Deptford is a harmonious multicultural area. This is signalled by one local resident who pointed out that a piece of National Front graffiti that had been left to fade on the wall – and not removed – was a metaphor for the declining appeal of organised racism in the area. In 1991 around 30,000 people lived in the district and 28 per cent described themselves as from 'ethnic minority backgrounds'. Those people considering themselves black, including Black Caribbean and Black African, made up 28 per cent of the total population, around 4 per cent identified themselves as Irish, 4 per cent identified as Chinese and less than 2 per cent as of Pakistani, Bangladeshi or Indian origin (Deptford City Challenge Evaluation Project 1997).

On the north bank of the Thames, the Isle of Dogs is almost literally an island. It lies on the inside of the meander of the River Thames that gives the district a tearlike shape. The origin of the name is not known although there are many myths about how it came to be known by its name. The district is on the inside of the meander of the Thames and it is where in the 16th century Henry VIII kept his hunting dogs. There is another older myth that the area gets its name from a medieval hunting trip, in which the huntsmen were killed leaving their hunting dogs to roam the Isle of Dogs and the ghosts of these dogs are said to still haunt the district. With the emergence of London as an imperial city the Island became the centre of the imperial dock construction with the formation of the West India Dock. The traces of these connections are everywhere embedded in the landscape in the form of maritime connections and place names. What's interesting about the Isle of Dogs is that it is both associated with global connections and an intense sense of locality.

At the time of the 1991 census the total population was around 11,000, the ethnic breakdown being 78 per cent White, 6 per cent Black African and Afro-Caribbean, 8 per cent Bangladeshi, 3 per cent Chinese/ Vietnamese and 1 per cent Indian and Pakistani. In the postwar era another series of folk demons has taken the place of the ghostly medieval hunting dogs whose barks were said to haunt the Isle. The Isle has also been viewed – particularly in the work of Phil Cohen – as a microcosm of the politics of nation and race (Cohen 1996). Chris Husbands argued in his seminal study that East End racism takes in a broad catalogue of incidents of local racism: from popular anti-Semitism which helped pioneer the Aliens Act of 1905 (Britain's first immigration control), through the Mosleyite agitations of the interwar years, to the dockers' support of Enoch Powell's 'rivers of blood' speech in 1968, and mounting harassment of the Bangladeshi community during the 1980s (Husbands 1983).

The victory of the British National Party (BNP) candidate Derek Beackon in local elections in 1993 was offered by some as the expression of the intrinsic nature of racist culture in East London. This also manifested itself in a version of ecological logic that located racism in particular places that provided its seedbed. The result is a kind of determinism that echoes early American urban sociology which itself was the product of a particular trans-Atlantic conversation. Chicago School urban sociologists like Louis Wirth and Robert Park took their inspiration from the early social explorers like Charles Boothe and Henry Mayhew both of whom conducted investigations into the urban poverty in London during the 19th Century (Kent 1981). This way of framing urban life was to a large degree repatriated through the publication of Young and Wilmott's classic study *Family and Kinship in East London* (1957). Understanding the social life of cities in this way results in a kind of ecological fallacy. The essential point is that 'community' is as much a narrative product as an organic achievement (Back and Keith 1999).

But this is not to be drawn to some relativistic abandonment of 'the real' in favour of the disembodied pursuit of discourse and urban story-telling. Rather it is a matter of working between the representation of space ('the conceived') and the spaces of representation (the lived) drawn from the work of Henri Lefebvre in *The Production of Space* (Lefebvre 1996). In this sense throughout our research we have tried to avoid slipping into the kind of intrinsic determinism that, like the myth of the nomadic howling dogs, haunts much of the public debate about youth in cities. It is precisely this sensibility about how to theorise urban life that has informed the methodology that we used to work with young people. The two districts are represented very differently: Deptford on the one hand is viewed as a place where 'race problems' have been supplanted by an emergent multicultural harmony; while the Isle of Dogs on the other is treated as an entrenched racist district. The research sought to probe and interrogate the adequacy of understanding racism and multiculture in this way.

In total the school sample consisted of 42 young people in Deptford (23 female and 19 male) and 47 in the Isle of Dogs (27 female and 20 male) and thus a total of 89 young people took part representing the diversity of ethnic groups present within these localities. The ethnic breakdown of the samples was as follows: 38 per cent of the total were white English (total of 35 young people – 18 female and 17 male); 17 per cent were black African or African Caribbean (total 17 – 8F 9M); 18 per cent were south Asian (total 18 – 10F 8M); 16 per cent were Chinese/Vietnamese (total 16 – 12F 4M) and 2 per cent of the young people were of mixed parentage (total 2 – 1F 1M) and there was one other young woman who was of South American parentage. The school ethnography was in the main conducted by the four research officers employed on the project during the first year. The research was completed in 1998.

The four researchers worked intensively in the school throughout the year. They kept fieldwork diaries and conducted secondary work in school and helped out with school activities in particular an anti-bullying initiative on the Isle of Dogs. For each of the research exercises interviews were conducted either in pairs or individually. One of the successes of the research was the implementation of a multimedia methodology that enabled young people to use a variety of representational strategies to construct their landscapes of safety and danger and included photography, written stories, art work, mapping and video. These research exercises generated a vast amount of empirical material totalling over 250 hours of tape-recorded interviews and 11 hours of video footage. What was immediately interesting about the material is that the multimedia nature of the self-generated representations allowed the young people themselves to find the medium they were most comfortable with; for some it was the photography exercises while for others the written exercises and audio diaries provided the most appealing medium. What follows is largely drawn from the photographic exercises and visual dimensions of the project.

'Youth gangs' and local patriotism 'talking big'

Much of the discussion about public safety is underpinned by common sense assumptions about the 'problem of male youth'. Young men in the inner cities are seen as urban interlopers, agents of street crime and violence. While, these young men *appear* spectacularly in news reports purporting to represent 'gang yobbery', 'football hooliganism' or 'race riots' they almost never speak: they are seen but not heard. Academic discussions have centred on whether such characterisations represent a realistic account of the situation or whether they form 'moral panics' whose origins lie elsewhere (Cohen 1972; Hall et al. 1978; Jefferson 1988; Robson 2000; Alexander 2000a). Since 1997 the policy agenda outlined by the Labour government has to some extent shifted the terms of this debate, paradoxically by drawing on some of the rhetoric if not the argument of the realist position, in order to exploit moral panics about ungovernable youth as a rationale for policies of 'zero tolerance' against crime and anti-social behaviour.

Tony Blair has also connected the issues of youth anti-social behaviour with tackling racism particularly in the aftermath of the murder of black teenager Stephen Lawrence and the inquiry into his death. At the Labour Party conference in September of 1998 he made this connection clear: 'From tomorrow kids can be picked up for truancy, young children alone in the streets can be subject to curfews, parents made responsible for their children's behaviour. From April anti-social behaviours can be taken to court and punished. Don't show zero imagination, help us to have a zero tolerance of crime ... When a young black student, filled with talent is murdered by racist thugs and Stephen Lawrence becomes a household name not because of the trial into his murder but because of an inquiry into why his murderers are walking free, it isn't just wrong; it weakens the very bonds of decency and respect we need to make out country strong. We stand stronger together.'[1]

The government's approach is focused on the management of *risk* through the mapping of crime hot spots and unsafe areas, child curfews and the invocation of a specific notion of 'safe' space. In this way highly *localised* micro public spheres become the focus of new forms of state intervention aimed in more or less repressive forms of policing and self-government (see also Claire Alexander, Chapter 11, this volume). While at the same time 'community cohesion' and other types of communitarian rhetoric become a catchall response for social problems that have radically different social qualities. Here white racist violence, the marginalisation of some sections of ethnic minority youth and 'black on black' violence are understood as manifestations of the same problem, that is, young men who are out of control.

At the same time, young people's own narratives, while they sometimes borrow from the vocabulary of policy elites, also draw on their own version of the state of play that is structured by their positioning within the landscapes that they draw for themselves. While young men appear but don't speak in this debate, it seems that the position of young women is completely absent from this discussion. Indeed, the language of community cohesion may conceal the regulating gendered dimensions of communitarian rhetoric. Iris Marion Young has argued what she calls the 'totalising impulse' of community precisely because it 'denies the difference within and between subjects' (Young 2002: 432). She privileges the city as an alternative theatre for difference that is open to 'unassimilated otherness' (ibid.: 437). In more prosaic terms, the appeals to 'community' in the multicultural contexts described here may be little more than a mechanism through which adult authority is exercised both inside localities and by state-sanctioned organisations. Our findings suggest that we cannot read off the factors that variously promote antagonism or intercultural dialogue from institutionalised structures of racial inequality precisely because the lived landscapes of Deptford and the Isle of Dogs disrupt the imagined territories of the social that have become the object of government intervention under current policy drives. The picture that emerged within the representations of young people is more complicated than current policy debate will allow. A good example of this is the way in which 'youth gangs' were discussed in the two locations.

In Deptford there was a strong sense that male youth gangs were distributed as distinct territorial units throughout south London. While talk about gangs was pervasive, only three of the young people interviewed had any direct connection to these gangs. It was claimed that mainly black young people initially formed youth gangs as a response to racism. These gangs were predominantly male but there were also a small numbers of female members. Gangs had emblematic territorial names like 'Ghetto Boys', 'Deptford Men', and 'Brixton Youth' and at one level they bore the marks of a 'racist mapping' linked to the popular iconography of black street crime and the moral panic surrounding 'mugging' (Hall et al. 1978; Keith 1993). At the same time, the incorporation of these spatialised gang labels was an attempt to recode these associations. In some of the accounts by young white people the stories about gangs were viewed as a diffuse source of anxiety and threat; at the same time there was a reluctance to racialise these feelings or focus them in some concrete way, for example by invoking the figure of 'the black mugger'. At the end of one interview in which a young white girl had talked extensively and quite fearfully about the threat of gangs, she was asked if there was anything else she would like to say; she replied, after a short pause: 'Yeah, about the gangs and that. It is true that they are mostly black boys involved but it's not because they're black'.

For the boys in particular the symbolic nature of these gang labels had to do with claiming as sense of place and identification with that place. To proclaim 'Ghetto Boy' status brought with it both a space of preferred identity and a claim to entitlement. The area around New Cross Milton Court Estate was referred to as 'Ghetto' and as one boy pointed out, 'To me now to be from Ghetto is an honour'. To recode the association as an emblem of pride changes the coordinates of racist mappings which criminalise both places and people. In a situation, these inner urban districts are the canvas on which racist fears and stigma are inscribed. What seemed to be happening here was that these inscriptions are turned back on themselves. Local patriotism is a response and a mirroring back of a negative urban imagery that is in turn recoded as positive. Such claims often projected masculine autonomy and also a sense of being placed in a landscape. For example young men would give the numbers of the local telephone boxes as if they were their own public/private home from home. The talk about gangs became a means through which these young men positioned themselves against the ways in which the places they lived were coloured by racist stigma. In this sense these forms of claiming and renaming place produces an alternative map of belonging. They are an alternative to the A–Z of racist geography but they do not completely break free from it. The ludic dimensions of the process could be limiting as well as empowering. The local patriotism expressed through such means is a kind of masculine choreography, a local pride that 'talks big' and responds to routine stigmatisation. The compensatory pleasures in moves of this kind are important to acknowledge because there is real fun to be had in countering snobbery and ignorance in this way. Yet, a local pride that 'talks big' may also carry 'hidden injuries' (Sennett and Cobb 1977). While spaces are reclaimed through 'gang talk', it accepts the territorial limits contained within the white racist mapping. Put simply it is a version of identity that remains held in the straightjacket of racist urban associations but simply turns it inside out.

A black girl complained of being labelled by her male peers in this way:

> Just because you know certain people doesn't automatically make you a part of a gang. Like saying I am like a Peckham Girl. I don't think so! I live in Ghetto and the Peckham Boys think I am a Ghetto Girl but because I was born in Peckham the Ghetto Boys think I am a Peckham Girl.

The association of a sense of identity through such naming initiations is a powerful rhetorical device for inscribing myths of origin and destiny in local prides of place. It can be very difficult to detach these labels once they have initially been made to stick. More than this, these identities can be a prison as well as a refuge. It was interesting that the young people themselves, and particularly the young women in Deptford, resisted being defined in this way. Nevertheless, while gang territories were acknowledged to be dangerous places it was generally agreed that the risk from gang violence was low. Yet at the same time there was an appreciation of the growth in gun crime and the incidents of 'black on black violence'. In the south London context, questions of violence and gang formation were being 'worked on' and assessed – often critically – within the context of peer groups that were multiracial in composition. There was great care here not to slip into generalisations about race or gender or claims that could be applied throughout the district. The assessment of gang formations and youth violence was both critical and cautious.

The situation on the Isle of Dogs differed considerably. A pervasive sense existed within white youth and larger community contexts that 'Asian Gangs' constituted the main threat. Here issues of crime, violence and risk were strongly racialised and associated with a specific gendered and ethno/racial category, that is young Bengali men. Claire Alexander has situated this shift with what she calls the 'rise and rise of the "Asian gang" '. A new folk devil has been constituted in which a 'complex inter-section of age, "race" and gender forms the perceptual baseline for the rise of the Asian "gang" ' (Alexander 2000a: 127, see also Chapter 11, this volume). The diverse experiences of young men from south Asian backgrounds get reduced to a grid of essentialised ideas about race and masculinity. These ideas were articulated forcibly amongst some sections of the white community activists on the Isle. One in particular had in his office collected examples of local and national press cuttings that reported 'Asian gang violence' on a noticeboard that he displayed to visitors.

What became clear in discussing youth violence on the Isle was the sense of a divide between black and white youth on the one side and Bengalis on the other. This distinction was kept very much alive in local circuits of rumour and gossip; this in turn enabled young white people to appeal to adult authority and 'common sense' in validating claims about violent Asians. Paradoxically, the Bengali young men that are pre-sent in the street or seen 'hanging around' are accused of mirroring the exact forms of masculine embodiment associated with some versions of the performance of white working-class masculinity. Yet these forms of embodiment, be it acting 'flash' or 'bowling' – to walk rolling the shoul-ders (see Desai 1999 and Robson 2000) – are also seen as threatening because they either challenge 'normal' (that is, coded white) claims to determine conduct, or establish exclusionary zones into which whites fear to venture. Some sections of the white population claim that 'Asian gangs' locally are the prime instance of urban violence. This has devel-oped to such an extent that it supersedes previous concerns over black male criminality associated with motifs of mugging or civil unrest. It was particularly telling that even local activists from the British National Party claimed 'black and white youth' were equally the victims of police 'double standards' when it came to urban violence (Back and Keith 1999), while Asian youth were seen to be getting away with attacks on whites and with violent crime. This shift is not complete and echoes of the 'black mugging' discourse are still registered but locally these formulations are increasingly faint.

For Tony Blair white racism is understood as the antithesis of 'com-munity' and viewed as the violation of common bonds of decency and respect. In the case of the Isle of Dogs white racism is articulated precisely through the language of community that is coded implicitly with a notion of whiteness and with an appeal to 'decency' and 'fairness' (see also Hewitt 1997). Similarly, Anthony Giddens points to the importance of creating a public sphere in which local democracy and community development can ameliorate dilapidation and engender safer cities (Giddens 1998). What is striking in both cases is that they appeal to some kind of intervention in 'local' affairs yet they lack any real sense of context and the complex struggles over belonging and inclusion taking place in particular localities. What I have tried to illustrate above is how the discussion of 'youth gangs' reveals the shape of some of these inclusions and exclusions. This is not to say that this contrast (that is, on the one hand the careful and complex interrogation of the meaning of gangs and on the other, a racist moral panic) is stable or an echo of underlying structural relationships. Rather, what it reveals are emergent patterns that may be reiterated but can also shift and be contested.

One of the limitations of the sociological work on youth is the preoccupation with spectacular behaviour that often focuses on young men. One of the concerns here is to give an account of what lay beneath the contours of the concern about conflict violence and youth crimes. Attention to the unspectacular disrupts some of the easy essentialisms that have dogged both public and academic debates about the position of young people in the postcolonial city.

Magic, escape and places of refuge

Neil Leach has commented that within cities 'symbolic attachments may be grafted onto physical form' (Leach 2003: 79). This process of 'symbolic grafting' came through clearly in the photoscape exercises conducted by the young people in the study. We gave them disposable cameras and asked young people to photograph places that they felt to be safe and those places dangerous by contrast. Once the photographs had been processed we then asked them to talk us through the decisions they had made and the stories contained in each image. Vikki Bell has shown belonging is 'performative', that is, attachments are established through actions and rituals that unfold repeatedly in any given context (Bell 1999). Through such actions places are carved and written into the fabric of the city producing specific meanings within urban space. As Caroline Knowles points out, 'Race is generated in the social texture of space, and so the analysis of space reveals its racial grammar as forms of social practice to which race gives rise' (Knowles 2003: 105, see also Knowles, Chapter 5, this volume). Parks, alleyways, playgrounds, and hallways were the environmental features most frequently catalogued as dangerous in both study areas. Sometimes these were connected with associations

Figure 1.3   *Cubitt Town Library*

with vulnerability to hateful or threatening behaviour and sometimes they were simply interpreted as unknown and unpopulated and therefore risky. They echoed the way Gail Lewis described how she moved through the chequerboard of the city at the beginning of this chapter. What was telling about the photographic exercise was that we requested a specific act of representation that in turn became a kind of performance of belonging. The images produced were sometimes on first glance surprising but as the young people narrated them they revealed the subtleties within the everyday maps of risk, danger and refuge.

Figure 1.3 shows a photograph taken by a Bengali girl from the Isle of Dogs. This first image shows the public library in Cubitt Town, East London. The library is a safe public space. 'I feel safe because there are people inside the library', she writes. This choice was common to all the Bengali girls for whom the library constituted a space where they both felt safe from harassment by boys and free from surveillance by their parents or members of the extended family. The second image taken by her friend shows her posing inside the library (see Figure 1.4). Visiting the library was viewed both as appropriate and approved by adults but the library itself became a space of freedom. Going to the library was both a kind of 'cover story' where girls could find a place to be 'hanging out' with friends and also sometimes to be meeting boys. It was a place

Figure 1.4   *'A safe place'*

to do homework and to work on the officially sanctioned school curriculum. The library was also a place of 'informal learning' where the young people expanded the curriculum on their own terms. Public libraries are places of self-improvement in London and contained in patterns of their use are subtle insights into desires regarding social mobility and 'respectable', or, perhaps more accurately, individual resistances to both adult authority and peer pressure. The library represented a cultural no-go area for the kinds of young people by whom these girls felt most threatened. It was off limits to the informal cultures of authority and recognition found in the street or the playground. In contrast the third photograph (Figure 1.5) shows a playground opposite this girl's home. She had experienced racist name-calling and harassment here: 'I feel unsafe because people there always make racist comments. This is opposite are [our] building.' It was safe enough to photograph from a distance perhaps, but the playground was a potential place of danger that needed to be navigated with care particularly during the daily journeys to and from school.

Most of the accounts by the young people from ethnic minority backgrounds showed a very sophisticated degree of local situated knowledge about high- and low-risk spaces as regards racism. These findings are very close to the pattern contained in Gail Lewis' account of growing up in London in the fifties (Lewis 1985). We also used audio diaries individually recorded by young people and group video walkabouts as ways representing and performing a sense of belonging. These exercises also provided similar insights into the strategies of precaution that were used to reduce the risk of racial attack. These young people sifted through a large repertoire of observations, stories, memories, and feelings. As a result their maps of their neighbourhood consisted of a shifting web of association that connected people in places, creating a highly textured choreography of safety and danger. As they travelled across this symbolic landscape, the crude coding of whole areas as either 'racist' or 'multicultural' broke

Figure 1.5   *Unsafe – playground taunts*

I FREL UNSAFE BECAUSE PEOPLE THERE ALWAYS MAKE RACIST COMMENTS. THIS IS OPPISTE ARE BUILDING.

down into a much more sophisticated and tactically useful map of the streets and public/private spaces they moved through.

To account for these patterns of habitation and exclusion it is necessary to understand the interrelationship between gender, racism and social class. Yet the interconnections between these lines of social differentiation are not mechanistic or straightforward (see Bhachu 1991). Avtar Brah has written that the search for a grand theoretical scheme for understanding these connections has been unproductive. She argued, "they are best construed as historically contingent and context specific relationships" (Brah 1996: 208). It is precisely these context specific contingent relations in which the interplay between structure and agency can be found.

Figure 1.6 is a picture of three white girls from the Isle of Dogs shown in an austere place that they refer to as 'Our landing'. For them this is a 'safe place' where they come to be together as friends in the winter and which they claim by scribbling their names on the wall, an interstitial space between home and street. During a video walkabout these three girls took us to this landing and they talked about the violence that occurs in the surrounding streets between groups of 'white' and 'Asian gangs'. The landing was a refuge, both out of their parents' jurisdiction and away from the activities of the boys. When asked if they were ever afraid of the violence between rival groups of white and Asian boys they answered 'No. Because they know us'. The young women disapproved

Figure 1.6   *'Our landing'*

of the violence but they also felt protected by the codes of local recognition. The 'white girls' were hostile to racism, yet at another level, their whiteness protected them – they were acknowledged and recognised as belonging to the Isle of Dogs. They were cast within a white territory regardless of whether or not that agreed with its terms or parameters of inclusion or exclusion. In this example whiteness, social class and gender intersect to produce an implicit set of parameters that calculate levels of danger and real risks.

The kinds of attachments that are spliced into the urban fabric are context and time specific. Put simply, the same physical structures can have very different cultural and symbolic grafts or cultural mapping. The quality of these cultural mappings is dependent on the social profile of the person making them. Figure 1.7 shows another picture of a stairwell taken this time by a Vietnamese girl called Ly who lives in Deptford. Here the landing and the area outside her flat are defined as a dangerous place, to be passed through quickly. 'This is my least favourite place downstairs from my flat,' she writes. It is a danger zone that needs to be crossed in order to reach the safety of home. In her interview she talked about the threats of harassment which she had suffered from neighbours and the vulnerability she feels in the immediate environs of her flat where Vietnamese families have suffered routine harassment. Through taking photographs these young people were able to record dangerous places from afar, or as in this case claim those spaces momentarily through being pictured within them. It is striking that Ly is pictured here in her least favourite place smiling back into the camera, happy and relaxed. In a sense, the research provided a context in which a performance of belonging could take place, in this case posing for a photograph. The photograph carries both a history of dread and feeling threatened in this place, yet also at the same time the act of photographic representation is itself an assertion of presence. The 'observational act' – controlled and conducted by the young person herself – becomes an assertion of belonging in an otherwise hostile place.

Nigel Thrift has argued that in order to understand the qualities of any given landscape is needs to be situated in time (Thrift 1996). The quality of the cityscape is transformed by night and day and these time geographies have different consequences for men and women (Rose 1993) and young and old (Skelton and Valentine 1998). For many of our informants the risk associated with a particular place was dependent on the time of day they passed through them. Parks could be safe during the day but risky at night; dangerous figures identified here were particularly drug users or alcoholics often associated with these places. Equally, young women reported being threatened and sexually harassed by older men at night around pubs and clubs. The gendering of these landscapes also intersected with issues of the position of young black people.

Figure 1.7   *Ly's landing*

For example, almost all the black boys from our Deptford sample claimed that they were vulnerable outside their area if they were alone, particularly in places that were constructed as predominantly white (such as the regions of Eltham and Welling). These accounts often cited the murder of Stephen Lawrence as evidence. This attack took place in 1993 in an adjoining suburban neighbourhood and Stephen Lawrence was travelling home with his friend Duwayne Brooks when he was killed by a group of whites. The same black boys claimed that this would not happen to a black girl in the same situation. Young black women, one of whom reported being chased and harassed in Eltham, contested these suggestions.

The accounts of the young people also disrupted some of the commonly held assumptions about the two districts in question. At the level of the neighbourhood, the young people in our samples identified specific micro-spaces of racism that did not feature on the official maps. This complicated the notion that particular neighbourhoods or districts were 'racist' while others were havens of 'multicultural harmony'. In the accounts offered by young people in Deptford it was routinely said that very low levels of racism were experienced in the district and that multi-ethnic friendship groups were the norm. However, within these accounts there was evidence of complex forms of racism that militated against intercultural dialogue and friendship. A young white girl spoke insightfully about the pressure that was applied through her parents to make her withdraw from multiracial peer groups and not have black boyfriends. This was despite the fact her grandmother was in a relationship with a black man and that her father had similarly been in a mixed relationship. This type of censure on mixed relationships was also manifest in the public spaces at street level.

The same young white girl spoke of an older white youth who worked as a local mechanic:

> He works down the High Street. I've got to walk past his place to [get] to my Nan's house. He's always standing there like looking me up and down and calling me a 'Nigger Lover' and things like that. He's been out with coloured people and still he calls me one as well. I've been out with three coloured people, and he must have been out with four or five girls and he's the one calling me a Nigger Lover!

Accounts like this question the existence of multicultural harmony. The pressure on this girl to disengage from her relationships with black people was palpable, yet to do so would also violate the norms of trust and association that had become established within the peer group. Here we can also find the disruption of racial categories by gender and the complex combination of anti-racist and racist sentiment.

When we asked her where she would call 'home', she did not choose the neighbourhood where she had lived in Deptford. Rather she projected herself into the adjacent areas of Brockley, Honor Oak Park and Forest Hill (where in fact she had never lived) because she felt that in these districts interracial friendships and mixed relationships were not viewed as problematic. Through an act of alchemy the place that she calls home, or what might be more appropriately thought of as a 'home from home', is created. She has never lived there but for her it is a place to be herself outside the surveillance and disapproval of adults and peers. It is also outside the circumscriptions of the domestic sphere crossed by racial contradictions and double standards.

This process of making home *out of home* is both banal and remarkable. In his little book *Sketch for a Theory of the Emotions*, Jean-Paul Sartre writes: 'When the paths before us become too difficult, or when we cannot see our way, we can no longer put up with such an exacting and difficult world. All ways are barred and nevertheless we must act. So then we try to change the world, that is, to live it as though the relations between things and their potentialities were not governed by deterministic processes *but by magic*' (Sartre 1962: 62, emphasis added). I think the process of making 'home from home' is part of this magic. In the vernacular the phrase is usually about replicating a home in another place. Here I am suggesting that home is made inside domestic or patriotic inhospitalities. In this sense, it is not a matter of replication or mimesis, it is also a matter of making new space.

In the two areas studied the linkage between place, identity and entitlement was ordered differently. In broad terms the youth community on the Isle of Dogs showed evidence of racial segregation in peer group formation, dating and relationships and other leisure activities. At the same time young Bengalis had developed a range of sophisticated strategies designed to make this ostensibly white racist place into a space that was both navigable and habitable. This involved constructing a series of 'boltholes', be it in the form of libraries or youth clubs, or other safe urban niches across which safe passage could be negotiated.

However, the position of young Bengalis was similarly complicated by the intersection of youth and gender identities and this was a particularly acute issue for young women. For them to be seen within the centres of Bengali community around Whitechapel or Poplar meant that they might become the object of gossip within adult spheres. While these places guaranteed 'safety in numbers' they were also the spaces of constant scrutiny and recognition. It should not be surprising then that a group of young Bengali girls chose to hang out on the Isle of Dogs in an area reputed to be a 'racist place' because its whiteness by definition meant it was beyond the sight of prying eyes and the sound of gossiping adults. If I am not comfortable where I am supposed to be safe, I will find comfort outside of those places even though this might mean going to the places associated with racial risk.

In Deptford, it seemed that the pervasive narratives of multicultural harmony provided another kind of resource to claim entitlement and belonging. It was telling that it was a middle-class boy from outside of Deptford who perpetrated the only incident of open racist name calling that occurred during our research period. In an extraordinary sequence of events, a multiracial male peer group elected one of its members to confront the boy about his record of racist abuse. Here the rhetorical assertion of 'harmony' was reinforced through policing peer racism. However, such claims and attempts to make safe non-racist youthful public sphere are always partial and temporary. The local homeland was subject to the palpable pressures of disapproving adults; suspicious members of the local police force. In this sense the stability of the notion of 'multicultural harmony' in Deptford was disrupted by the presence of racism inside and outside of the area. The example of the young white girl who is forced to find a 'home from home' outside of Deptford because she had a black boyfriend and was involved in a multiracial peer group is an illustration of this uneven complexity.

Conclusions: 'damaged homes and places to be'

I want to return to the question I posed at the very beginning, namely, how do young people make the postcolonial city a home? Before addressing this directly I first want to reflect on the different associations contained within this notion. John Berger has commented that the notion of 'home' is quarry to very different kinds of moralists. On the one hand there are those who claim ownership to the definition of 'home' in order to wield power. 'The notion of home became a keystone for a code of domestic morality, safeguarding the property (which included women) of the family. Simultaneously the notion of homeland supplied a first article of faith for patriotism, persuading men to die in wars which often served no other interest except that of a minority of their ruling class' (Berger 1991: 55). This sense of homeland is profoundly resonant with our current situation in the world after 11 September 2001 and the succession of wars that have come in its wake. Berger points to another reading of the meaning of home. He says that beneath these dominant interests there is an antecedent meaning. Here home is 'the center of the world – not in a geographical, but in an ontological sense ... the place from which the world can be founded' (ibid.: 55–6).

Young people make the city a home precisely through producing a kind of phenomenology of home in line with Berger's notion of home as a way of centring a sense of place in the world. The maps that are produced to document the contours of safety and danger cannot be reduced to typologies or clunking correlations between ethnic categories or gendered identities and the social qualities of a given place. Each individual young person combined available forms of social knowledge to project a map and find a way through. This is an attempt to name something close to what is *Umwelt* in German, in other words the world of our desires, our needs and of our activities. As Sartre puts it, this world is 'furrowed with straight and narrow paths' (Sartre 1962: 62).

These landscapes are complex, they cut through time and space but they are also complicated in the ways in which the interplay of habitat and habitation works. Equally, they are produced through the interplay between the attribution of social identities and the coding of the urban landscapes with cultural and 'racial' grafts. The results can produce remarkable and counterintuitive things, be it young Bengali girls who go to a 'racist place' to make a 'home from home' or young men who give the numbers of public telephone boxes as 'home contact points'. We have to listen and look carefully to recognise these remarkable things and find experimental ways for them to be observed and recorded. The *Finding a Way Home Project* was such an experiment and for all its undoubted faults it enabled its participants – however incompletely – an opportunity to be observers, to grind their own lens and to draw their own map of their lives. Inside cities there are still further invisible and mute cities. They are places that give space *to be*, not places of identity or unitary or fixed notions of selfhood, but a space to perform and claim belonging amid the inferno of contemporary city life. Despite the damage done by urban geometries of power and exclusion, young people find refuge and ways through the cityscape and in so doing homes are grown out of home.

Note

1. Labour Party Conference speech, Blackpool, 29 September 1998.

Chapter 2

Diaspora Politics through Style: Racialized and Politicized Fashion in Global Markets

PARMINDER BHACHU

In this chapter, I want focus on the gendered global micro-markets which have emerged through the racialized and politicized aesthetics of the diaspora as asserted by Asian women in London. From the margins, they have created culturally mediated economic spaces – diaspora voices expressed through improvisational style and fashion. Firstly, I will narrate the story of the Punjabi suit or *salwaar-kameez* (a tunic, trousers and long head scarf), henceforth, the suit, and its reimagination by second-generation, London-based Asian women entrepreneurs and designers. A formerly denigrated economy has moved to the mainstream with suits being worn by high-status fashion icons such as the late Princess Diana and high-profile political women like Cherie Booth QC, wife of the British Prime Minister, Tony Blair.[1]

Secondly, I want to describe the hybridizing diasporic aesthetics[2] that constitute the source codes of these economies, which have their origins in the politicized and racialized sensibilities of immigrant mothers. I want to refer to the *sina-prona* – sewing and stitching – cultures and the improvisational aesthetics of co-constructing[3] clothes in a continuous borrowing from and raiding of multiple sites of local and global media, the street, and suit retailers. All this is combined with an inherited diasporic culture, which remains vibrant domestically and commercially. From this have emerged the leading design entrepreneurs who have taken their suit designs into new global markets.

Thirdly, I want to refer to the disruptive markets these women have created from the margins, a product of their ability to deal with dissonance and conditions of disequilibrium. Their politicization in the locales in which they do their design and retailing work, whilst being in globally connected commercial zones and production sites, gives them an edge in new capitalist markets. These new markets are largely defined by the aesthetics of co-construction and customization. They pay heed to the

42

authentic voices of individuals in micro-communities, selling them products that encode their individualized consumer desires. I want therefore to suggest that the British Asian women designers' cultural moment of improvisation and co-construction is perfectly in synch with the contemporary market moment, which is defined by the very same characteristics. I want to argue that, for a change, it is their position of ethnic and racial disadvantage which gives these designing, retailing and stitching women their position of comparative advantage: as niche-marketers who are super-responsive to their local customer bases, the areas in which they live, politic and do their cultural and commercial work.

This is complete contrast to the elite India- and Pakistan-based designers who 'want to make it in the West' but who are not racialized in the same way and who do not care for the hybrid agendas of British Asians. These nationalistic designers set up shops in London in the 1990s which failed,[4] though there is a current attempt to ply again their recontextualized ancient heritage, arts and crafts design.[5] These elite design agendas, encoding the ancient heritages of India and Pakistan in the products they sell in London, have not succeeded precisely because their 'national products' – albeit beautifully crafted, designed and embellished – have been out of tune with the market moment of co-construction and dialogic improvisation[6] of individualized customer desires and local markets needs. I want to develop this argument beyond that which I presented in *Dangerous Designs* (Bhachu 2004), by looking at the recent treatment by Western fashion houses of Indian designers such as Ritu Beri and the general vulnerability of Indian design to Western whim, despite the best efforts of the Fashion Design Council of India (FDCI).

So let me firstly present the background of the Punjabi suit economy and the cultural and commercial dynamics that have made it a mainstream trend. What is the cultural, racial and political groundwork behind these movements which have made it 'hip to be Asian'?

Narratives of the Punjabi suit[7]

The Punjabi suit represented the clothes worn in Britain by immigrant women, mostly from the Punjab in North India and Pakistan, in the 1960s and 1970s. It was also worn by multiply migrant women who had come via East Africa, the twice-migrant communities who had left India almost a hundred years before migration to Britain. In the 1960s and 1970s the suit was negatively coded, considered the garb of low-status, working-class immigrants who were not welcome in Britain. These were the women connected with the labour migrants whom Britain recruited to fill labour shortages after the Second World War and who had British citizenship and passports as residents of the former British colonies.

To many of the white British, the suit represented a threat, incontrovertible evidence that the colonized had come to the land of the colonizers. The negative coding of the suit also applied to the turbans worn by Sikh men. The early fights in the 1950s and 1960s with British employment agencies had been around the turban: the fights by Sikhs to be allowed to wear the turban as bus conductors, on motor bikes, in the public spaces of banks and post offices. As late as the 1980s Sikhs still had to fight for the right for their sons to wear turbans in private schools, as illustrated by the famous Lee versus Mandala case.[8] Many Sikhs cut their hair and gave up their turbans until they became more culturally confident, with their own community infrastructures, and had established a critical mass of turban-wearing people to buttress their ethnic and sartorial confidence. The tale of the suit has many similarities.

The heroines of the tale are the older immigrant women who kept the suit economy alive by adhering to the timeless styles they had migrated with, suit styles they had worn for years which they often stitched themselves and which they reproduced once more in the changed diasporic context in Britain. They maintained their cultural and sartorial (tailored) frames despite the racial slurs and taunts. They were told they were 'Pakis' wearing 'nightsuits' and 'pyjamas' despite the fact that many were not from Pakistan and many from East Africa had never been to the Asian subcontinent in their lives. The older women in classically styled suits are precisely the ones who socialized their British-raised and British-born daughters to wear the suit. The mothers provided their daughters with a cultural framework that legitimized suit wearing. In many cases they stitched suits collaboratively with their daughters, taking account of their subcultural and class styles, their personal fashion idiosyncrasies and the trends in vogue at the time. In this way, my own mother persuaded me to wear a suit in the overtly racist 1970s when there were few stylish young Punjabi women in London who wore 'young fashionable suits' as opposed to 'mummy-type suits'. In my late teens and early 20s my mother lovingly stitched suits for me, co-constructing them as we went along. She paid full heed to my own style and incorporated it in the suits she made for me. She also taught me to cut and sew suits for myself. Thus, she gave me a sartorial template of cultural confidence through clothes denigrated in the public realms at that time. She gave me the confidence to be racially myself on my own terms regardless of the terrain I found myself in. There are many similar narratives of astute mothers who socialized their second-generation daughters into wearing trendy, fashion-conscious suits with pride against the racial and sartorial odds. Their daughters subsequently further developed their own British subcultural and subclass style, both in the domestic domain and – significantly, for this chapter – the commercial.

The most innovative design entrepreneurs in London are products of the *sina-prona* economy which was highly elaborated as it was reproduced and recontextualized in diasporic settings such as East Africa where it was a need-based economy. Both Geeta Sarin, the pioneer fashion entrepreneur and Bubby Mahil come from this background of *sina-prona*, which refers literally to sewing and beading. It is really a metaphor for a command of domesticity which is often generationally transmitted, a required skill for the running the household in a diasporic setting where there are no professional service providers to meet the household demands of clothing your children, yourself, and the men. The sewing machine was and remains a critical piece of technology for this culture. Women inducted into this culture were highly skilled in many stitching, craft and food-making processes. In reproducing their cultures after migration, these diasporic women were innovative in their improvisation in responding to the dislocated contexts. I suggest that second generation Asian women have translated these domestic skills, elaborated and reimagined in a previous diasporic setting, into commercial domains of their London fashion markets. Their diasporic sensibilities of innovation and improvisation were and are the hallmark of domestic *sina-prona*, which is encoded in their highly negotiative entrepreneurship of co-construction of clothes they sell to their customers in their London shops (see Bhachu 2004 for details).

In the following, I want to focus first on two diasporic designers from this background, both born in Kenya and raised in London. They are Geeta Sarin, who came to London as a teenager and pioneered the suit trend in London – she is in an older generation, now in her mid-50s; and Bubby Mahil who came to London as a two-year-old, and who is now in her late 30s.

Geeta Sarin: the pathbreaking diasporic designer of 'one-to-one design dialogues'

Geeta represents the professional end of the *sina-prona* diasporic sewing culture (Bhachu 2004). She says her mother:

> ... was an excellent seamstress and in Kenya, all the girls were supposed to know something about stitching or tailoring. My mother and other women in the joint household constantly emphasized that all the girls should know sewing, stitching and cooking, apart from anything else. This is how I learnt. Also I had a bit of talent and I always loved good clothes.

Geeta identified a market niche from what she saw at the Indian social functions she attended in the early 1980s:

> There were beautiful young Asian women who were wearing ready-made *salwaar-kameez* but they were not the right cuts or the right colours ... I could see that there was a definite need for the younger generation. Obviously they had no choice but to tell mum 'Alright fine, you are making me a *salwaar-kameez*, I will wear it because this particular function requires me to wear a *salwaar-kameez* ...

The ready-made suits then available in Britain were badly cut, shoddily sewn and made with no understanding of the clothes codes of British Asian women in their different subcultural locations.

Geeta, in contrast, offers fusion elements in her clothes – this is what is attractive to diaspora markets; the locally based British Asians and transnationally based Indians and Pakistanis who are her clients, along with a significant minority of white Europeans.[9]

One-to-one design dialogues

Geeta's way of working is through 'a guided dialogue' between herself and her clients. She is there herself in her shops to deal with customers directly and is absolutely hands-on in her design enterprise. She negotiates patterns with customers all the time. She describes this as 'the engineering of an outfit'.

Her manufacturing unit in India enables her to get the British-conceived, India-manufactured suit in London within as short a period as four days. The unit is primed for her design processes and instructions. She can expedite the manufacturing process in India by doubling the money she pays the tailors and workers, who work overtime to complete urgent orders. She has had suits delivered to clients within two days.

The ideas for each design come from many sources, her inputs and her clients' suggestions and desires, including ideas from fashion magazines. Geeta is a mediator, both a design consultant and a guide who moulds these ideas through drawing and sketching. The sketch is the powerful instrument of negotiation that allows her to be more democratic in her designs. Although there are stylishly displayed clothes in her shop and many people do buy off-the-peg, the major sector of her business is that of individually cut and tailored suits for men and women. She says:

> You pick a Lucknow *kurta*, a Lucknow *kurta* is a Lucknow *kurta*. It's a *kurta* with no shape ... In my design ... it's a little bit more tapered. It has more shape and it's better cut. ... The cut makes a lot of difference.

This emphasis on the 'cut' is what gives Geeta's clothes their diasporic edge. It encodes their 'Western-ness'. The shape and the silhouette indicate their British Asian registers.

Racial and cultural pride design sensibilities

Geeta emphasizes the importance of her cultural background and racial experiences to her design aesthetics. She makes the point that when the British ruled India, they took away with them many of the finest Indian crafts and attacked the most highly skilled craftsmen:

> We still let them keep doing this to us here and in India. Why are we ashamed of our culture? My inspiration is cultural. Absolutely. Most Indians from India living abroad were ashamed of their background. I have seen that wealthy Indian elites would wear only [European] designer clothes and shoes like Louis Vuitton, Versace, Cardin, a whole bunch of other designer names. Now the people who can afford to buy designer clothes also wear the *salwaar-kameez* and with confidence and pride. They can afford both European designer clothes and also wear our own clothes.

Geeta is emphatic in her assertion that she has:

> ... stuck to my roots. I stuck to my cultural heritage. I have never been ashamed of it. I have not moved away from my cultural background. People like us are making their mark now. People don't bother with all these others who were ashamed of their cultures. These are the people who are behind. They were culturally ashamed and never spoke their language to their children, who were so confused, they didn't know where they were coming and where they were going.

She also says that she never imagined when she started that suits would be worn by leading fashion icons. She had wanted to provide well-designed clothes for British Asians like herself, who were into clothes and wanted to dress well. However, her strategy in developing her style was to negate the racism that denigrated the suit as 'Paki' dress and instead to emphasize cultural pride:

> Today, every high street store has outfits that are and look like a long *kameez* with *kaajs* on the side and trousers, sometimes straight-cut ones. The *salwaar-kameez* has come a long way.

Geeta Sarin's articulation of how and why she defined her own style comes from her ability to sustain herself on the strengths of her diaspora roots and cultural heritage, all the more ingrained through the East African experience in Kenya. She has developed an anti-imperialist and anti-racist discourse around clothes. Her interpretation of her clothes and her enterprise is explicitly couched in terms of cultural pride and its maintenance. Geeta's commercial projects and cultural statement are political acts. Her recoded designs of traditional Indian clothes are inserted into the European and international markets to create new commercially and culturally subversive spaces. Thus, the market is used not just as a straightforward mechanism of exchange but also as a means of negotiating a diasporic style, a material form that encodes complex battles of cultural and racial pride.

Second-generation diasporic hybridizer: Bubby Mahil

> 'Young Asians and Europeans don't want something that is totally Asian: they want something with an Asian element,' opines Bubs Mahil, who designs Indianwear for the British Prime Minister Tony Blair's wife Cherie.
>
> *India Abroad* 22 September 2003

Bubby developed the diaspora *sina-prona* sewing culture to literally stitch and tailor an identity for herself that is absolutely reflective of her context and biography. She reworks traditional designs more radically than Geeta, involving a greater fusion of different elements. The *salwaar-kameez* features but is not central.

Bubby narrates this incident of when she was seventeen or so. Her cousin was getting married and she and her sister needed suits for this occasion. They went all over the shops in all the main ethnic shopping areas in London but could not find anything they liked. Bubby then decided to stitch her own outfit. She bought pink chiffon and a matching lining fabric. She made a dress with a short bodice, attached the rest of the frock-style dress by ruching the chiffon and finally made a *churi-dhar* (leg-hugging trousers) to go with it – the result, a dress worn with a *salwaar*. She said this looked stunning and earned her many compliments at the wedding. Many younger women wanted this type of outfit. Soon after, she made a fusion-style wedding dress for a white friend. It was a combination of an English wedding dress in an Indian silk fabric which she got embroidered in India as she happened to be visiting there. This was another path-breaking outfit that got her peer group excited and wanting more of her style. Initially, she did all the stitching herself and sold her products at suit parties organized in other people's houses, until she became so busy that she decided to open her own shop. Now she designs in the UK and the clothes are made in India.

A racially initiated cultural battle becomes a commercial space

Bubby was politicized by her white friends' racist comments and decided to respond to them defiantly. She says:

> In those days, I didn't have any Indian friends, all my friends were English, and if you were walking down the road going down somewhere and you saw an Indian girl wearing the *salwaar-kameez*, my friends would automatically say 'Paki', just because they were wearing a *salwaar-kameez*. That is when it offended me and I thought ... 'Why am I ashamed of wearing what we do? That is our culture but I have got to do it in such a way that they accept it as well.'

Bubby's fusion style is reflective of her context and also captures the youth consumer styles of her time. This encoding of the complex cultural textures in clothes is continuous and not static. It is ever responsive to local and global fashion trends and individual idiosyncrasies of her customers. She improvises and co-constructs and therefore captures the new and what is not-yet-spoken all the time as she dialogues with her customers to produce a design that is eloquent in its becoming. She achieves a voice through the clothes and asserts her own version of her ethnicity and culture and, at the same time, creates a distinct commercial space. She is determined to adhere to her own style and she emphasizes vehemently:

> Because of things I experienced when I was young, which I was ashamed of, I do not want to lose it now. Wearing *salwaar-kameez* and the way everybody always used to look at us and our dress, you know, I just do not want to lose that.

Micro-designing through dialogic sketching

Like Geeta, Bubby negotiates her designs with her customers and the pencil sketch is the first stage in a sophisticated global process of production, as I witnessed during my fieldwork:

> A plump woman comes into the shop. Bubby draws a simple sketch with her as the client describes the type of neckline she wants, the shape and the collar, the embroidery and the extent of it, using some of the styles already in the shop. The client decides on a *lungi* suit with a short just-below-the-hips *kameez*. Bubby convinces her that a *lungi* suit, with

a straight, ankle-length skirt rather than a sarong, would be flattering for a plump person, giving her height, especially with a shorter top. A rough sketch is drawn by Bubby as they discuss the various possibilities and finalize the style, fabric and embroidery. At this stage the woman leaves.

Bubby later elaborates the sketch, now number 153 in her order book, into a fully fledged drawing with instructions for all the various details, elaborating the conversation with the outline sketch. She faxes the drawing to India that day. She also talks the sketch through on the phone to India to clarify the instructions, and makes several subsequent calls to check on the progress of the outfit as it goes through the various stages of being made. The outfit is ready for the customer in the shop within three weeks at a price of £225.

Racially encoded diaspora designs[10]

Bubby uses skills developed elsewhere in her family's earlier phases of migration to create a style that represents her own hybrid experiences. She combines different elements to produce something that makes sense to her customers who buy from her and whose context and subcultural tastes and norms she shares, represents and incorporates in her clothes. The processes by which she does this reflect precisely the ways in which diaspora cultures are created through constant negotiation and transformation in new spaces. Displacement and rupture are sutured through recontextualization.

It is this process of negotiation which gives the British Asian designers their dynamic edge. They are continuously engaged in market conversations and pay heed to their customers' voices whilst mingling and matching their own ideas and suggestions with those of their clientele. The process of hybridization is not binary – pure to impure – but a continuous one, that borrows and raids multiple economies of signs, that constantly reinterprets inherited traditions and formulates itself through complex, multiplex connections. It is not straightforward, but webbed, networked, rhizomic, borrowing both horizontally and vertically from many sources of knowledge. The designers working in this way are thus best placed always to respond to the new, the moment.

Selling India to the 'West': revivalist Indian designer Ritu Kumar

'Indianness' was also very much the theme for Ritu Kumar, the doyen of Indian fashion.

'Everything works as long as we, as Indians sell it as Indian and not try to sell it as something else' said Kumar, among the most respected Indian designers, after showing off slinky tops replete with Hindu iconography.

News India 1 August 2003: 28

Ritu Kumar is described as the 'grand lady of revivalist ethnic fashion' and 'the high priestess of traditional *zardozi*' (*Galaxee* May–June 1996) – *zardozi* being the embroidery of the royal courts of India done with pure gold and silver thread and now also in lurex, a less glamorous aesthetic than the original form developed in the Mughal courts. Ritu Kumar has innovatively revived many languishing embroidery and craft traditions. An executive member of the Delhi Crafts Council, she knows leading Indian artists and crafts people as well as the influential and powerful decision makers in the state-sanctioned arts and crafts institutions and handloom industries. She trained in museology in the United States before embarking on her career of reviving traditional arts and crafts in India. Her estimated annual turnover from her Indian domestic enterprises is 10 billion crore rupees, higher than any other Indian designer (*Outlook* 20 April 1998: 63). Having been supremely successful in India, she clearly wants to go 'global' and become an international designer.

Representing India: a window to the East

Ritu considered her London shop was:

> ... very much a window to the East, and in particular a window to India. What I always thought was there was a reflection of India in various ways, one was from the Indian film industry, which was very strong ... The second is you would get some merchandise that is available already in different shops, even in Mayfair. But there was a certain thing missing there. There wasn't one *defined design identity* that was coming in with the merchandise. It was assorted merchandise. Accompanying it, what I wanted to do so very much was to have a reflection of contemporary Indian art. (Interview with Zee TV, May 1996)

Her idea was that she was selling 'top-of-the-range' India, the 'ancient traditions of Indian craftsmanship' and not kitsch India. Her commerce in highly crafted clothes represented sophisticated Indian products as designed for elite Indians. These chic products were further transferred, primarily for a market of the white elite in Britain. Her publicity stated: 'Creator of the first chain of exclusive boutiques in India, she has added one in the UK which is the haunt of queens, princesses and celebrities who aspire to acquire garments... .' Ritu emphasized that in presenting a window on the East she wanted to stress India's dynamic modernity as played out through a revived 'contemporariness' and its location in an international arena. She stated this was 'not folklorish India, it's not ethnic India, it's contemporary India'. Her discourses are about representing India as a country that has been and is evolving a contemporary hand-writing that 'Western audiences' are not familiar with since Bollywood images have dominated India's representation abroad.

Ritu wanted a defined design identity (which she saw as missing from the British scene) which would be designed to educate exclusive 'Western' markets about classic chic India and its sophisticated contemporary design economies regulated by influential design professionals like herself. The products she sold in the UK were the same as the ones in her shops in India:

> We haven't changed. We are coming with our own identity. More than perceiving markets, I think there is an education process that there is an alternative. We are not slotting ourselves into what the market needs ... We are saying this is what we are, this is what India is, we will not change. How we are perceived in the market we do not know. (Ritu Kumar, interview with the author)

Her posture of commercial disinterest in the market occurs despite her huge commercial success in the Indian market. As I have indicated earlier, she is a famous and successful market leader, and commercially more suc-cessful than any of the other competing Indian designers who barely reach half her annual turnover. She centrally uses the market for both commer-cial and cultural exchange, even though the explicit agenda of her joint enterprise with the ARKS gallery had the subtext of educating the 'West' about the sophisticated high chic and arts and crafts aesthetics of India. Her understanding of the market is obvious from her sophisticated web-site and her recent entry into hi-tech cyber-marketing techniques.[11]

In the past the revival work that she has done successfully for com-mercial domains had originated in the arts and crafts domains, the revival of which was initiated by people involved in nationalist freedom struggles and then became government-sponsored. This government sponsorship for the 'apparel sectors' of the Indian economy still continues. For example, in 1998 the Indian government, under the aegis of Apparel Export Promotion, sponsored the Oorja-Indian fashion show in New York, where Ritu was among the exhibitors. Similarly, in July 2003, the 4th Lakme India Fashion Week was sponsored by the Fashion Design Council of India (FDCI) whose purpose is to 'professionalize' the Indian fashion industry. (Such government sponsorship is in marked contrast to the position of the British Asian designers, who have had to develop their own markets and commerce without any state or institutional help.)

Ritu's design agenda is couched in a nationalist and anti-imperialist discourse about the revival of tradition. The statements about high arts and crafts do hide market interests, which this supremely class-conscious commercial sphere caters for. The implicit agenda is of selling to the 'West' which is, from the perspective of Ritu and others like her, populated by the wealthy elite whites and transnationally located South Asian elites, and not locally based Indian immigrants living in and produced by racialized contexts.

Ritu stated in my interview with her:

> But what comes out of the country and what represents India to a lot of people who live abroad, especially to the Indian who has kind of lost touch with India … For them unfortunately, it's still a limited gypsy clothing culture. And I think they are looking for something to identify with and there's a great deal of confusion there outside the country as to who people are; particularly, I see it through the clothing.

I do not think hybridizing British Asians are so confused after all with 'a limited clothing culture' and do not need 'something to identify with'. These negative attitudes about British Asians are pervasive amongst many members of the subcontinental elite. Those Indians who occupy an elite class position in India do not want to forgo their privileged placement as Indians, as it accords them enormous local advantage. If they were to identify themselves as British Indians, they would have to assume a whole different class and race location, and relinquish the hierarchies of their country of origin in which they have positions of power. Therefore they refuse to acknowledge the local Asian scene. A diasporic Asian intellectual also suggested that:

> They do not want to be seen as people of color and are not going to be denigrated immigrants, as British Asians. There is a very racialized consciousness among South Asians from India. They do not want to be identified as people of colour, racialized subjects in very racialized countries. So by keeping to their India label and being transnational psychologically and otherwise, they do not have to fall into racialized hierarchies.

Racialized hybridization versus elite national purities

All these fashion entrepreneurs are making strong political statements – their commerce and commodities are highly politically charged. All of them engage in a discourse of cultural pride. In the case of Bubby, the damage done by racist taunts and stereotyping galvanizes her to create a defiant hybrid style that is both true to its context and responsive to the youthful sartorial mores of her subcultures. Geeta Sarin responded to English racism by being 'proud of our culture' in a British context. In Ritu's case, her design agendas emerged not out of hostile encounters with racism, but through responses to the damage of imperialism and also through her own transformative personal experiences of being educated in the West, which prompted her to learn about her own cultural background and the arts and crafts of her country. This background determined her revivalist arts and crafts agenda, the hallmark of her design identity. Ritu makes a nationalist design statement, intimately connected with the Indian nationalist movement whose influential members spearheaded the revival movement. She is a dynamic national actor with design aesthetics that are about an ancient nation, a past-orientated discourse of contemporizing an ancient nation's languishing craft skills and design vocabularies. She talks of representing India, of performing ambassadorial function to present 'a unique style reflecting the ancient traditions of Indian craftsmanship in a contemporary vocabulary' as stated in their publicity material. So she makes the already significant more significant.

Diasporic fashion entrepreneurs like Bubby and Geeta, on the other hand, are engaged in future- and present-orientated dialogues of forming the nation as they go along. In contrast to Ritu, they are in a way, anti-nationalist. For them there is no national heritage and ancient past to preserve and revitalize, only a new nation to be formed and an emergent national space to negotiate. They celebrate the syncretic forms which are true to their biographical experiences, the migration trajectory and their racialized cultural locations and which they assert in the market. They are not trying to capture 'Western' markets. They are creating their markets by 'doing their own thing' in the communities in which they live and have been part of since their childhoods. Their commercial agendas, which come out of their own cultural locations, naturally have a close fit with the market moment. They do not negate market interests, nor engage in an arts-and-crafts agenda. Bubby and Geeta do not adopt a 'teaching' approach, because of their egalitarian co-designing and the fact that they are market-driven. Their assertion of hybrid styles and often subversive designs are transformative, transformative of the nation, shifting the sartorial, cultural and commodity landscapes of Britain. They are generating new forms of Britishness and new identities of Europeanness through the clothes economy of locally negotiated diasporic designs, which are themselves tempered by and transferred through global economies. Elite designers lack the negative principle of co-construction and improvisation that defines the design vocabularies of diasporic design entrepreneurs, even though they sell beautifully crafted clothes. They are static and bereft of any design input from the people who wear them.

Moreover, subcontinental elites seem quite divorced from the ethnicized cultural battles that diasporics have gone through and now assert in commercial domains. The diasporic encode these ethnicities, hard fought for as public registers of their recognition. The elites have entered the market recently and do not know what has gone on before. Their understanding of local racialized settings in which they want to initiate their markets comes not from local experiences acquired over time, but from superficial class-coded knowledge commonly articulated in their class circles. They did not do the cultural and commercial groundwork for the suit economy to develop. British Asian immigrants and their second-generation progeny did this having opened up suit shops a decade and more prior to the arrival of elites. It is not British Asians but the Indian elites who are quite confused about how to respond to new markets in fast capitalist situations in a global city like London, in which they have much less familiarity and genuine self-confidence and little political and cultural clout. The diasporic fashion entrepreneurs, on the other hand, are absolutely clear about their market messages, which they assert strongly and which emerge from their own experiences as locally based British Asians and as the second-generation progeny of immigrants.

Pandering to the 'White West': an elite racialized discourse

But the Indian fashion industry, as a whole, remains keen to expand into Western markets. 'The fashion industry has potential; I want it to be Rs.10 billion [$212–217 million] powerhouse in 10 years,' says Vinod Kaul, the Fashion Design Council of India (FDCI)'s executive director (report in *India Times* 1 August 2003). The current market share is Rs.1.8 billion ($39 million). The hope is that India's fledgling fashion industry could become as big and powerful as the information technology (IT) sector.

According to the same report in the *India Times*, Kaul was greatly excited by the visit of UK designer John Galliano to Ahmedabad and actress Liz Hurley's announcement that she might wear a sari for her wedding designed by an Indian designers (she chose Versace to design her clothes in the end). When the fashion buyers from prestigious New York, London and Parisian department stores arrived to buy clothes in India, there was absolute delight because of the potential they represented to increase Indian exports abroad.

However, in responding to outsider agencies and interests, and in wanting to make it big in the 'West', Indian fashion entrepreneurs are forced to accept control from precisely those 'Western' agencies against whom they fought their decolonization battles. In selling to the 'West' on Western terms, they are in some ways surrendering to the ex-colonizers, a form of neocolonialism in design and commercial agendas. The India-based fashion industry remains dependent on high-profile European stars like Liz Hurley wearing Indian fashion in order to legitimate and develop their fashion industry.

In 2003 London's Selfridges ran a Bollywood season extending throughout the store, generating £3,000,000. They took a batch of Indian fashion designers, to showcase their work, but, according to *India Today*, 'ripped it apart'. One designer was quoted as saying, 'They took my basic patterns and made me restyle the outfits in keeping with what they said was the silhouette of the season so that in the end I felt it was not my work completely' (*India Today* 22 September 2003).

Ritu Beri went down a storm at the Paris Fashion Week in 2003, with the Western media gushing about 'the newness and freshness' in her designs. But the fashion house who recruited her sent its own teams to organize production in India. Thus, her honeymoon with Paris lasted just a few seasons, a clear reflection of her enforced dependency on outsider agencies and their design templates through which she is expected to filter her own. Indian designer Suneet Verma who is the 'Indian ambassador' of Moet Chandon of the Louis Vuitton-Moet Hennessey group paints a similar picture in stating 'I would say that there is a sort of noise out there, and we are making a noise together, so we are being noticed ... To be honest, I don't think we're very successful yet. You could say we are making inroads.'

It seems that this is the price Indian designers have to pay if they want to make it in the West. There is a great deal of control exercised by the buyers and design controllers of European and American fashion houses. The agenda is set not by the India-based designers but by the people who buy from them. They are in a way ruled by New York, Paris, Milan and London-based design personnel and their economic agents.

This is a very different scenario from that of the London-based diasporic designers who have set their own agendas. They have fought for their local moments. Their authentic agendas endure because they are not pandering to outside agencies. They do not submit to pressures to conform to the design desires and requirements of outsider agencies. They do their own thing and sell on their own terms in domains they have helped to produce and know intimately, in landscapes in which they have struggled and in which they have politicked and fought their cultural and also commercial battles. None of the local Londoner diasporics are responding to the desires and diktats of outsider agencies. Since they are of the 'West', constituting it dynamically as its citizens, none of them engages in a discourse of making it in the 'West'. Such a frame is irrelevant for these racialized and politicized locals whose British cultural and racial politics are about asserting their own cultural frames and about representing themselves as British Asians.[12] They create and respond to their own moments with the new that is about representing their own agenda in their own countries of residence on their own terms. They have had to negotiate dissonance all their lives, mostly from a position of disadvantage. Lester Thurow (1999: 33) points out that market success goes to people who can negotiate conditions of disequilibrium in fast-changing economies.[13] Multiply moved diasporics have to deal with fracture and dislocation and disequilibrium on a daily basis. It is their modus vivendi and operandi as reflected in their improvisational aesthetics. This ability to improvise is what is reflected in their markets. They have the skills to capture the new and the moment. Having fought in hostile terrains to represent themselves on their own terms, to create new licences of participation, this is where their power lies.

Notes

1. This reimagination of the suit has parallels in other Asianizing trends in Britain (and America): the enormous popularity of Indian food – curry surpasses roast beef as the food the most commonly eaten by the white British; the ubiquitous fashionability of *pashmina* shawls; the uptake of British Asian *bhangra* music by mainstream stars like Madonna, Jennifer Lopez, Britney Spears and Ricki Martin (see Aljazeera.net section on Culture: 'Bhangra turns the tables on UK pop.', article by Arthur Nelsen in London, 28 September 28 2003).
2. 'Hybrid'/'hybridizing' refers to the complex and continuous mixing and fusion of different cultural and sartorial (tailoring) forms and also performances: the combining of new and old connections and new and newer connections that innovatively produce emergent cultural and commercial spaces. 'Diasporic aesthetics and sensibilities' refers to the defining characteristics and core values of those with migrant biographies in the diaspora, whose lives, cultural practices and social networks are cast across different nation state borders and continents.
3. 'Co-construction' refers to the negotiation of a design, the product and the cultural forms from which these things are derived, incorporating the inputs of colleagues and customers. For example, the creation of a design or an outfit-taking account of the customer's inputs and suggestions – a jointly discussed process that produces the garments.
4. Libas and Yazz, subcontinental high-status London shops like that of Ritu Kumar, selling high-craft India- and Pakistan-produced fashions, all closed within a couple of years of each other during the late 1990s. Yazz and Ritus

stayed open for around three years and Libas was open for over a decade and is now run as a by-appointment-only studio. The shop itself in Mayfair in central London closed.

5. For example, the much-noticed group show by Rina Dhaka, Tarun Tahiliani, Manish Arora and Vivek Narang at Lord & Taylor at Saks, Fifth Avenue, New York in August 2003; the Bollywood month at Selfridges, London, August 2003. These events were reported in the US-based weekly newspapers, *News India Times* 9 May 2003 and 1 August, 2003 and also *India Abroad* 17 October 2003.

6. 'Dialogic improvisation' is similar in substance to the above explanation of co-construction: an object or a design produced by two people who have taken account of each other's suggestions and have incorporated them in the making of the 'thing'. This is a dynamic process of improvising to produce a cultural or music form or an outfit – something that has emerged from a conversation between two or more people.

7. 'Narrative of the suit' refers to the stories about the suit that are told through the making and the wearing of the suit.

8. The Mandla versus Lee case was a famous case in the early 1980s which led to a successful classification of the Sikhs as a race after much legal wrangling. This classification recognized Sikhs as a distinct racial group with specific cultural symbols that they had the right to adhere to and observe. This much-publicized case in 1983 was sparked off by the refusal of the white headmaster of a private Catholic school in Birmingham, England, to allow an East African Sikh boy, Gurinder Mandla, permission to wear a turban as part of his school uniform. Lord Denning, a renowned British high court judge, ruled not to allow the Sikhs to be classified as race, a ruling that was later overturned by the House of Lords. As a result, the Sikhs were legally allowed to wear a turban in many public sites. Mr Mandla, the father, who was himself a solicitor, won this case for his turbaned son.

9. Geeta estimates that her clientele is roughly 80 per cent Asian, 20 per cent white British.

10. 'Racially encoded designs' refers to designs that reflect the racial experience and identities of the person who is innovating, interpreting and wearing them. These are styles that respond to and incorporate the racial experiences and identity of the person who makes and wears them so that they become forms of politicization. For example, negative racial experiences are played out through a style and the choice of clothes.

11. They are replicating the design and marketing processes of the pre- and post-industrial era. Cf. Christopher Locke: 'Ancient markets were full of the sound of life: conversation. They dealt with craft goods that bore the marks of people who made them. But the internet – unmanaged and full of the sound of the human voice – is proving that the Industrial Age is nothing but an interruption as the conversations resume, this time on a global scale' (Levine et al. 2001: v; see also: Searles and Weinberger in ibid).

12. In an article in the magazine *India Today* 22 September 2003 headlined 'Ready to Bear' it is stated, 'However, what Indian designers may be lacking in, the British-Asian fashion industry is optimizing to the hilt … One reason

for the seemingly dichotomous degree of success between Indian designers and their British counterparts could be that the latter have a distinct style and attitude, 'British-Asian fashion is not as different in cuts as it is in styling' says Mani Kohli, a leading British-Asian designer. 'People have to blend the ethnic background with the environment and enhance it to blend with the mainstream.' Ahmed Sarwar of *Asian Women*, a leading British-Asian fashion magazine agrees. 'Asian fashion in Britain has its own direction,' he says, pointing out that most clothes are designed in Britain but manufactured in India.

13. Lester Thurow, writing about quite different market contexts, points out 'Disequilibrium conditions create high-return, high-growth activities. The winners ... have the skills to take advantage of these new situations' (1999: 33).

Chapter 3

Global and Local Articulations of Asian Identity

MIRI SONG

Ethnic identities in a global context

We live in an increasingly 'global' world. Globalization entails the increased interconnections of social and economic life, and has resulted in the spread of capitalist market relations and a truly interconnected global economy (Reich 1991; Robertson 1992; Waters 1995; Boli & Thomas 1999). Another key aspect of globalization is the way in which information and communications technology has resulted in the 'time-space compression' which links distant lands and lives together (Harvey 1989). There are many competing arguments made about the effects of globalization in every sphere of life, but one commonly cited argument is that globalization is a dialectical process, meaning that rather than resulting in a uniform set of changes, globalization consists of mutually opposed tendencies (see Featherstone 1990; Giddens 1990, 1991).

For example, this dialectical process can be illustrated by the tendencies toward cultural homogenization *and* cultural differentiation (Hall, Held and McGrew 1992). Globalization is sometimes interpreted as a process of gradual homogenization dictated by the West, whether it be in the clothes we wear or the food we eat (see Latouche 1996; Ritzer 1996). At the same time, globalization can engender emotionally laden forms of nationalisms (Smith 1990) and a return to the mythic certainties of the 'old traditions' (Morley & Robins 1995) which refute any conception of a genuinely representative and collective identity and experience.

Yet others have argued that while national identities are declining, new hybridized identities are emerging (see Appadurai 1990; Pieterse 1994): 'By compressing time and space, globalization forces the juxtaposition of different civilizations, ways of life, and social practices. This both reinforces social and cultural prejudices and boundaries whilst simultaneously creating "shared" cultural and social spaces in which there is an evolving "hybridisation" of ideas, values, knowledge and institutions' (Hall, Held and McGrew 1992: 75). As a result of these processes, more and more people are said to be involved with more than one culture (Hannerz 1990).

The dynamics associated with globalization, and modernity more generally, are said to destabilize established identities (Giddens 1990; Calhoun 1994). Increasingly, people's sense of their ethnic identities and affiliations are said to be relativized and shaped by our greater consciousness of the interconnections of people and societies around the world (Featherstone 1990; Robertson 1992). Globalization and the shifting and multifaceted nature of ethnic identification in many Western societies is especially relevant in relation to second-, third-, and fourth-generation 'diasporic' minority people, who are negotiating their senses of home and belonging within multiethnic societies, such as the USA and Britain (see Bhachu, Chapter 2, this volume).

Although there is much debate about the concept of diaspora (see Vertovec 1997; Anthias 1998), it can be defined as 'the (imagined) condition of a "people" dispersed throughout the world, by force or by choice. Diasporas are transnational, spatially and temporally sprawling sociocultural formations of people, creating imagined communities whose blurred and fluctuating boundaries are sustained by real and/or symbolic ties to some original "homeland" ' (Ang 1994: 5). Clearly, people's real or imagined attachments to a distant 'homeland' are conducive to the creation of new identities. In diverse ways, diasporic people inevitably impact upon and transform the cultures and societies they pass through (Gilroy 1993).

There is now a bewilderingly large literature about globalization, diaspora, and transnationalism – which span many different disciplines and fields. Peggy Levitt and Mary Waters (2002) capture the wide remit and multiple meanings associated with these terms:

> At present, vocabularies of 'diaspora' and 'transnationalism' are both used to describe the ways in which globalization challenges social organization and identity construction. Scholars using these terms are interested in how heightened social, economic, and political interconnectedness across national borders and cultures enables individuals to sustain multiple identities and loyalties, create new cultural products using elements from a variety of settings, and exercise multiple political and civic memberships. (2002: 6)

Contemporary international migration is significantly different from that of previous periods, and this is most evident in studies of transnationalism, which emphasize the economic, cultural, political, and familial networks and links between two or more locations (Gold 2000). 'Transnational communities' refers to communities linking immigrant groups in advanced capitalist countries with their respective sending nations and hometowns. These communities are groupings of immigrants who participate on a routine basis in a field of relationships, practices, and norms that include both places of origin and places of destination (Portes et al. 1999).

Thus people's sense of 'belonging' and identity are complicated by mass migrations and transnational ties. For example, it is not unusual to be 'twice migrants', such as the people who immigrated from India to East Africa, then from East Africa to Britain (Bhachu 1985), or those who immigrated from India to the Caribbean, and then to Britain (Vertovec 1994). Given the complicated trajectories of many ethnic minorities, in terms of moving from one place to another, one's ethnic identity and affiliations need not be bounded territorially to one's birthplace in Britain, Pakistan, Tanzania, or Hong Kong. Thus the conceptualization of transnational identity requires the decoupling of cultural identity from national identity.

The diversity of transnational experiences

In the context of globalization, immigrants and their children today are much more *able* to maintain a variety of transnational ties with their 'homelands'. In many major metropolitan areas in the USA and Britain, diasporic people may encounter a geographical density of other co-ethnics. Transnational ties are made possible by relatively inexpensive and quick air travel, and also by technological advances in communication and the mass media. Many groups have access to various forms of ethnic media, such as ethnic daily newspapers, weeklies, radio, and 24-hour television stations. Furthermore, second-generation children, such as Korean American children, can learn their parents' ethnic languages through language programs offered on ethnic television stations, and Korean immigrant parents commonly send their children to Korea for summer holidays in order to help them learn the Korean culture and language (Min 1999).

Some second- and third-generation individuals may embrace forms of diasporic cultural practices and identities. For example, young Black people may exhibit a strong identification with a global and diasporic Black culture, which traverses the 'Black Atlantic' (Gilroy 1993; Alexander 1996). Certainly there has been a great deal of cross-fertilization of African American, Black Caribbean, and Black British cultural forms in the fields of music and literature. In the case of Asian Americans, in addition to trends in panethnic Asian identification and partnering, there is growing evidence of a global Asian popular culture. For example, the pan-Asian magazine *Giant Robot* is heavily 'plugged into' youth cultures in Japan, Hong Kong, and Korea. Though they are in the minority, some second-generation British Chinese young people have chosen to move to Hong Kong (from where their parents emigrated) in order to live and work there (Parker 1998). In addition to the attraction of good jobs, the BBCs (British-born Chinese) who go to Hong Kong tend to evidence a strong interest and connection with various forms of Hong Kong popular culture, such as popular films and music, which they consumed while living in Britain.

However, it is not possible to generalize about the transnational ties and experiences of disparate minority groups; nor can we assume a homogeneous experience within a group, without reference to individuals' specific settlement histories and class locations. Although there is some evidence of Chinese American interest in exploring their Chinese heritage (see Louie 2002, as discussed below), in another large study of second-generation groups in New York City, the Chinese, who are often attributed with an enduring notion of Chineseness by the wider society, exhibited low levels of transnational practice, as indicated by the possession of language skills, the amount of contact with their parents' national-origin country, interest in parental home countries, and the sending of remittances 'back home' (Kasinitz et al. 2002). By comparison, second-generation Dominicans and South Americans (Ecuadoreans, Peruvians, Colombians) manifested the highest levels of transnational practices in New York City. Many questions about the nature, depth, and experiences of such diasporic ties still remain. For example, what forms do transnational ties take, and how 'deep' or significant are such practices and ties (Levitt & Waters 2002)?

An over-optimistic discourse?

In some of the literature on globalization and diaspora (though these terms encompass an admittedly diverse array of writings), the postmodern emphasis on fluid identities and positionings is far too celebratory, emphasizing the freedom with which diasporic minorities – the 'subject' or 'subaltern' – are able to fashion one or more positionings, or to mine connections and identities in relation to their real or imagined 'homeland' (see Bhabha 1990, 1994; Featherstone 1996). For example, Mike Featherstone (1996) points to the 'extension of cultural repertoires and an enhancement of the resourcefulness of groups to create new symbolic modes of affiliation and belonging ...'.

For Homi Bhabha, marginal, betwixt-and-between postcolonial migrants are a real force to be reckoned with, and diasporas are liberating forces against oppressive state structures and exclusionary nationalisms. Some also argue that new, more contingent forms of allegiance and identity are making the nation state largely obsolete (see Appadurai 1996; Glick-Schiller 1999).

There is no question that contemporary understandings of cultural and ethnic identity must be anti-essentialist and capable of conceptualizing change and multiple forms of affiliations which can transcend national borders. While I would agree that agency and the choices made about ethnic identity are extremely relevant for ethnic minority peoples (Song 2003), the politics and dynamics of diasporic peoples' ethnic affiliations and identifications are far more constrained and subject to negotiation than suggested by the rather breezy and celebratory writings about diaspora and hybridity. Not all diasporic people may be equally successful in their efforts to assert hybridized identities, or occupy and enunciate a 'third space'.

Andrea Louie's study of second- to fifth-generation Chinese Americans in the USA documents Chinese Americans' interest in investigating their family histories and genealogies, which culminates in their 'return' to their ancestral villages in China. This passage 'back' is achieved through their participation in a program evocatively called 'In Search of Roots'. One key reason why Chinese Americans, many of whom speak no Chinese dialect or know little about China, may participate in this program is that, 'Chinese Americans legitimize their identities within a U.S. racial and cultural politics that forces them to be associated with essentialized views of China and Chinese culture' (Louie 2002: 313). While many Chinese Americans cannot easily, or at least comfortably, claim roots with China (given their lack of language skills and cultural knowledge about China), they cannot claim their status as bona-fide Americans either – given their racialization as Asian or Chinese (see also Tuan 1998). In fact, Louie argues that many Chinese Americans – though they may be middle-class and university-educated – 'find themselves at the margins of global flows. For the most part they lack the social, cultural, or economic capital to participate skilfully in cross-border flows' (Louie 2002: 319).

Some of the theoretical writings on globalization and diaspora lack concrete articulations of the specific local and national structures which shape and constrain diasporic groups and individuals around the world. In addition, much of this writing obscures the differential ability of post-colonial peoples to realize their desired positionings and identifications. This is because the 'subject' is rarely discussed in sufficiently concrete context, and often seems to be floating around in an ether of endless possibilities.

It is important to weave together a framework which takes into account both the analysis of cultural politics and the political economy of specific histories and geopolitical situations (Ong 1999). In the remainder of this chapter, I will examine, within the context of diasporas and transnational flows, the ways in which the understandings and embodiment of *Asianness* are increasingly diverse, contested, and subject to discourses about *ethnic authenticity*. I will also look at the ways in which these contested understandings of Asianness (as generated by diasporic Asians, the wider societies in which they live, and 'native' Asians residing in Asian societies) shape, constrain, and transform the cultural, social and economic opportunities of diasporic Asians. The occupation of these liminal diasporic spaces is surely mediated by not only the wider societies which racialize them, but also the politics of 'sending' societies, from where discourses of ethnic authenticity are also generated.

Through a discussion of particular studies of diasporic Asians, I will also examine how discourses of Asian authenticity can create tensions and social divisions among Asian and Asian-origin people and their co-ethnics. The category 'Asian' is both broad and fluctuating across disparate societies. In this chapter, I will focus specifically on East Asian diasporic people, with ethnic origins in countries such as China, Korea, and Japan.[1]

Ethnic authenticity and the meanings and boundaries of Asianness

What it means to be Asian, or to claim membership within a particular Asian ethnic group, such as Chinese or Korean, and the boundaries around who is and is not Asian, are now more contested and blurred than ever – not least by Asians (both 'diasporic' and 'native') themselves, who are highly aware of the diversification and complexities surrounding the different positions and articulations of Asianness. 'Native' Asians are known to draw distinctions between themselves and their co-ethnics abroad.

As someone who was born in Korea (of Korean parentage), I moved to the USA just before my sixth birthday. I call myself both Korean American and Asian American. Several years ago, I was struck when a visiting Korean scholar at my university said to me, 'In my country [Korea] …'. This scholar knew of my Korean heritage, and her use of the 'my' pronoun made me wince, even though I knew that it was not intended to be malicious. The drawing of this distinction between us is reminiscent of Ien Ang's account of her '(troubled) relationship to "Chineseness" ', in which she tells us of her first journey to the People's Republic of China. Ien Ang was largely treated as one of the White

Western tourists in her tour group. Ang reveals that she had hoped that the Chinese guide would say something to her as an acknowledgment of an affinity between them, but Ang is disappointed. The debates concerning the meanings and boundaries of Asianness, including the changing markers of Asian identity, often refer to essentialist beliefs about ethnicity.

There is some evidence of inclusive pan-Asian identities and groupings in societies such as the USA (see Espiritu 1992; Tuan 1998) and Britain (see Alexander 2000), but there is also substantial evidence of ethnic boundary keeping and differentiation among various Asian-origin groups, which results in concrete inequalities in treatment and status for various kinds of Asian people, wherever they may be situated in the Asian diaspora. While there has been a great deal of research on the social exclusion and marginalization of Asian-origin people (and non-White ethnic minority people more generally) in White-majority societies, there has been much less attention given to the ways in which forms of differentiation, exclusion and boundary keeping arise in different subgroups of diasporic Asians residing in one society; and between diasporic Asians and 'native' Asian people who reside in Asian societies.

As discussed below, there is some evidence that both 'native' and 'diasporic' Asians subscribe to essentialist beliefs about an 'ethnic core' (Smith 1990) – something which is not specific or exclusive to Asian-origin people. Louie's study of Chinese Americans, discussed above, found that Chinese Americans evidenced their preoccupation with ethnic authenticity through their usage of expressions such as 'not being very Chinese' or 'being too Chinesy' (Louie 2002: 328) in their descriptions of one another. In addition to White discourses about 'the other' and the racialization of Asians as foreign, both 'diasporic' and 'native' Asians can be complicitous in propagating essentialist discourses about Asianness – even when they may be aware that these are typically reductive and essentialist formulations.

'Multigeneration' Asian Americans and new Asian immigrants

Mia Tuan's (1998) study of third-, fourth- and fifth-generation ('multigeneration') Chinese and Japanese Americans in the USA provides very interesting documentation of some of the tensions which can arise between multigeneration Asians who have been born and raised in the USA and newly arrived Asian immigrants, with whom multigeneration Asians often have little in common.

In fact, the broad pan-ethnic group known as 'Asian Americans' comprises a very wide diversity of Asian-origin people, of varying settlement histories and class backgrounds, and coming from a multitude of different nations. This is important to note in the contemporary USA because various arguments about the quasi-White status of Asian Americans have gained prominence in recent years (see Hacker 1997; Gans 1999 – but see Song 2001). The discourse of Asian Americans as 'honorary Whites' tends to characterize them as an undifferentiated mass, who increasingly share the privileges, status, and even values, of many White Americans.[2] But, as discussed here, it is problematic to lump together all Asian Americans, given their great diversity.

In her study, Mia Tuan found that although many multigeneration Asian Americans had adopted largely Americanized lifestyles, they still tended to be seen as foreign immigrants by many members of the White majority. Many White Americans expected these Asian Americans to be ethnically authentic, as demonstrated by certain markers of ethnicity, such as the knowledge of an Asian language or the consumption of Asian foods. As a result, in addition to resenting White people who made such assumptions about them, some multigeneration Asian Americans wanted to distinguish themselves from newly arrived Asian immigrants, who were regarded as being unfamiliar with American practices, language and lifestyle. These newly arrived immigrants were seen to stigmatize the status of third- or fourth-generation Asian Americans as bona-fide Americans by behaving in ways which were considered to be '... clannish, selfish, rude, aggressive, unwilling to assimilate, nerdy, and overachieving' (Tuan 1998: 148).

As illustrated in the quote below, some Asian Americans themselves may exhibit nativist hostility toward new Asian immigrants:

'I thought I would never say this. But these new immigrants are ruining things for us,' Jim Yamada, a third-generation Japanese American, said in disgust. 'Asian Americans fought for decades against discrimination and racial prejudice. We want to be treated just like everybody else, like Americans. You see, I get real angry when people come up to me and tell me how good my English is. They say, "Oh, you have no accent. Where did you learn English?" Where did I learn English? Right here in America. I was born here like they were. We really hated it when people assumed that just because Asian Americans looked different we were foreigners. It took us a long time to get people to see this point, to be sensitized to it. Now the new immigrants are setting us back. People see me now and they automatically treat me as an immigrant. I really hate that. The worst thing is that these immigrants don't understand why I am angry.' (quoted in Cheng & Yang 1996: 305)

Although he is by no means representative of most Asian Americans, established Asian Americans like Jim Yamada are frustrated by many new immigrants' lack of understanding or even concern with the racial dynamics in the wider society. Long-settled Asian Americans' distancing of themselves from new Asian immigrants may be an attempt to shield themselves from the racial abuse and taunting which is aimed at Asian immigrants who are characterized as foreign and speaking little English. Such efforts to disidentify from new immigrants can also be interpreted as an attempt to retain what social standing and prestige they may accrue as Asian Americans who were born and raised in the USA.

More established Asians' affiliations and relationships to the wider society are likely to differ considerably from those of new Asian immigrants, and new immigrants may understand their disadvantaged or marginal status quite differently from their Asian American co-ethnics. According to Jeremy Hein (1994: 285): 'Where a "native minority" can attribute inequality to a racial and ethnic hierarchy, a "foreign minority" may attribute inequality to their status as newcomers adjusting to life in a host society.' A migrant orientation perceives prejudices to be unintentional and to be the result of natives' ethnocentrism, rather than outright racism.

Such differences in perceptions arise, in part, because newly arrived immigrants and native-born minorities tend to encounter different kinds of concerns in their everyday lives. Generally speaking, recent immigrants are likely to view problems of a rather practical nature – such as finding housing and jobs, learning English, saving money (or sending it back to relatives) – as more pressing than the racial discrimination they may encounter in the wider society (Lopez and Espiritu 1990: 206; Feagin 2000). For instance, the experiences and needs of refugees from Vietnam, Cambodia, or Laos, who started arriving in 1975, when the American involvement in the Vietnam War ended, differed, not surprisingly, from those of third-generation Japanese Americans who were born and raised in California, and who, by comparison, were largely 'Americanized'.[3]

In effect, recent immigrants, particularly if they have come from poor countries, such as Laos, are willing to endure some racism and marginalization as the cost of being an immigrant. These different understandings of racial marginalization and discrimination, in turn, affect new Asian immigrants' senses of ethnic identity, including their perception of whether a broad Asian American identity makes sense, or means anything to them. Given all these potential differences, whether in terms of length of settlement or the ethnic diversity contained within the rubric 'Asian American', the term 'Asian American' holds no automatic resonance for many of the people officially included in this category.

While some second- and third-generation Asian Americans may feel a kinship with newly arrived Asian immigrants, tensions can arise in relation to Asian Americans' histories of settlement. Multigeneration Asians are highly aware of and reject essentialist discourses about the foreignness and cultural distinctiveness of all Asian Americans. A key concern for many multigeneration Asian Americans is to gain acceptance as 'real' Americans. Their sensitivity to racist depictions of all Asian Americans as 'fresh off the boat' may consciously or subconsciously lead multi-generation Asians to differentiate themselves from recently arrived Asian immigrants, and, however unwittingly, to reproduce discourses of Asianness which rely on crude and static markers of Asian ethnicity. The imposition of homogenizing discourses of ethnic authenticity by the wider society – involving the characterization of all Asians as pidgin-speaking foreigners – fosters social divisions between multigeneration Asians and recent Asian immigrants.

'Return-migration' to Japan

Up to now, most studies of diaspora have shown that it is usually immigrant parents who sustain a 'myth of return' to their homeland, whether it be Pakistan (Anwar 1979) or Korea (Min 1998), rather than their children or their grandchildren. However, it appears that, even several generations removed, disparate articulations of a 'myth of return' can appear and motivate people to investigate an ancestral homeland (see Ang 1994; Gardner & Shukur 1994; Parker 1998; Louie 2002). In the case of second-, third- or even fifth-generation individuals, an awareness of global diasporas and transnational communities can influence and generate interest in their ethnic ancestry and some real or imagined 'homeland'.

Japanese Peruvians are largely acculturated in Peru, after a century there. Most speak only Spanish and are Catholic. Yet their status as ethnic minorities and their racialization as Japanese has resulted in their feeling more Japanese, rather than Peruvian. This is borne out by their high rates of endogamy and their propensity to maintain ties with ethnic Japanese associations in Peru.

Migrants use their transnational ties as a strategy to maximize their opportunities. Ayumi Takenaka (1999) documents the experiences of Peruvians of Japanese descent. Over 20,000 Japanese people initially migrated from Japan to Peru from 1899 to the 1930s. Almost a century later, the descendants of these migrants began to migrate from Peru to Japan to work mostly as factory workers. This 'return-migration' to Japan has been comprised of predominantly third-generation Peruvians of Japanese descent (aged 20–35). In the early 1990s, the Japanese government needed contract labourers and allowed Peruvians with Japanese ancestry (going back up to three generations) to work in Japan on a temporary basis. The preferential treatment of Japanese Peruvians as contract workers was based upon an essentialist assumption that, because of their Japanese heritage, such workers would be relatively easily assimilated into Japanese society.

Japanese Peruvians invoke their Japanese ancestry as a strategic resource in order to migrate to a country with a much stronger and stable economy. Their motivation to go to Japan stems from not only their marginal status in Peru and their desire for greater social and economic mobility, but also their ethnic attachments to Japan, as an ancestral homeland – even though they have never been to Japan, nor speak the Japanese language.

This 'return-migration' to Japan has not been easy for them. Upon arrival in Japan, these Peruvians of Japanese descent (typically third-generation young Japanese Peruvians) find that they are not treated as Japanese people, but rather, as foreigners and as an undesirable ethnic minority group who are treated as 'more Peruvian' than Japanese – despite having a 'Japanese face and name' (Takenaka 1999). The fact that many Japanese Peruvians do not speak Japanese, and the fact that they engage in forms of contract labour, have also hindered their ability to mix with the wider Japanese population.

As a result of their marginal status in both Japan and Peru, some of these Japanese Peruvians aspire to move to the USA – a place which they perceive to be more open to them. In the course of their migration to Japan, and subsequently, to the USA, they have forged transnational ethnic ties spanning Peru, Japan, and the USA. Most significantly, Takenaka found that Japanese Peruvians create their own ethnic identity as 'Nikkei' – thus distinguishing themselves from both Peruvians in Peru and Japanese in Japan.

These Japanese Peruvians went to Japan with positive expectations instilled in them by their grandparents in Peru (the initial immigrants to Peru), only to find that the Japan they encountered was 'cold', 'rigid', and 'too Westernized'. The dashing of expectations and the experiences of alienation then result in an 'ethnic denial' of being Japanese. Thus Japan ceases to be the reference point for the Nikkei community. Interestingly, these Nikkei distinguish themselves from Japanese people by saying that the Nikkei still maintain 'good, old Japanese traditional values' (such as the spirit of mutual help, respect for the elderly) which are seen as absent among the 'native' Japanese in contemporary Japan, but which are regarded as 'the fundamental essence of being Nikkei'! Ironically, direct interaction with the 'native' Japanese has resulted in the awareness of differences, rather than similarities, between Japanese Peruvians and 'native' Japanese. Nikkei values, as Japanese Peruvians describe them, which are articulated in terms of an authentic

Japaneseness which is now seen to be lost in Japan, belong exclusively to Japanese *descendants* (Takenaka 1999).

Ethnic ties in Korean transnational corporations

In a study of the workplace relations between Korean immigrant employees and their Korean national managers in Korean transnational corporations (TNCs) in the USA, Jo Kim (2004a,b) found that while globalization unites Koreans and Korean Americans and promotes solidarity between them, it also fosters a workplace environment where distinctions between the two groups can be sharply drawn.

Kim examines the complex roles of ethnicity and co-ethnic ties in the context of a global workplace – a Korean transnational corporation in the USA. In particular, Kim focuses on the workplace relationships between the national managers from Korea (the 'jujaewon' – JJWs) and their US-based Korean American employees. Korean TNCs in the USA are subsidiaries, and their headquarters in Korea monitor them regularly through their Korean managers, who are dispatched every three to five years. Because many of the JJWs possess limited English-language skills and lack familiarity with American social and cultural norms, these TNCs recruit Korean Americans (of differing settlement histories) who are bilingual and university-educated.

As in the case of the Japanese Peruvians, Korean American employees are recruited by Korean TNCs partly because of the assumption that they share some degree of cultural affinity with the Korean managers. However, the workplace actually differentiates the two groups, and this differentiation exacerbates the tensions between Korean American employees and Korean managers from Korea.

Kim finds that understandings of ethnicity (and perceptions of Korean American employees as either more 'Korean' or 'American') become the basis for the rationalization of biased work practices. Employees in the TNC which Kim studied were differentiated in terms of their degree of assimilation or history of settlement in the USA: for instance, 'the first generation', the '1.5 generation', and the 'second generation' were each associated with particular degrees of 'Korean-ness' or 'American-ness'. The JJWs assumed that first- and 1.5-generation Korean Americans were more like themselves socially and culturally than second-generation Koreans.

The Korean managers expected their 'more Korean' colleagues to work longer hours and to carry out special personal favours for them – as is commonly done by work subordinates for their bosses in Korea. By comparison, the Korean managers were loath to ask the 'Americanized' second-generation Korean Americans (or White Americans) to do such extra work – citing their different cultural and social sensibility and norms. Thus the stereotypes that JJWs held about their 'more Korean' and 'more American' colleagues tended to generate expectations about their loyalty and work ethic. Indeed, the degree of assimilation into American society was given more validation for employee behaviour than were other explanations concerning individual attributes and abilities.

On the one hand, the Korean managers were critical of the 'more American' Korean American colleagues for being lazy and not being as committed to their jobs, and they appreciated the perceived loyalty and commitment of their 'more Korean' employees. On the other hand, because they could relate to their 'more Korean' colleagues, they expected more of them, and they took these colleagues' hard work more for granted. Thus the 'more Korean' employees were disadvantaged by the obligations which accompanied perceptions of ethnic solidarity and similarity in a workplace in which Korean-ness was articulated in varying ways and degrees. Again, the Korean managers sent from Korea operate in such a way as to reveal their preoccupation with ethnic authenticity: Korean-ness and American-ness, and the seemingly disparate markers for each. The global TNC, which has thrown together 'native' and diasporic Koreans, illustrates the variable and in some cases inequitable status and treatment of the transnational workforce.

Conclusion: the specifics of global and local intersections

According to some key authors, the so-called interstitial spaces between cultures, which are inhabited by diasporas, migrants, refugees, and exiles, can be empowering locations in which boundaries and essentialised ethnic and racial identities can be challenged (see Bhabha 1994; Pieterse 1994).[4] The celebration of these interstitial spaces is problematic because they tend to obscure the ways in which the material specificities of both geographical location and the racialized body mediate one's ability to negotiate one's belonging and status in a given society. Place, class, sex, 'race', and nationality all intertwine in complex ways in constraining the opportunities available to diasporic individuals (see Knowles, Chapter 5, this volume).

True, globalization and diasporas have resulted in a proliferation of culturally hybrid Asian identities, but not all hybridized subjects occupy the same social and political space. In this way, the key idea – that with globalization comes the relativization of identities – is overstated, in that it tends to overlook the very real consequences of racialization, and the differential embodiment and status associated with different kinds of Asianness.

The diverse embodiments and meanings of Asianness discussed above threaten the legitimacy of the term 'Asian', at least in any meaningful sense. Discourses of Asian authenticity, as articulated by diasporic Asians, the societies in which they live, and 'native' Asians, encourage forms of social differentiation, which result in the emergence of new ethnic boundaries and new ethnic identities. While their diasporic status can accrue benefits, such Asians can find themselves in situations in which they are subject to expectations that they be authentically 'Asian' by the wider societies in which they live, as well as being regarded as inauthentically Asian by their co-ethnics residing in Asian societies. These sorts of expectations of one another go far beyond issues of identity, and can impact upon a wide array of economic and social opportunities.

In many settings, awareness of generational 'remove' (from the 'homeland') is significant in the ways in which 'native' and diasporic Asians assess one another – for example in Japan, being of Japanese parentage was not sufficient to make 'native' Japanese people see the Nikkei as 'really' Japanese. In Mia Tuan's study, third- or fourth-generation Chinese and Japanese Americans were highly aware of how different they were from newly arrived Asian immigrants.

While ethno/national distinctions are not irrelevant for diasporic Asians, they are much more likely to recognize and forge an Asian panethnic identity and ties, on the basis of being second-, third- or fourth-generation Asians, rather than claim an affinity with a co-ethnic who is either a newly arrived immigrant or 'native' of their ancestral 'homeland'. In the United States, ethnic distinctions among third- and fourth-generation Asian Americans of Chinese and Japanese heritage may be diminishing, in favor of a more generalized Asian American culture and forms of panethnic association (Tuan 1998: 166).

In the global context, what is interesting is that these many different kinds of interactions between 'native' and 'diasporic' Asians will become increasingly complex, with the identification of finely graded categories of people. With the settlement of people like the Nikkei, who are Peruvians of Japanese descent (but who have again resettled in places like Canada and the USA), diasporic peoples are generating new terms of belonging and group membership. In future, even myths of return may not easily or straightforwardly hark back to one specific 'homeland'. Perhaps the trajectory of 'twice migrants' or multiple migrations will become more common.

All of the studies we have discussed above can lead us to question any easy assumptions about the nature and durability of what we call ethnic ties or the benefits which accrue from ethnic ties. While an ethnic connection to an Asian homeland may provide an entrée of sorts, this ethnic tie can also involve liabilities as well as opportunities – demonstrated in the studies of Korean TNCs and 'return-migration' to Japan.

Will ties and affiliations to Asia remain important in the future for multigeneration diasporic Asian peoples? Will processes of racialization in predominantly White Western societies mean that Asian origin people will be unable to 'shake' expectations that they be authentically Asian by prevailing societal norms? There is a dialectic to the processes concerning globalization, transnationalism, and diaspora. While there is significant and undeniable evidence of new hybrid forms emerging, what often seems to underlie their formation is an engagement (whether forced or voluntary) with concerns and debates about ethnic authenticity and essentialist understandings of 'difference', culture, and 'origin'.

In sum, the contested negotiations of what it means to be Asian, and the identification of many different kinds of Asians (both by the wider society and by Asians themselves) reflect the power struggles and inequalities underlying assertions of ethnic identity and 'difference'. Because much of the theorizing on globalization is too celebratory in its emphasis on the emancipating possibilities of diasporic, interstitial subjectivities, it is necessary to consider the material locations and positions of specific subgroups in explorations of what it means to be Asian.

The meanings and symbolic markers of Asianness will continue to fluctuate and be renegotiated by both 'native' Asians and the increasingly complex array of diasporic Asians. Given the tremendous diversity of diasporic trajectories, even in relation to one originating 'homeland', differences in the class backgrounds and histories of settlement abroad are likely to enhance and propagate discourses and beliefs about the significance and manifestations of ethnic authenticity.

Notes

1. The 'place' of South Asians in 'Asian American' is ambiguous – they are certainly on the margins, but if so, they are a privileged group (Prashad 2000). Conversely, in Britain, the term 'Asian' refers predominantly to people of South Asian, not East Asian, heritage.
2. There appear to be two main bases for such an argument: First, Asian Americans as a whole constitute a relatively privileged group in terms of socioeconomic indicators (Song 2001). Second, there are substantial numbers of Asian Americans, especially women, who are partnering with White Americans.
3. Even among immigrants from Southeast Asia, there were two waves of immigration: while the first wave, from 1975 to 1980 was comprised primarily of

South Vietnam's elites, the second wave included the 'boat people' who had escaped from concentration camps and great economic hardship (Cheng & Yang 1996).

4. In a typically brilliant observation, Stuart Hall (1991) notes that, 'Paradoxically, in this world, marginality has become a powerful space. It is a space of weak power but it is a space of power, nonetheless' (34).

Chapter 4

Comparing New Migration with Old: Exploring the Issue of Asylum and Settlement

KATE REED

There has been a significant amount of interest in the issue of asylum in Britain over recent years within public, social and political and academic realms. As the number of asylum seekers reaching British shores over the last 20 years has increased questions have been raised as to which migrants should and shouldn't be allowed to stay. The current influx of asylum seekers has also prompted a renewed interest in immigration in the academic realm and a 'moral panic' exacerbated by the media. According to Cohen (1972), certain groups have periodically been the focus of moral panics. They are labelled as being outside the core values of society and as a result pose a threat to these. The groups investigated by Cohen were the Mods and Rockers – today, asylum seekers can be seen as their modern-day equivalent. Asylum seekers are depicted as state scroungers and characterised as 'new' and troublesome migrants. According to Karpf (2002), the tabloid press uses the language of "invasion" to talk about the current influx of migrants, as if they are the enemy. Such language of panic has occurred many times before regarding previous migrant groups to Britain. As Karpf (2002) and others have pointed out, asylum is not a new phenomenon. Despite attempts by the media to separate asylum from previous flows of migration to the UK, as authors such as Schuster and Solomos (2004) and Sivanandan (2001) have pointed out, we can see clear parallels with previous treatments of migrant groups throughout the 20th century.

While there has often been a tendency within the media to see asylum as a 'new' phenomenon, there has been a failure within some of the most important academic research on asylum to fully connect the settlement experiences of asylum seekers in Britain with those of other settled ethnic minority groups (for example Pirouet 2001). This is because much academic writing and research focuses on the process of migration and the sociolegal implications of this, failing to look at what actually happens to people once they have been in the UK for several years as many asylum seekers have been. While some issues such as citizenship have been explored comparatively, other points of comparison have been ignored. Research has neglected to explore asylum fully within the context of concerns with race and ethnicity, ignoring issues of belonging, generation and identity among asylum seekers. As Castles (2000) argues, over time new migrants settle and live their lives within the context of the 'host' society. They feel the same contradictions and conflicts as earlier, more settled, migrant groups. This has often eluded debates on asylum. Furthermore, asylum seekers have come to be seen as a homogenous group and such homogeneity often exacerbates their 'otherness' from other ethnic minorities within the UK. The diversity among them is ignored and any *difference* that is recognised is between them and other ethnic minority groups. This failure to recognise difference within the category of asylum means that we underestimate the experiences and needs of particular groups. Asylum seekers have different needs and experiences depending on where they have come from, and how they were persecuted in their country of origin. This should be acknowledged if we are to develop research and policy which is sensitive to their needs.

The aim of this chapter is to highlight comparisons between the process and experience of asylum and the past migration and experience of existing ethnic minorities within the UK. In doing so, the chapter aims to show firstly that asylum is not a novel phenomenon and bears many similarities to past experiences of migration and settlement, and secondly that by drawing on the experience of existing ethnic minorities in the UK, our understanding of the experience of asylum can be enhanced.

The chapter will explore these issues in three sections. The first will focus on exploring correlations in patterns of migration, paying particular attention to the treatment of migrants both 'old' and 'new' by governments in the UK. In particular I will focus on the political semantics of economics and culture that operate to vilify and exclude today's asylum seekers in similar ways to the old racisms of colonialism and other historical periods. In doing so, I will highlight the ways in which the treatment of asylum is not something new but has many similarities with previous patterns of migration to the UK. Secondly, I will draw on empirical work to explore similarities in experiences of settlement between asylum seekers and other settled ethnic minority groups. Such comparisons move our attention away from short-term settlement issues, which tend to dominate the asylum literature and enable us to prepare and recognise the importance of long-term settlement strategies for asylum seekers. Thirdly, drawing on past debates about diversity among Britain's existing ethnic minorities, I want to emphasise the diversity of the category 'asylum seeker' itself. Asylum seekers are often presented as homogenous. As a homogenous group they are then cast as different from other minority ethnic groups and consequently become 'othered'. Again drawing on earlier debates in ethnic and racial studies (Reed 2000), I want to argue that we must recognise that these are highly diverse groups who cannot be lumped together in what Goldberg (1993) calls an 'ethnic reductionist' approach.

The chapter will conclude by exploring why it is so important to make these connections between past experiences of migration and settlement. The case for a comparative approach will be made on a number of grounds. Firstly, it will be argued that the recognition that asylum is not a novel phenomenon may help to challenge some of the myths of 'invasion' surrounding the media hype on new migrants. Secondly, it will be argued that we can learn from the past experiences of migrants in order to build more sensitive and diverse research and policy frameworks on asylum. Finally, such an approach enables us to develop debates about racial categorisation. Bulmer and Solomos (1999) argue that almost everyone is talking about the role of ethnic and racial categorisation in the construction of social and political identities. However, according to them, it is paradoxically the case that there is still much confusion about what it is that we mean by key terms and concepts like 'race' and 'racism'. Exploring the issue of asylum in terms of existing forms of racial categorisation challenges and develops our understanding of the social and political constructs of race and ethnicity.

Migration, past and present

Britain has a long and varied history of migration. Since World War Two and until recently, immigrants from the former colonies have dominated immigration in the UK. In particular during the 1950s, immigrants came primarily from the Caribbean and India. Immigration during the 1960s and 1970s was mostly made up of people from India, Pakistan and Asians who were expelled from East Africa (Alexander *et al.* 2004). In recent years asylum seekers and refugees have entered Britain from regions such as Eastern Europe, Africa and the Middle East. In the standard typologies of migrant groups, asylum seekers are people who move across borders in search of protection but who may not fulfil the strict criteria laid down by the 1951 United Nations Convention (Castles 2000: 563). The criteria relate to those residing outside of their country of nationality and who are unwilling or unable to return because of a well-founded fear of persecution on account of race, religion, nationality, membership of a particular social group, or political opinion. According to recent national statistics on immigration, there were 8,605 applications for asylum in the UK in the third quarter of 2004 (July to September). The top five nationalities applying for asylum were Iranian, Chinese, Somali, Zimbabwean and Iraqi (National Statistics Online 2004).

Much of the recent media interest on asylum presents it as a new phenomenon, a type of migration that has never occurred previously, which is restricted to the late twentieth and early twenty-first century. Koser and Lutz (1998) in their book *The New Migration in Europe* discuss the ways in which migration since 1989, including asylum, is conceived of as new. They claim it is seen as new in the sense that there are now more people seeking asylum due to the increase in ethnically motivated wars. They also argue that it is often seen as new in the sense that current flows of migration are much bigger than previous ones. Other aspects of newness that they highlight relate to new migrant locations, new types of migration (intensified short-term movements for example) and new migrant profiles (for example increased clandestine migrants and asylum seekers). Moreover, the nature of current hostility to asylum seekers in the media is clearly unprecedented in its intensity (Kushner 2003). This also marks out asylum as a somewhat novel phenomenon, despite the efforts of historians like Kushner who trace it back into the nineteenth century.

However, despite the recognition of new aspects of current asylum-types of immigration, there are many correlations with the past. Certainly the current treatment of asylum seekers by the UK government, emphasising the management of immigration, resonates with past treatments of other migrants. Authors like Bloch (2000) and Solomos and Schuster (2004) have highlighted the ways in which government treatment of asylum seekers in the UK is nothing new. According to Schuster and Solomos (2004: 267) for example, when looking at the development of New Labour's policy agendas on race and immigration in Britain, there are correlations between present and previous policies from Labour and Conservative governments. They argue that there have been shifts in policies on race and migration under New Labour, from multiculturalism to social cohesion. They also note a movement towards the promotion of selected migration and tightening of attitudes towards asylum seekers. These shifts, however, are nothing new but rather remain consistent with a belief shared throughout the postwar period, and across the political spectrum, that social cohesion and harmony depend on limiting and controlling the migration of certain groups into Britain. According to Bloch (2000), the justification put forward by Conservative and Labour governments for the curtailment of social welfare benefits has been to deter 'bogus' asylum seekers who abuse what is perceived to be a generous welfare system.

Asylum seekers are excluded and expelled from British society. This results from being located at the crossroads between two different political semantics: those based on economic issues on the one hand, and those based on culture, identity and tradition on the other (Ray and Reed 2005: 222). On the one hand, cost is used to rationalise stricter border controls. On the other hand asylum is placed as a threat to British national culture. In this sense immigration controls become matters of national security that we need to defend (ibid.: 223). This process of exclusion through economics and culture however is not a novel phenomenon or specific to asylum. As Sivanandan (2001) shows, we can see this process occurring through countless waves of migration. Whether it is economics or culture that holds sway in a particular epoch depends on the economic system of that epoch. Thus according to him, in the period of primitive accumulation, it was the religion of the Catholic Church that gave validity to the claim that the native Indians were inferior and born to be slaves and exterminated at random. With the development of industrial capitalism and colonialism, the racialist ideas of the previous epochs were synthesised into a racist ideology to condemn all coloured peoples to racial and cultural inferiority (Sivanandan 2001: 1). In contemporary society, global capitalism with its continual pursuit of profit has fostered ethnic wars and displaced people. In contemporary society, the tradition of demonisation and exclusion of the 'other' through economics and culture has become a tool in the hands of the state to keep out the refugees and asylum seekers on the grounds that they are aliens and scroungers come to prey on the West and threaten its national identities (Sivanandan 2001: 2).

Thus according to Sivanandan (2001: 2) historically blacks were demonised to justify slavery, then 'coloureds' were demonised to justify colonialism. In contemporary society, asylum seekers are demonised to justify the unequal process of globalization. In this sense asylum seekers are, in different ways, an epitome of mobile modernity onto which anxieties about cultural subversion and 'invasion' are projected (Ray and Reed 2005: 230). The exclusion of asylum seekers in the UK today is not so different from that of previous migrant groups. The only difference between the past and present treatment of asylum seekers is that their exclusion is no longer colour-coded (Sivanandan 2001).

Overall, rather than seeing asylum as a 'new' phenomenon, we can see that it resonates with past migration and must not be treated as a separate phenomenon. Discourses on the perceived 'newness' of asylum form part of what Foucault (1972) calls the 'regime of truth' in a particular society. Regimes of truth, routinely elaborated in the media, establish what may be known and how. These regimes of truth are overthrown by other new and powerful discourses over time. Asylum discourses will in time disappear and be replaced by new panics about a different wave of immigrants. However, as shown within this section of the chapter, these regimes of truth operating in the context of asylum have operated in similar ways to the past treatments of immigrants.

The experience of asylum and settlement

In this section of the chapter I want to move on from the comparative experiences of migration to explore experiences of settlement of new immigrants and compare these with the experience of existing ethnic minorities. Again, in the emphasis on the 'newness' of asylum in the media and academic research, there is a failure to link experiences of asylum seekers with those of existing ethnic minorities. Academic research regarding issues of settlement is often split between those working on issues relating to existing ethnic minorities[1] and those working in the area of asylum. This separation is unhelpful as insights could be gained on the current experience of asylum seekers from experiences of ethnic minorities who migrated previously and settled. This oversight in research is often a result of the failure to connect debates on asylum with broader issues associated with long-term settlement, more specifically neglecting to tie debates on asylum with those on race, ethnicity and identity. While there are obvious differences between those recently migrated and settled groups, there are also marked similarities, which again reinforces the argument that asylum is not a new phenomenon.

This section of the chapter will draw upon the findings of a research project conducted by Larry Ray, at the University of Kent, and myself. The project focused on exploring the experiences and needs of a sample of ethnic minority groups in East Kent, UK, in relation to their experience of harassment, policing, community safety and structural needs for support, housing and advice (Ray and Reed 2005: 217). The research was based on a series of group and individual interviews with several ethnically diverse groups of respondents during 2001 and 2002. The study included respondents from ethnic minority groups and also asylum seekers. Within the research we interviewed a group of men and women Romany who had lived in East Kent all their lives. We also interviewed a group of men and women Czech Roma asylum seekers who had left the Czech Republic due to racial persecution and had lived in East Kent for three years but were still waiting to find out if they would obtain leave to remain. The study included a group of South Asian Muslim men, who identified first and foremost as Muslim, and who either studied or worked at the University. We also interviewed a group of Muslim women. We interviewed two groups of Chinese respondents; the first group were first-generation migrants who worked mostly within the Chinese restaurant or takeaway business. The second group included those who were British-born and who were students at the University. Both of the Chinese groups were made up equally of men and women. Both the Muslim and Chinese respondents were relative newcomers to the area (Ray and Reed 2005: 217).

The asylum seekers within our study had all been living in Britain for at least three years. They were, however, still waiting to find out whether they would be granted exceptional leave to remain so they were still living in the country illegally. These asylum seekers were obviously leading very transient lives and the fact that they didn't know whether or not they could stay meant that they were fearful of putting down roots. In fact, one of the male respondents, Maracek, said that if he didn't find out whether he could stay soon, he would actually try and move his family again, this time to Canada as he felt they would have more chance of being granted leave to remain there. He was tired of waiting around in the UK living illegally. However, while the asylum seekers in the study were obviously living somewhat dislocated lives they also had to settle to some extent and put down roots in the local area. Their children went to school and learnt English and mixed with a wide variety of other children. In fact, Maracek's son was deaf and much effort was made both by the family and asylum aid groups in the area to find him a place in a school that included children with hearing impairments. The asylum seekers within the study made friends with non-asylum seekers who were members of the broader regional community. They also made friends with people from other non-white ethnic groups. Within our study asylum seekers got involved in local cultural events, teaching the wider population of the area about their culture. In particular, the respondents in our study played traditional gypsy music at various events in order to publicise both their culture and position as asylum seekers.

When we look at these issues of settlement and the experience of living lives day to day in the UK, we can see that the experiences of asylum seekers are similar to those of existing migrant groups. These are perhaps most obviously recognised when we think about issues such as low (or no) incomes, experiences of racism, poor housing and so on. The asylum seekers in our study couldn't work because of their asylum status and so barely had money to live on. They were living in poor accommodation, although this had improved for two of the asylum seekers in the study as they had been moved from an overcrowded flat to a small house. The asylum seekers in our study said that they had suffered some racial abuse from the local white population. The abuse that they identified was verbal involving mostly name calling (Ray and Reed 2005).

The asylum seekers in the study also often had difficulties making themselves understood both within the local community and with the authorities because of language barriers.

Within the study, these experiences were not so different from those of the existing ethnic minority groups interviewed. For example, linguistic barriers were identified as a key problem for asylum seekers on moving to the UK; similarly this was a key problem identified by some of our Hong Kong Chinese respondents who had lived in the UK for a long time. Also, within the study with regard to sense of community, the Muslim South Asian respondents and Canterbury gypsies who had both lived in Kent for some years all had a globalised sense of community. They had crossnational and transnational ties rather than a local sense of community. This was the same as the asylum seekers who had recently arrived in East Kent. Furthermore, the groups within the study apart from asylum seekers experienced similar experiences of racism; particularly in the form of verbal abuse such as was the case for the Chinese respondents. In fact those who suffered most significantly from racial abuse were another 'white' group, the Canterbury gypsies who suffered racist abuse both on an individual level and institutionally.

These comparisons have yet to be fully explored within the asylum literature. Within asylum literature much work has focused on exploring policy issues relating to the immigration process (Bloch 2000), or on the ways in which states develop policies in order to prevent long-term settlement (Hassan 2000). Research is only just starting to focus on postmigration issues relating to asylum seekers (for example Ager et al. 2002). Settlement issues relating to the experiences of existing ethnic minorities have long been explored in research. For example, research has been conducted extensively in the area of racism (for example Solomos 1988; Solomos and Back 1996), on issues of housing and income (Modood et al. 1997; Pilkington 2003) and on issues such as health (for example Nazroo 2003; Reed 2003). While a few studies are starting to take a comparative approach, (for example, Alexander et al. (2004) highlighted the language needs of both existing ethnic minorities and asylum seekers in a recent study on interpreters) mostly studies on asylum seekers fail to note similarities between their circumstances and those of settled ethnic minorities.

Additionally, certain areas explored within the context of ethnic minorities have remained completely unexplored within the context of asylum. Migration creates transnational communities in which people maintain extended networks over long distances across the globe and with these form 'hybrid' identities and senses of belonging (Ray and Reed 2005). One example of this is the emergence of 'hyphenated' identities such as 'British-Asian' and 'African-American', which express not so much a dual sense of identity as new forms of combined identity. There have been many explorations around these issues of identity among existing ethnic minority groups (for example Parker 1995; Reed 2003). However, they seem to have been neglected in the context of asylum. The experience of migration, especially forced migration that produces asylum seeking, is one of the key issues for the early twenty-first century created by globalism and intersecting identities of ethnicity, religion and migrant status (Ray and Reed 2005: 214). Such a fluid and global sense of identity should be explored in the context of asylum seekers, some of whom have been in the UK since the 1980s and have begun to create multiple forms of identity.

Diversity in the context of asylum

So far then, I have explored the ways in which asylum cannot be seen as a new phenomenon but has many correlations to past patterns of migration and experiences of settlement. In doing so, I have highlighted the importance of connecting asylum with past patterns of migration and experiences of existing ethnic minority communities in the UK. I now want to argue that it is also important to recognise that the category of asylum seeker itself is a heterogeneous one. In East Kent alone there is a vast array of asylum seekers ranging from Czech Roma to Turkish Kurds who are grouped together as being the same 'types' of people with the same experiences and needs. Again in exploring issues of diversity among asylum seekers I will be drawing on past theoretical debates and experiences of existing ethnic minority groups in the UK.

Research on asylum often tends to falsely categorise asylum seekers as a coherent group. However, the experiences of asylum seekers are actually incredibly diverse, in terms of ethnic, geographical and cultural backgrounds. Their experiences of persecution and their reasons for seeking asylum are equally diverse. Again this highlights the separation of discourses on asylum from those on settled ethnic minority groups, as debates on diversity and *difference* have been running in the humanities and social sciences since the 1970s. Postmodernism with its critique of universalism and emphasis on deconstruction fosters the importance of relativity and difference. According to authors such as Skeggs (1997), with postmodernism, the concept of difference has come to stand in for inequality. In terms of race and ethnicity, this emphasis on difference has led to a shift away from essentialist notions of race to a deconstruction of ethnic and racial categories.

This moves us beyond what Goldberg (1993) calls an ethnically reductive approach in which all minority ethnic groups are lumped together and viewed as the same. It can also, according to Alexander (2000a), lead to the fragmentation and 'othering' of ethnic minority groups. Minority ethnic groups are also separated according to ethnicity and labelled as different. In particular Allen (1994) argues that a persistent stress on difference may lead to marginalizing those that do not fit into any particular category, for example people of mixed race. Furthermore, according to Alexander and Alleyne (2002: 544), the fetishism of both 'culture' and 'difference' has proved inadequate for conceptualising or challenging the resurgence of racist movements and ideologies.

Despite problems with the theoretical concept of *difference* it can be used to recognise diversity in the context of ethnicity and asylum. Asylum seekers in the UK form an extremely heterogeneous grouping originating from a diverse range of geographical locations. In the UK they range from Tamils, Turkish Kurds and Somalis to Kosovar Albanians and Czech Roma and so on. As such their cultures, experiences of racism and settlement needs are multifaceted and variable as are their reasons for migrating to the UK. Such diversity is highlighted in a recent study conducted for the Home Office by Robinson and Segrott (2002). In their study which included a range of interviews with 65 asylum seekers from varying contexts, they found that there were differing reasons among asylum seekers for seeking asylum in the UK; while some from ex-colonies may come to the UK on the basis of colonial links, others came to the UK simply because they saw it is a non-war zone. The authors thus saw asylum seekers as agents each adopting differing strategies and each with different goals. This recognition of diversity in their work is underpinned by the realisation that the process and experience of asylum is rooted in individual biography. Within this section I will focus on highlighting three key issues relating to diversity among asylum seekers: gender differences, diversity in experience on coming to Britain, and ethnic diversity.

According to Mason (1995), when looking at ethnic and racial groups we need to be conscious that all social groups are gendered. The ways in which relations between men and women are constructed in social groups are central aspects of how ethnic identities are conceived and experienced. Therefore it is important to recognise diversity between women and men within social groups. As others have pointed out (Crawley 2001; Reed 2003), the experience of asylum is unequivocally gendered; with the experiences of male and female asylum seekers being far from identical. Organizations such as the Refugee Women's Resource Project (a project providing resources and research in the area) have outlined some of the specific problems faced by women seeking asylum. They have shown that women seeking asylum often face forms of persecution such as rape, sexual violence, forced sterilisation, genital mutilation and domestic violence in their countries of origin, from which they are unable to get state protection. They have also highlighted the ways in which women's experience of torture and violence are diminished by the Home Office which fails to listen to them (Ceneda 2003). As care givers within the family women face further isolation, often becoming situated in poor housing with little opportunity for education and work. In addition, women are also affected badly by recent changes in legislation affecting refugees, for example, by family dispersal and new support arrangements, which destroy whatever networks they have managed to generate. This highlights the need to recognise that asylum and refugee experiences are mediated through gender.

We must also recognise the diverse array of experiences among asylum seekers on migration to the UK. Research on asylum often portrays asylum seekers' experiences of the authorities or of racism as exactly the same. This claimed homogenous experience does not ring true if we look at evidence. Going back to our comparative research project on asylum seekers and settled ethnic minority experience in East Kent, a diversity of day-to-day experience is shown. While undoubtedly respondents within the study shared the common experience of seeking asylum and all aspired to gaining refugee status, their experiences in this process were also very varied. For one person living in East Kent housing had been the biggest problem. They had been situated in poor housing and felt isolated. Another person felt that housing facilities had been very good and language barriers were what caused them the most anxiety. Within the study, respondents also had different experiences of racism. Some of the respondents experienced verbal racism from their immediate white English neighbours. However, others felt that English society was actually very racially tolerant, particularly in comparison to their places of origin. The Romany asylum seekers in the project came from the Czech Republic and had had to leave their country due to extreme racism. Some talked about the ways in which in the Czech Republic people are mostly white and in contrast any gypsies are persecuted. They argued that in contrast in the UK there are a diverse range of people with a variety of nationalities and ethnicities and as a result they felt that people in the UK were much more tolerant. This, however, was far from a uniform experience among the respondents. Finally, asylum seekers vary in terms of racial categorisation. For example, there are asylum seekers from the former USSR that identify as white, asylum seekers from Sudan who identify as black and those such as Czech Roma who vary in their racial and ethnic identification.

Despite the diverse array of asylum seekers that arrive in the UK each month, explorations of this diversity, and what that means for existing forms of racial categorisation in academic debates, are ignored. Consequently many academic studies fail to paint a detailed enough picture of the experiences of asylum seekers and these, in turn, feed into broader public and policy representations. At the very least it is important to recognise that asylum seekers in their heterogeneity problematise our existing forms of racial categorisation in research. Many of the key studies on race and ethnicity in Britain concentrate on issues relating to being black, white or South Asian (for example Alexander 1996, 2000a; Back 2002). While such research often explores the role of ethnic and racial categorisation in the construction of social and political identities, few people have explored this in the context of asylum. They have neglected to focus on the way asylum challenges existing understandings of the social and political constructs of race and ethnicity. This is particularly true of those asylum seekers such as the Czech Roma who are viewed as 'not quite white' and thus do not fit neatly into existing forms of racial categorisation but rather, transcend them.[2] As Parker and Song (2001) write with regard to the issue of mixed-race people, it is important to recognise the insights offered by mixed-race people to the multi-faceted nature of identity. The rethinking of 'race' through mixed-race disrupts the certainty of a key social category, as Parker and Song point out. For them the very notion of 'mixed-race' confounds the ideal of pristine, pure 'races' with the undeniable historical truth of mixture, while simultaneously highlighting the inescapable fact of racialisation. We must also recognise the potential of asylum in its heterogeneity and blurring of racial identification to be able to do this too.

Conclusion

In this chapter I have focused on linking debates on asylum seekers in the UK with issues relating to other types of migrants past and present. In doing so I have highlighted the importance of recognising that asylum is not a new phenomenon but has many similarities to past experiences of migration. Furthermore, I have highlighted the connections between past experiences of migration and settlement. In this last section of the chapter I want to conclude by looking at why such comparisons should be made. Firstly, making such comparisons is beneficial at a public level. According to Robinson and Segrott (2002) much of the general debate about migration has focused on the economic value of labour migration to the UK, or on celebrating ethnic diversity and the achievements of past migrants. Relatively little has been said about the positive aspects of asylum, which continues to be cast by the government and media as a problem, burden and cost (ibid.: 64). If academic research on asylum focused on highlighting the ways in which asylum is similar to past migrations, emphasising the positives of the past this could perhaps filter into the public realm. By underscoring asylum with previous experiences of migration some of the media panic on asylum could be addressed. Of course as argued, there will always be panics about migrant groups and new entrants into the UK; furthermore, it would be difficult to challenge the media and public perception of asylum seekers as state scroungers. However, by recognising that these are not new panics, we can perhaps challenge some of the myths of 'invasion' surrounding the media hype on new migrants.

Secondly, comparing the experiences of asylum seekers with past experiences of migration and settlement is also important for developing research and policies in the context of the settlement of asylum seekers. In drawing on the past experiences of existing ethnic minority groups, we can prioritise what is important in the context of settlement. We can learn from their experiences to develop more directed and sensitive research and settlement policies that speak to the needs of asylum seekers. We must apply caution here in mapping experiences of existing ethnic minorities onto asylum seekers. We must highlight (as argued in this chapter) diversity of experience. However, exploring the experiences of past ethnic minorities may enable us to be more sensitive to the needs of asylum seekers.

Thirdly, comparing the experiences of asylum seekers and ethnic minorities is also beneficial at a conceptual level. A comparative approach offers a contribution to current theoretical debates that address the issue of ethnic and racial categorisation. As mentioned, many of the key studies on race and ethnicity in Britain concentrate on issues relating to being black, white or South Asian. The issue of asylum with the diversity of racial identification and categorisation and in particular the inclusion of those deemed as 'not quite white' (Neal 2002) serves to challenge our existing thinking about race. This relates in particular to gypsy asylum seekers who may be white but who are often racialized as non-white perhaps in similar ways to Irish travellers (Ray and Reed 2005). Comparisons of the process of categorisation between asylum seekers and ethnic minority groups and between colour-coded and not-so-colour-coded experiences of race and racism, serve to highlight a novel process of racialisation, one that needs to be furthered explored in the context of race and ethnicity.

Overall, the current experience of asylum seekers in Britain is one of various forms of social exclusion. They remain social outcasts through government policy and media panic. Popular opinion sees asylum seekers as a drain on society. Rather then capitalising on the skills of asylum seekers and celebrating the cultural diversity that they bring to the UK, they instead become scapegoats. As a nation we need to reflect on the current situation and relate it to a not-so-distant past. We need to look at our history of migration and focus on what immigrant groups can bring to the UK not just in terms of professional skills but also in terms of culture. Only through such a process of reflection can we appreciate the current experiences of asylum seekers and hopefully build more sensitive research and policy initiatives, which address their needs and recognise what they can add to the nation.

Notes

1. 'Ethnic minority' is widely understood in Britain to denote a category of people whose origins lie in countries of the new Commonwealth and Pakistan; in other words in former British colonies (Mason 2000: 15). The term often denotes homogeneity, however diversity must be recognised between and within these groups.
2. The same case could be made for UK Romany and Irish travellers who are also deemed to be not quite white (Ray and Reed 2005).

5

ng Whiteness: British Lifestyle Migrants in Hong Kong

CAROLINE KNOWLES[1]

(photographs by Douglas Harper)

This is about the production of whiteness: a modest contribution to race formation theory. Whiteness is about race *and* ethnicity;[2] things which have different conceptual uses and intellectual histories, but which nevertheless operate in tandem and in connection with other forms of social distinction. Race formation theory (Winant 1994) tells us that race is socially constructed, but rarely reveals *how* race is *made*. I want to conceptualize race in terms of the social mechanisms of its production. Race (and ethnicity) – in this case whiteness – is made by *bodies' social and spatial practices*.[3] Why whiteness? In geopolitical terms whiteness is insignificant. But if we are trying to understand the *power geometries*[4] of globalization and in the operation of racism – processes that structure the world in which we live – then whiteness needs closer analysis. I will argue that whiteness is *made* in the power geometries of globalization, specifically in the operation of global migration: made in the ways in which people operate, move through, and in the terms on which they occupy, and use *space*. This insistence on examining whiteness comes from critical white studies[5] where whiteness is named, marked and located as a tapestry of advantage, acknowledged as a badge of racial privilege and exclusion (Cohen 1997: 245–6), but its composition and production are not explained. Whiteness comes in many varieties. Which white people are we talking about? Where? White studies literature has often overlooked these specifics. Dyer (1998), for example, skilfully establishes the contours of an amalgam he calls 'white' and 'Western'. Others are really talking about America's industrial heartland (Roediger 1992, 1994) or East London, so we need to be clear about specifics and to note that race making is *always gendered* (see Noble's and Ali's chapters, 7 and 8, this volume).

In this chapter I will focus on the mechanisms making *white Britishness* in the context of some case studies based on my research in Hong Kong. In moving from 'white' to 'white British' there is a shift from race, to race and ethnicity as a specific conjunction of social relationships and processes. Whiteness can be studied more or less anywhere, but Hong Kong[6] is a particularly interesting place for many reasons. We'll just take two of them. It is, despite recently fluctuating circumstances, both a significant player in the global economic networks of the Pacific Rim (Skeldon 1997: 265), and it is also the most recently evacuated colonial space. The British are no more interesting than any other tribe of white folk, but they (we) are bound up with a forceful argument about the significance of empire in the making of whiteness in postcolonial literature (McClintock 1995; Dyer 1997; Rutherford 1997). As this argument forces us to review the status of the past in the making of the (racial and ethnic) present, it is worth thinking about the manufacture of white Britishness in a place like Hong Kong. If empire still matters, as postcolonial theorists[7] claim, then we should be able to detect it mattering in Hong Kong. I'll say a bit more about Hong Kong as a postcolonial landscape later. As migrants they have connected themselves with culturally unfamiliar landscapes and people, and these are processes they easily reflect in interviews. My account of whiteness is therefore both very specific and highly qualified; but, as I hope to convince the reader, opens onto broader landscapes and raises bigger issues than the conduct of an insignificantly small number of British lives in Hong Kong.

Concern with the social mechanisms making whiteness obviously extends well beyond the things that social and cultural theorists call 'race' and 'ethnicity'.[8] Trying to pick race or ethnicity out of a set of circumstances is like tracing a thread through an intricate tapestry: the thread has no special meaning on its own, but it forms a vital constituent of the overall picture which would not make sense without it. The world is composed through thousands of social mechanisms, but for the sake of clarity I want to highlight two kinds of mechanisms that play a significant part in race making, those centrally concerned with *space* and *human agency*, with people and places. I am concerned with individuals' local/global spatial practices: the movement of bodies in space – corporeality and comportment. The circumstances I have chosen to investigate in Hong Kong connect with contemporary debates in globalization – particularly its racial grammar, an issue on which globalization theory has been determinedly silent – and postcolonial literature's concern with the status of the past in forming the present. The material I work with is derived from an empirical investigation of people's relationships with places, albeit on the most micro of scales, but it is also a modest attempt to contribute to bigger debates and to the theorization of race and ethnicity in the context of postcolonial, global landscapes. Individual lives are a window onto bigger social processes. People have been overlooked in the development of race formation theory which is firmly focussed on macro elements of social structure, rather than micro–macro intersections. People, and their lives and movements and racial categories need to be placed in the same analytic frame.

This chapter begins with the smallest and most concrete units of analysis, people and places, and moves onto bigger landscapes, onto migration and globalization, and more abstract issues such as space, the conceptualization of race and subjectivity making: individual lives connect with these bigger social landscapes and issues. We enter this abstract territory of race making through the stories of two British expatriate men – John and Bill – living in Hong Kong at the beginning of the 21st century. The stories of John and Bill are stories about people and places and regimes and the networks connecting these things: things which are important in pursuing the kind of grounded, *materialist* account of race – concerned with the details of lives and the actual movement of bodies in space – we need to develop (see Back, Chapter 1, this volume). Biography and place are windows onto the racial organization of the global order of things: big and small things are always connected.

Hong Kong

John's and Bill's stories are *Hong Kong stories* and Hong Kong is important in shaping their identities as white British migrant men. We begin with a discussion of Hong Kong and its particular character as a *postcolonial landscape*: people make places which make people in a cycle of place/subjectivity formation. Two of the most serious problems with postcolonial literature are that it relies on some highly generalised accounts of the character of (the British) empire, when, in fact, forms of imperialism were unique in each place; and secondly they pay little attention to the (equally diverse) social and political contours of postcolonial societies.

Hong Kong was a unique bit of the British Empire seized from China in the 1840s and 1850s Opium Wars to secure the shipping routes for opium grown in British India. Its British administration had little impact on local custom (Flowerdew 1998: 13) and operated, as in northern Nigeria, through indirect rule (Chun 2000: 434). The outcome of negotiations from the mid 1980s meant that when Britain's 99-year lease on the colony expired in 1997 it would revert to China as a Special Administrative Region (SAR) with its own mini-constitution (the Basic

Law) and what amounts to municipal government – in the bigger political context of China – under a chief executive, a post occupied by the increasingly unpopular Tung Chi Hwa from 1997 to 2005. Its prosperity at times surpassing that of the colonizer (Man and Wai 2000: 291–2), Hong Kong entered globalization under colonial rule. It is both newly industrialized, part of Asia's 'economic miracle', and newly deindustrialized as it was catapulted into the kind of service economy, off shoring (with China) and banking, insurance and corporate HQs that characterizes global cities (Skeldon 1997: 265). There is a close mutual political and economic interdependence between China and Hong Kong with investment flowing in both directions (Lam 1997: 440). Hong Kong's mutating urban landscape is built on a shifting, accelerated, set of global economic circumstance. Its architectural aesthetic is visibly moulded by global corporate interests, and its banking and insurance towers are the signature buildings of some of the world's leading modern architects. A fabulously modern city with a state-of-the-art public transit system, its central walkways and plazas are *corporate* space that presents itself as *public* space (Cuthbert and McKinnell 1997); and a close relationship between the local state (as landlord in chief) and the corporate elite (who lease and develop land) has played a significant part in shaping the city (Bell 1998).

Densely populated and built on, space itself is a major issue, as the many land-reclamation projects and dense high-rise living show. A mega city in the making, the Hong Kong, Shenzhen, Canton, Pearl River Delta, Macau, Zhuhai metropolitan system is set to become the largest urban area in the world (Abbas 1998: 194). Abbas (1997: 298) describes Hong Kong as a fractal city, a city that expands not through suburbs but self-replication in which new districts repeat the structures of the city centre. Abbas (1998: 190) also suggests that migrancy and disappearance are part of the form and substance of Hong Kong urban architecture: '... the city is changing daily, right in front of our eyes, though not necessarily in ways that we can see. Whether one goes or stays, the experience of migrancy is inescapable' (ibid.: 185–6).

John, Bill and the others are migrants in a city of migrants. With no official border restrictions with China until 1949, Hong Kong has hosted layer upon layer of Chinese dissidents, refugees, and those in search of new lives (Flowerdew 1998: 22). Refugees and migrants in Hong Kong are a living archive of political, economic and social change in China itself. Later waves of migration brought an elite flow of transnational workers, colonial functionaries and poorer immigrants servicing the elite (Skeldon 1997: 266). International migration, of course, is important in establishing the global status of a place (Li, Findlay and Jones 1998: 131). As the last British Governor, Chris Patten said, 'Hong Kong represents the kind of Asia in which both West and East are comfortable' (Yeung 1997: 255). Hong Kong is the West's kind of East, and this makes it possible, even easy, for John, Bill and the others to live and work there.

Hong Kong has echoes of (British) familiarity for an 'exotic' location. Elements of the ethnic and racial grammar of this mutating postcolonial landscape are burned into the built environment. British and Irish pubs pepper the landscape, there's an outpost of the British Council discharging its usual functions in spreading 'British culture'. There is Government House, the old residence of the Governors, now tied in with a different set of (Chinese) functions. There are recognisably British post boxes, now painted bright green. There are London-styled double-decker busses and trams. You can still get high tea or a steak and kidney pie. Visually recognisably British things still mark the Hong Kong landscape, some of them serving new purposes and new contexts: '... colonialism is both the most obvious fact about Hong Kong and that which produces the most elusive effect' (Abbas 1997: 300).

John and Bill

John and Bill are lifestyle migrants. It is important to note that migration *out* of Britain is quite different in character from migration *into* Britain by the economic migrants of the 1950s and 1960s from the Caribbean and Indian Subcontinent; and the African, Middle Eastern and East European asylum seekers of today. These differences, of course, are about race, ethnicity and gender but not in any straightforward way. John is a *second-generation* lifestyle migrant. I am using this term 'lifestyle migrant' loosely to refer to those who weave together bits of what they 'need' or demand in life from different places, and who use this form of *bricolage* to think about belonging as the satisfaction of needs. Lifestyle migrants do not 'need' to move, they seek a change of place in order to upgrade their circumstances: they are economic migrants. Need is a problematic concept. You could say that even refugees do not *need* to move. Many stay put and suffer the consequences. But the concept of *need* has a different valency in their lives, which are organized by more basic forms of survival. All forms of migration ultimately bleed into each other as Clifford (1994) suggests.

John

If the term 'diaspora' were used to refer to the circumstances of white British people like John – which it isn't[9] – then John's circumstances could be described as part of a diaspora of privilege. John grew up in

New Zealand between the ages of five and seventeen, when his family returned to Britain. In his late thirties at the time of interview, he has lived in Hong Kong for 14 years and sees it as '... my home. I have no particular desire to go back to Britain at all.' I can report that for John and the others, New Zealand and Australia, but rarely Britain, were favoured retirement spots. This is John's story:

> I came on holiday and stayed! Life was so much easier then if you were British, whereas now they've quite rightly made the immigration status the same as for any other national ... I arrived to see my then girl friend. I'd just folded up my light engineering business in Britain, and I was at a loose end and she always said 'Come to Hong Kong, come to Hong Kong' and I came with the intention of staying two weeks, a month or so ... and I never went back, basically ... wandering up and down the little back alleys [was what made him want to stay] ... people were making it happen [His admiration for this unfettered enterprise is clear and linked with the red tape which stifled his business in Britain. His departure was about] ... all the violence and unpleasantness in Britain. I mean Britain is the only place where I've ever been badly beaten up for no reason ... you don't see graffiti [in Hong Kong], you don't see cars that are vandalised, petty crime virtually doesn't exist and that's due to police on the streets. And the police don't have the 'them' and 'us' mentality that's certainly been growing up in Britain over the last 30-odd years. Where they feel besieged so the police then tend to cleave to themselves ... it's one of the marked differences, is the attitude towards the police here and their attitude to the public.

He doesn't say so, but this is clearly part of a racialized narrative on the street-level operation of British multiracial coexistence. He gives a 'classic' example of public-order policing Hong Kong-style in the handling of protest during the handover ceremonies in the pageant marking the end of empire in 1997 in which the police drowned out the protest with loud Beethoven played on the public address system rather than arrest the protestors in front of the world's TV cameras. He moves on to reflect on examples of the British Government's handling of empire. All of our informants position themselves in relation to empire, without being invited to, at some point in our interviews:

> ... a lot of it has been shockingly inept, shockingly isolationist and in a lot of cases, spineless. If you make a decision, stick with it. That was one of the reasons why I was quite fond of Margaret Thatcher because, right or wrong, she'd make a decision [the Falklands, of course, was the loss of empire in contrast to the Hong Kong pageant of honourable withdrawal] ... Britain saddens me. Because I see so

potential, that is just getting lost. Wasted … now you are reach-
a different culture of haves and have-nots, based on education. In
ot of cases the state schools are shockingly inefficient; and it's a case
f dumbing-down, which is not good. Man was meant to look up, not
down. It's got man where he is today: the ability to look at the stars
and wonder. You have to set standards and this is why my sister has
struggled to put her kids through private schools [which are good at
standards and] … discipline. [Would he live in Britain again?] Not
unless you undo 40-odd years of social engineering. You've got a very
slow breakdown in society from the point of view of education and
the bureaucracy that is supposedly there, for the people, in law and
order. I mean one of the few blessings still in Britain is that the common law system is basically intact. And the judiciary is politically
independent [Ironically he is drowned out by a police siren outside!
But this gives him time to pause and feel superior to Americans, and
feeling superior to Americans is an important feature of British white-
ness] … I have more attachment here. Here is my home …

John, interview at his office
in Hong Kong, 2000

John, like other lifestyle migrants, sees Britain as sliding into a social
and political abyss of disintegration and decline from which he has
escaped. He is a fierce social critic, he wants, expects, things to basically

Figure 5.1 *John's island home* (Douglas Harper)

operate for his personal convenience and betterment. His life and his requirements are the vantage point from which the world is judged. He is able to comparison-shop in other countries and in other lifestyles and make choices. He is a knit-your-own-world global citizen, and his actions are a form of globally organised individualism. John belongs, not in a country, but in a set of circumstances that promote, or at least do not impede, the things he wants to have and do: things he regards as entitlements. While British multiracialism gets in his way and annoys him, living as part of a small ethnic minority himself – the British make up 0.3 per cent of the Hong Kong population according to the 2001 census – brings many of the things he wants in life. He and his (British) wife have bought an apartment on an island off Hong Kong and it is a *good life*. It contains elements of old (colonial) Hong Kong: the more exotic landscape of junks and fishing huts which are, elsewhere in Hong Kong, replaced by the glass and steel tower blocks of major corporate players on the global scene. Aesthetically John's island could be in Greece or part of coastal Spain. Have the landscapes of vacation become the template for the ideal everyday life? What John wants from his life is about those forms of private pleasure that come from living a certain way, and he seeks a political and social context in which this can take place. Ironically – given his right-wing libertarian political views on democracy and fears of social disintegration – he finds his particular brand of 'freedom' and the 'good life' in a temporary bubble in the People's Republic of China.

Figure 5.2 *Fishermen's houses* (Douglas Harper)

Circumstances of *arrival* and *departure* provide a more useful way of thinking systematically about forms of migration than *categories* of migrants advanced in the literature on migration, and inevitably combine personal and political circumstances. John the lifestyle migrant doesn't encounter any difficulties in moving to Hong Kong. As a British citizen, at that time he has no immigration problems, he simply gets on a plane, arrives, and soon gets a job. His lifestyle is not threatened although he doesn't speak Cantonese, he can get by because so many Hong Kong Chinese speak English. He can go back to Britain when he likes, although generally he chooses not to. Like other expatriates he uses particular parts of the city. He knows a number of Chinese people, but only in his public/professional life. He socialises with other 'Gweilos' (whites) as he refers to them by the local name. Last time we spoke to his wife she had been unemployed as a result of the localisation programme, and John, who was trying to develop another business, was becoming frustrated by the red tape and noise-pollution regulations. John and his wife will leave Hong Kong soon. They will go to Australia, Shanghai or Singapore.

Bill

Bill, who has been in Hong Kong 25 years, is *left over* from the apparatus of empire. Unlike John, who arrived when the future of Hong Kong as part of China was all but settled, he came to swell the officer ranks of the colonial police force in the 1970s when he'd finished university and was casting about for a job. His circumstances of arrival were very simple. He was recruited in Britain through a national press advertising campaign aimed at young men in Bill's position, and his passage to Hong Kong was organised by the government. He vividly remembers his arrival in Hong Kong; he remembers who else was on the flight (a batch of new police officer recruits all came together), the drinking during their delay in a European airport, the men who missed the flight on to Hong Kong, his early days in his new home and the initiation ceremonies and pranks played on new officers by those with more experience. His memories betray a work culture steeped in some very traditional versions of masculinity. Unlike John he is not from a family of lifestyle migrants. His parents live in the same house they have lived in all of their married life, the house where Bill grew up and from which he left for his foreign adventure. His parents, horrified by his move, forbade him to go to Hong Kong because it was so far away from their world.

Most of the people Bill knew left Hong Kong in 1997 when he decided to stay. He moved onto 'local conditions' of employment and learned rudimentary Cantonese. Like John he is a self-confessed lifestyle migrant who moved in order to upgrade his life circumstances, disposable income and leisure opportunities, not to escape persecution and death like a refugee.

Bill says: 'Hong Kong has been a very good deal for me, for my family, I've got a lot out of it. I'm very, very grateful to the Hong Kong Government, it's a very, very good employer ... these jobs no longer exist ... .' Bill's youngest son plays rugby for Hong Kong. There are frequent, exotic, holidays: opportunities, money and climate are all significant elements of lifestyle migration. For Bill Hong Kong is a *workplace*. He will not remain beyond retirement: 'I can bear it to work, but to retire and live, I don't think I could ... .' He reveals some of the boundaries of lifestyle migration: the other side of the salary – and things it buys – equation is the polluted environment and lack of space some people find intolerable.

As a way of telling us about his life, Bill agreed to take us to places that were significant to him. Walking, and not just talking, through people's lives is a useful research technique in developing a material analysis (see also Back, Chapter 1, this volume for a discussion of visual techniques in mapping racialized use of space). I thought this would reveal Bill's sense of *space* and specific connections with Hong Kong in a more embodied way. Bill's 'tour' was a threading together of places and time. He focussed on the period from the mid 1970s to the mid 1980s when he was part of the Police Tactical Unit (PTU) which is trained in riots and emergency situations and operates to support local police as a mobile patrol and in

Figure 5.3   *Policing the New Territories* (Douglas Harper)

swamp duties in the New Territories which abut the border with China. Hong Kong is also the space behind Hong Kong, the New Territories and China: and those were the boundaries – between China and Hong Kong, between Communism and the British Empire, between illegal immigrants and those who had a right of entry and abode – Bill was enforcing. The main job of the Police Tactical Unit in that area was dealing with illegal immigration: 'IIs' as Bill refers to them. On the border we stand and look at the barbed-wire fence that separates Hong Kong from mainland China with the Shenzhen special economic zone as a backdrop and a steady flow of trucks in both directions containing the produce of Hong Kong's off-shoring arrangements with China.

Bill's wife, Lisa, comes on the trip too. She came to Hong Kong in the 1970s, as a maid from the Philippines, another slice of (more pressured) migration by women as domestic workers with limited entry conditions, supporting an extended family network at home on minimal wages, and with marriage as a means of improving financial and migration circumstances. Maids work on two-year contracts which do not accumulate to meet residence requirements. Hers is also self-evidently a gendered story. Doug, the photographer, and I get to see how Bill and Lisa negotiate their memories of this area, which is simultaneously a place of leisure – as the biggest unbuilt-on part of Hong Kong – and, for Bill, work. In geopolitical terms this border was also, in recent memory, one of the world's hotspots; a listening post into China.

Our tour is a bit like one of Bill's patrols. This is obviously a police and military term that involves a particular sense of place as territory – land to be reclaimed or retained – wrested from alternate uses (Feuchtwang 1992). In this case territory is being defended from the occupation and (illegal) activities of (illegal) immigrants who, lacking alternate avenues of subsistence, involved themselves in crime and prostitution, Bill tells us. Patrol also involves particular kinds of bodily movement in space: covering, observation and surveillance: in this context a mechanism of colonial governance. Bill took us to high places – which is where some of the police stations and substations he was associated with were – so that we could look down over great distances. This hilltop fortification allowed easy observation of the conduct of people within the territory, and enforcement of the boundaries between states by controlling the flow of people from one to the other. He tells us that the Hong Kong police are more like the Northern Ireland Police Force (another, unresolved, colonial conflict closer to home) than any mainland police force in Britain in being armed and trained in riot and crowd control. Bill 'sees' in macro terms, pointing to great tracts of land and discussing population movements, across borders, and internally as the population grows through migration and the government struggles to house it. He tells us about the densely populated estates of apartment blocks in the

New Territories, vertical communities of 50,000 which present particular problems for the high-rise police patrols he now manages.

Bill's IIs – the objects of his patrol – came in two varieties. Most were Chinese, but there were also Vietnamese refugees in the period following the end of the Vietnam War. He doesn't generally use the term 'refugees', preferring instead to refer to them as 'illegal immigrants' as this makes it clearer what must be done with them:

> We had Vietnamese illegal immigrants … [at the end of the Vietnam war, many escaped to China then tried to get into Hong Kong] … and the authorities wanted them back … we did one or two operations whereby we had a sealed train provided by the [Chinese] mainland authorities … filled them up with Vietnamese and we guarded the train … [he admits this was politically sensitive, that they loaded up their trains at midnight] we put them on the sealed train and cordoned the area … and it used to be. … single-line railway line covered over, and there was this gap that marked the border … [He elaborates later] My idea … for transporting the Vietnamese back on the sealed train, was to use cattle trucks [which were particularly secure with no windows] … but no way [he is told] can you do this, its too politically sensitive. There is no way, we just have too many newspaper reporters. [He pauses to explain that the Hong Kong police winter uniforms looks particularly militaristic]

Figure 5.4   *The border between Hong Kong and China*
(Douglas Harper)

Nazi regime of Hong Kong transporting Vietnamese refugees [he admits this is what they are] in cattle trucks! That's a no no …

Being returned to China after having escaped as Vietnamese refugee would a dangerous position to be in. Chinese returnees were in an equally dangerous position, and it was Bill's job to send them back too. He points in to the distance as he explains to us:

We would have to go through here when we were picking them up off the marine launches [that picked up those escaping from China in leaky boats or walking over the oyster beds at low tide lacerating their feet] … and loading them into lorries and bringing them back along here … following the road that runs parallel to here … the holding centre for illegal immigrants, they'd gather so many, then they'd have a day they'd move them across the border, so we'd pick 'em up in lorries, take the lorries with us, from there take them … and they would only allow certain police drivers to go across the border, so you might have ten trucks but only two drivers, so you'd wait there with them while the drivers took them across, and the markings would have to be taken off the police vehicles, Royal Hong Kong Police as it was then, markings would have to be taken off and we'd always have an immigration official with us … We just watched the lorries … [Two of his Chinese IIs in the lorries are still remembered 20 years later]. Walking up and down the lorries and 'Excuse me sir, excuse me sir' from the back of one of the lorries. A Chinese lad speaking better English [the 'Queen's English'] than I did, educated in Beijing and wanted to get out. Amazing.

He also tells us categorically, as though it is a point of principle, that he has 'never set foot on Chinese soil' and, of course, as a colonial police officer he was not allowed to. His wife, on the other hand, goes there regularly to shop. His second example of the returnees on the trucks is still more disturbing:

We met this beautiful Chinese girl, pleading not to be sent back, because once they were out there [in China] they were put on a train and taken inland to a detention centre, and she was pleading with us not to put her on the train and she knew once she got on the train the guards would rape her, she knew what was going to happen to her.

Did he feel bad about this?

No ... it's a job, alright yes ... you were upholding the law of Hong Kong, you were, when we arrived we swore allegiance to the Queen ... and the people of Hong Kong, to uphold the laws of Hong Kong ...

The land border is covered by a fence, barbed wire ... now they have motion detection centres, CCTV everything up there ... villages on the Hong Kong border were losing three and a half thousand people a day ... so we had a massive flow of IIs coming in ...

The allotment of *legal* migrants into Hong Kong today from China is 150 a day, or 54,750 people a year, which dwarfs the arrival of asylum seekers in Britain in much lower numbers and more distressing circumstances (see Reed, Chapter 4, this volume, for a discussion of the British context). These are economic migrants.

White Britishness

The lives of these two men reveal quite a lot about the broader social and political landscapes on which their lives are set. We see in Bill's comments the interface between people and the regimes they serve. He remembers these two incidents years later because they demanded that he operate counterintuitively as a kind and compassionate man. We see the collusions between the Britain and China over the treatment of refugees. If race operated as a mechanism used by Bill in thinking about his job, then the Chinese officials on the other side of the border would have thought about refugees using other terms. What do we learn from these two men's stories about the nature of male migrant white Britishness on this particular postcolonial landscape? This, of course, hints at some fundamental questions about how race and ethnicity are *made in these circumstances*, in the connections people establish with places through bodily movements. *Whiteness*, like other versions of race (and gender) making, *is made in* where people go, how they get there (arrival and departure) and how they comport themselves once they are there. You are not what you eat, but the sum of your journeys!

White Britishness is produced and sustained in how John and Bill came to Hong Kong in the first place, in whom they are able to be and the kinds of lives they can lead once they are there. It operates through global migration and the ways in which white folk are able to operate locally. Both of these things are evident in the stories John and Bill tell, stories that have bigger contexts connected with the past of empire, not in a residual left-over way, but in an active contemporary sense. This is important in settling the contemporary significance of empire in making the racial contours of the present, global, world in which we live.

Global migration

Migration is part of the dynamic between dwelling and displacement, the rhythms composing human life. International borders are more difficult for some than others to cross. They are also borders between lifestyles, forms of consciousness and ways of being in the world, of subjectivities (Breytenbach 1991). Migration displays what Massey (1999) calls the power geometry of globalization. Gross disparities between lifestyles, wealth and opportunity are produced and maintained in the operation of migration. John and Bill moved easily to Hong Kong; their passage smoothed by the apparatus of empire and the promise that even after Hong Kong returned to China things would continue much as before for lifestyle migrants with relevant skills to offer on the local labour market. We lack systematic taxonomies of migration which tells us who moves where, when, and in what circumstances (Hesse 1999: 136, drawing on Massey). A global geography of migration, which addressed some of these taxonomies, would settle the place of John and Bill among other migrants, and, having established the basic contours of migration, attention to arrival and departure stories – imagine if you will the arrival and departure stories refugees would tell if we asked them – would add further important detail. Migration literature conceptualizes people as 'labour' moving between jobs and supplies none of this kind of detail which establishes important social difference between people and circumstances, things that are connected with gendered versions of race and ethnicity, although not in straightforward ways we can easily identify and generalise about. John's and Bill's circumstances are quite different from each other, but they have more in common than the migration circumstances of Bill and Lisa, or Lisa and the Chinese IIs Bill patrolled.

Global migration is a complicated business: its geographies are evidently connected to, and actively reconstruct and reconfigure, some of the geographies of empire (see Bhachu, Chapter 2, this volume). The feet and bodies, activities and social practices of people in boats and aeroplanes have carved the migration routes of the global order. The ways in which people occupy and move through space, connecting spaces together, is fundamentally important in establishing the character of global (and local) space, and the social character of its users and occupants. John's and Bill's connection with Hong Kong is carved through the conduits of globalization's reconfiguring of empire. I suggested earlier that John and Bill belong in bigger stories, and this is one of them.

This is not the racial grammar[10] of empire as Hesse (1999: 127) has it, but a new reconfigured version of it: walked and talked by bodies with new (and old) purposes operating in time and space.

Local connections: people and places

Lives are, of course, lived locally. New attachments to place are formed and constantly remade. Local space and people making activities are important social, habitual, mechanisms. People make themselves and their lives as they make space, so that space is the practical accomplishment of human activity. It tells its own stories about the making of people and places in gendered, racial and ethnic (and other) terms. Space is an active archive of politics and individual human agency (see Back, Chapter 1, this volume). The lives, activities and social relationships of people, past and present, establish the social character of space. Hong Kong's relics of empire, from social and administrative practices to signs and street furniture, will remain until the Hong Kong Chinese remove them.

John and Bill live in different kinds of places and do different things with their time: they use Hong Kong in quite different ways. The connections people establish with places are about the reasons why they come to Hong Kong in the first place, and the manner in which they conduct themselves once they are there. They tread particular pathways through the city. John from his office to the ferry and his island and the pubs and restaurant and sports bars it contains; Bill, from his tower block to his office and back to his club with its sports and social facilities. When he walks (or drives) as part of his job he patrols, overseeing the movements and activities of others. John and Bill are comfortable in these places and these movements which have become part of who they are. Mapping personal topographies in this way reveals finely textured social distinctions etched by race, ethnicity, class, lifestyle, gender and more besides. John and Bill likely share aspects of their personal topographies with relatively well-placed Hong Kong Chinese men. Their topographies show similarities with those of their wives, but they are not exactly the same. Expatriate women's personal topographies often take in activities with friends, shopping and journeys servicing the activities of children. We also see a concrete example of empire structuring the present in the making of white Britishness. John has managed to find employment despite his lack of basic Cantonese and the localisation of workplaces. There is still a (closing) space marked out in which colonial privilege is reconfigured. The same goes for Bill. All regimes and not just colonial ones need patrolling – what a fabulous transferable skill – and Bill has been promoted, with only the top three jobs in the police force being reserved for Chinese citizens.

How do John and Bill comport themselves as lifestyle migrants – note the pathways connecting work and leisure activities for both men – in Hong Kong among their Chinese hosts? How white British people operate when *they* are an ethnic minority is an interesting sociological question. Both men are modest and respectful of their Chinese hosts. Both have tried to learn rudimentary Cantonese but without much success, and this cuts them off from the people whose lives compose the bustle of the streets they tread in all but the most superficial of terms. Consequently their connection with this place is mediated by a partial grasp of what is going on around them. Their access to Chinese people and the Cantonese press is restricted. They live in what one of our informants called 'the expatriate bubble' of partial understanding and half-meaning. They also know that their connection to this place will end and that they will move on somewhere else: they are in transit. Their social networks centre on other expatriates, many of whom are white if not British. Both men's connection to this place is structured by their feelings about Britain and a reluctance to (Bill) or determination not to (John) return there. Both have a global sense of place. They live modestly, but with a sense that they are entitled to be here and entitled to and grateful for a 'good life'. They carry a sense of choice and opportunity with them as they walk the streets. You are *how* you walk as well as where you walk! Would a Hong Kong Chinese man walk around London this way? And what would have been his experience of getting there in the first place?

Conclusion

In this chapter I have outlined a materialist, compositional theory of race generated from empirical study of people's relationships to places which holds micro and macro social processes in the same analytical frame and traces the connections between them. I have taken issue with race-formation theory because of its failure to reveal the social mechanisms of race making. Race is neither a myth nor an objective condition of descent. It is made in gendered terms in mundane social practices and I have pointed to people's spatial movements – global and local – as being important social mechanisms (of course there are others) in race making. It is materialist in being about the spatial practices of bodies. It underscores the importance of performative aspects of race (ethnicity and gender) focussing on the details of corporeality and comportment. As I said earlier, people's global/local movements are coloured by empire and I have hinted at how this works. Let me say a bit more about this in bringing matters to a close. It is important to challenge the kind of post-colonial theory that doesn't grapple with the concrete details of colonial lives and governance or consider the specifics of place: that treats empire as a left-over residue in the collective mentality of nations and its popular culture. '*Was* empire significant in making white Britishness?' is a different question from '*Is* empire significant in making white Britishness today?'. The supposition, in postcolonial literature, that empire coexists with global landscapes of the present, and plays an active part in forming white Britishness is, I think, correct, but the mechanisms by which empire operates, its contemporary forms of inscription – the present salience of empire – are matters requiring investigation. How *does* this work? Do the social practices and subjectivities – ways of being in the world – of empire survive? In what forms do they survive? What are their new surface of emergence, their new practices and their new purposes?

In the lives of Bill and John we see some clues. Empire survives as a feeling of choice and opportunity, (divergent) forms of entitlement, facilitated by a (racialized) geography of routes already carved out and traversed by others. White Britishness is made in there being a place marked out in which daily life is feasible, in language and in other terms too. And it is made in the details of that daily life, using particular routes and places in the city – the routes and places of privileged, lifestyle migrants – in particular ways. It is made in the ways in which John and Bill conduct themselves in Hong Kong; in their routine movements around the city, in where they go and why; in the texture of their relationships with others – whom they mix with and for what purposes – in the ways in which they position themselves locally; in the ways in which they cast themselves through new forms of belonging; the character of that belonging, and the adaptations and accommodations they make in pursuing it. White Britishness is also made in the relationships which John and Bill and the others maintain with Britain (often brokered by women), and in the ways in which they position themselves in relation to the legacies of empire. It is made in the details of the ways in which they connect themselves with this bigger story. Some of these things are legacies of empire, but they are actively sustained and reformulated by present activities: by the movement of bodies in space.

What I am saying is that the place of empire in the making of white British subjectivities can be settled empirically and biographically, and through a tapestry of biographies it can be settled more categorically, and circumstantially. If empire still matters and makes whiteness then we should be able to say how. Because this particular piece of empire remained into the dying years of the twentieth century, Hong Kong became a 'last justification for imperialism itself' (Morris, cited by Tambling 1997: 364), raising uncomfortable questions concerning the place of empire in British history and the place of empire in making

Britishness. It is our unresolved relationship to our racial past-in-the-present that makes white folk problematic participants in contemporary multiracial societies.

It is the urgency with which we must resolve this that makes this materialist, compositional, people-centred, spatial, social-process-centred, performative, joined-up micro/macro approach to race theory more useful than others. The first advantage of approaching things this way is that the kind of mapping I suggest displays finer social distinctions – as well as similarities – between people. A mapping of routes shows the fine texture of race, ethnicity and gender etched by other forms of social difference. It shows what these things mean and where they overlap. I suggested earlier that John and Bill share routes with similarly well-placed Hong Kong Chinese men, that there are differences between men and women, and between women. One of the biggest differences between women lifestyle migrants is about work. Released from the obligation to contribute to the family budget and with substantial domestic support from servants, many expatriate women pursue a life of hobbies and leisure at the club or by the pool. Others work very hard.

The second advantage of the approach I advocate is that conceptualised in this way race acquires some political leverage it doesn't otherwise have. It makes it possible to ask – through what kinds of lives, routines, conceptions of the self, sense of the world, social relationships and use of global and local space could less problematic forms of whiteness be made? Forms of whiteness that are adaptable, flexible, non-exclusionary, that appreciate what cultural adaptations are made in migration, which know what it feels like to be an ethnic minority, that are ready to give up rather than lean on old privileges and forms of entitlement, that are critical of empire and reflexive about its substance in the present global order of things. If racial categories are made, then they can be remade. For whiteness to operate fairly and openly without advantage, disadvantage or exclusion in multiracial contexts, we white people, and the social and political mechanisms of our making as racialized subjects, must change.

Notes

1. I gratefully acknowledge financial support for this research from the British Academy and from the University of Southampton.
2. Concepts, ideas, referring to social and political (but not biological) distinctions made between people. Race and ethnicity are arbitrary social inventions, which form part of the broader social context in which they have meaning and a force in practice. Their power lies in the force they have in people's

thinking, actions and practices, and in their effect on the way things are organized. This volume emphasizes these things as part of a materialist analysis. Referring to the arbitrary character of race Mason (1994) says that there are no races but there is race. The same is true for ethnicity: there are no ethnic groups but there is ethnicity. Mason continues that it is racism that establishes the social character of race. And by extension it is the nature of the forms of meaning, differentiation, exclusion and annihilation that establishes the social character of ethnicity. Ethnicity is often used to carve finer social distinctions than are referred to by race. And for this reason it is more closely aligned with individual notions of identity. Anyone interested in following these things up should read Miles (1989), Miles and Torres (1996), Back and Solomos (2000), Goldberg (1993) and Hall (1991).

3. 'Social mechanisms' is an attempt to unpack the bigger category of social structure and get at some of the micro-details through which race is made. Social mechanisms include routine activities, forms of social organisation and interaction: they are about people's spatial practices and forms of association and individual and collective action.

4. 'Power geometries' is a term used by Massey (1999) to discuss the ways in which individuals and social groups are placed in relation to global social processes. The term 'power geometries' points to globalization's social inequalities which operate around the things we refer to as race, class and gender. These social inequalities do not occur in a neat pattern that is easily described but need to be uncovered, situation by situation in the kind of interconnection I hinted at in the tapestry example.

5. In critical white studies whiteness is named, marked and located as one, privileged, position among others, thereby unmasking it as an undeclared central position from which the world is judged. It is, of course, important to note that whiteness does not involve a single position, but a matrix of related positions. It is *unmasking* and *naming* that characterize the present attention to whiteness. In critical white studies whiteness carries an admission of racial guilt and culpability, a reckoning with history, and recognition that anti-racism requires whites to transcend their racial significance (Cohen 1997: 245–6).

6. Now a Special Administrative Region of the People's Republic of China, with its own constitution, the Basic Law, Hong Kong operates as a local state, which is a subnational state of China (Cuthbert & McKinnell (1997: 296). Under the 'one country two systems' formula Hong Kong retains its 'way of life' until 2007.

7. By 'postcolonial theory' I refer to the seminal work of Said and especially his classic text *Orientalism* (1978) and much excellent work which followed and developed Said's insights. Chun (2000: 433) criticizes Said for focussing on 'the texts of high colonialism' and the 'production of metropolitan knowledge' and because 'he has said much less about the institutional realities of colonialism'. These are valid criticisms and I fully endorse them. It is important to look at processes and practices and not just texts and colonial writing.

8. Ethnicity is seen as something which is made and not something primordial in the work of the anthropologist Fredrik Barthes (1969) and developed by

Anthony Cohen (1994), Eugene Roosens (1989) and Katherine Verdery (1994) who see ethnicity as the product of social organisation and forms of consciousness as well as an important way of calculating political difference. Roosens (1989: 13), an anthropologist in the Barthes tradition, develops this political point further, arguing that ethnicities are animated around the political landscapes of social disadvantage, and this is usefully seen as one of the mechanisms producing ethnicity. In the dialogues between ethnic selves and the political landscapes animating them we derive important clues about *whose* experience counts and *how*.

9. Diasporas are not clearly distinguished from transnationals or from other sorts of migrants. They are part of a political claim which asserts that anyone can belong anywhere, that it is routes not roots that are significant, and that there is no primordial connection between race and place. They are also part of a claim about marginality and displacement that is enduring over time. Jews are the archetypal diaspora: their historic displacement is continued in a present set of circumstances flecked with anti-semitism. See Clifford (1994) for a more detailed discussion.

10. By 'racial grammar' I do not mean the underlying principles by which race operates; there are no underlying principles by which race operates, but the social practices to which race gives rise. I mean the things race (and ethnicity) make(s) happen.

PART II

THE BODY AND SUBJECTIVITY

Chapter 6

Brilliant Bodies, Fragile Minds: Race, Sport and the Mind/Body Split

BRETT ST LOUIS

I'd like to begin, if I may, with a brief story. The 1994 film *Hoop Dreams* chronicles the American sporting dream and tells a poignant tale of thwarted ambition and frustrated desires. Nowhere is this more apparent than in the moving story of Curtis Gates, the older brother of William, one of the two young basketball players featured in the film. A local basketball legend as a result of his elaborate skills embroidered by competitive intensity, Curtis went to Colby College in Western Kansas on a two-year scholarship because under National Collegiate Athletic Association (NCAA) regulations his grade-point average was not high enough for him to accept a four-year playing scholarship at Marquette University. After his spell at Colby, Curtis was courted by large schools and full scholarships and chose the University of Central Florida. However, in this bigger pond Curtis was expected to conform to the team pattern. He could no longer dictate the plays or practice when he wanted and was moved from centre to guard, spending most of his time on the bench. Disenchanted with his peripheral role, Curtis left Orlando during the first year of his scholarship and returned to Chicago. Like people that many of us know, he was someone who could have 'made it'. Living with his wife's family and their four-year-old daughter, he got a security job at a hospital and rarely played basketball again.

This story provides fuel for the ranks of social and cultural critics who recognize professional sports as a mirage that attracts black youth with its seductive promise. Even former NBA all-star Charles Barkley promotes this view:

> For every David Robinson, Shaquille O' Neal, Hakeem Olajuwon and Patrick Ewing, there are countless names who will never make it ... There are so many guys I know who had the intelligence to do almost anything, but all they thought about was basketball.

And when basketball didn't work out, they had nothing to turn to. (Barkley 1996: 9)

The lure of professional sport does indeed consume the minds and ambition of many black youngsters at the expense of their consideration of alternative career options. We also know that for those 'lucky' enough to gain an athletic college scholarship not only are their chances of signing professional contracts minimal,[1] but they may not even receive the academic education promised by their enrolment and attendance (Eitzen 1999). It is widely recognized in the US that participation in varsity sport affects the educational experience and commitment of student-athletes (Adler and Adler 1991; Snyder 1996; Coakley 1998; Putler and Wolfe 1999) and the almost professional demands of practice and competition adversely affect the time and energy left for academic study. This is compounded by the anti-intellectual environment within many major male collegiate sports programmes that encourages student-athletes in certain institutions to give academic study a low priority (Coakley 1998). And finally, the educational outcomes of student-athletes also suffer in terms of their lower and slower rates of graduation in comparison with the larger student body (Eitzen 1999; Snyder 1996).

The case of US collegiate sports, therefore, provides a clear example of the uneven social relationship and disparities in power between educational institutions that participate in intercollegiate sports and student-athletes. For D. Stanley Eitzen (1999) the popular notion of college sport as an extension of the academic pedagogical domain where student-athletes learn and develop valuable life skills obscures the systematic exploitation of black student-athletes (amongst others) through the reproduction of a series of myths about college athletics as providing a free education, an opportunity to earn a degree, a foundation for a professional athletic career, and the chance to escape poverty and achieve life-long financial security. However, this useful understanding of sport as a formal mechanism for disciplining racial groups that reproduces a dominant *material* social order is analytically limited in its ability to explain the relative autonomy and compelling voluntaristic force of sporting *ideals*. Therefore, it is important to note the subtle qualitative hierarchy between the intellectual and the physical that exists alongside the material-structural formation of sport. This is illustrated in the strategic rendering of the Cartesian mind/body problematic within Curtis Gates's story. Despite his undoubted physical abilities Curtis's basketball career is restricted by his intellectual limitations; firstly in his failure to gain the necessary grade-point average to attend Marquette University and secondly because of his lack of the requisite 'work ethic' that underscored his failure at the University of Central Florida. Therefore, to apply the philosophical dichotomy, while Curtis as *appearance* is 'body' he is, in *essence*, 'mind'. His athletic successes as body are transient and insubstantial while his ultimate athletic failure is prompted and compounded by his mental and intellectual weakness.

This chapter focuses on high-performance *modern* sport as distinctive, for example, from Classical games and medieval folk pastimes.[2] The point of departure for the argument below is the premise that the recognition of racial sporting participation as a social 'problem' is, in itself, analytically problematic. The synergy between the intellectual and the physical that is often played out within sport is deeply profound inasmuch as the two are presented as antithetical and antagonistic.[3] And this incompatibility does not simply enumerate a categorical mind/body difference but, given the distinctively physical social space that sport occupies in strict opposition to the cerebral and scientific (Bourdieu 1990), also reflects a social and cultural hierarchy. Therefore, this chapter argues that the differential conceptualization of body and mind within sport reiterates a broader ontological hierarchy that places the intellectual as the higher faculty and the physical as the lower which tacitly reinforces the production of uneven social relationships and opportunities that restrict life chances. Furthermore, the tension between academic achievement and athletic endeavour and the social stakes of privileging intellectual or physical capacities is heightened when articulated with race.

This chapter explores the articulation of Cartesianism[4] with racial athletic participation and assesses its injurious impact on the regressive racialization of black physicality *and* the ostensibly progressive critical responses to this athleticization of black life.[5] Accepting sport as physical activity, this means that the distinctions between cerebral and muscular sports and concomitant hierarchical values ascribed to them signify deeply meaningful social processes: this is especially – although not exclusively – the case in relation to racial patterns of sporting participation where the predominance of, for example, black athletes in activities characterized as based on a muscular physicality lends itself to the familiar zero-sum equation of high physical competencies as equivalent with lesser intelligence as evidenced within race and IQ debates (cf. Alland 2002). In developing this approach, this chapter examines the strategic use of a form of Cartesian dualism as the conceptual basis for recurrent descriptions of human species (racial) variation throughout the modern human sciences. I then explore its function as part of the descriptive framework for explanations of physical and intellectual racial differences alongside what is referred to as the Darwinian 'law of compensation'. In addition, I consider how this has informed the contemporary voluntaristic acceptance of racial athletic stereotypes that supports the miseducation and unrealistic sporting ambitions of black youth and contributes towards the invisibility of the professional successes of the black middle class. I conclude by unpacking the Cartesian thread within the purported African American 'sports fixation' (Hoberman 1997) and dominant critiques of sport as encouraging anti-intellectualism and providing a distraction from social engagement and academic and professional development. I argue that there is a problematic assumption of the intrinsic regressive character of sport that is situated antithetically to the progressive value of the life of the mind and suggest the critical need to (re)consider the progressive potentialities of sport alongside its inescapable disciplinary function.

Racializing the mind/body distinction

In building the philosophical principles underlying the modern era of science, as opposed to the prevailing dominance of clerical and supernatural thought, the impact of Descartes on the natural, physical and human sciences is deep and enduring. As far as the question of race is concerned, Cartesian dualism often implicitly provides the conceptual basis for the racial distinction between intellectual reason and physical passions. Without the mind/body opposition, racist philosophy, geography, and anthropology would have had to find another framework capable of describing the qualitative differences between racial types. However, while Descartes notes that reason distinguishes humans from beasts he carefully removes the possibility that human populations might descend into the bestial; 'reason', he famously writes, 'exists whole and complete in each of us' (Descartes 1998a: 21). This is not another empty Enlightenment promise of human universality that obscures claims to racial particularism. Descartes' concern with establishing principles of epistemological certainty asserts the exercise of reason as a distinctively human enterprise and the alternative views found in disparate lands demonstrates the various applications of reason as opposed to an indication of barbarism or savagery. Forms of thought and knowledge specific to local tradition and custom are superficial manifestations of rational activity that emerge through an indubitably human rational capacity: therefore, 'the same man, with the same mind, if brought up from infancy among the French or Germans, develops otherwise than he would if he had always lived among the Chinese or cannibals' (Descartes 1998a: 28). In other words, for 'ardent Cartesians', the empirical phenotypical markers of race are irrelevant in the formation of human character and simply represent an incidental and accidental difference between peoples (Eze 2001: 54).[6]

If the capacity for reasoned thought separates the human from the beast, Descartes then points to a desirable objective of thought;

that the thinker masters themself in the attempt to change their internal desires rather than the external world. Given that some philosophers were 'able to escape from the dominion of fortune and, despite suffering and poverty, rival their gods in happiness' (1998a: 33), Descartes asserts that the mastery of thought elevates the thinker above the vagaries of fortune and nature. This mastery allows thinkers to regard 'themselves richer, more powerful, freer and happier' (ibid.: 33) than the unthinking who are favoured by accidents of chance and nature. Therefore, thought is oriented towards self-mastery for its own sake but also contains a moral purpose; the pursuit of human perfectibility. And it is the appropriation of this moral code that informs the racial division of the human species: the human capacity for 'constant reflection upon the limits prescribed for them by nature' (ibid.: 33) forms the conceptual basis for subsequent racial typologies. What Descartes understood as different *expressions of reason* that did not constitute demonstrations of savagery or barbarism would be recast by some as *alternate behavioural patterns* that indicate an (under)developed cognitive faculty. Therefore, reason separates human from beast as species but the internal variations in human rationality are observable in the distinction between primitivism and civilization.

The development of analytical insights – and judgements of value and quality – into the primitivism/civilization dichotomy along racial lines can be quickly traced within the racial imagination exercised by many eighteenth- and nineteenth-century human scientists in 'properly' cataloguing the varied mental and corporeal characteristics of the human species. Perhaps demonstrating the 'racial unconscious' within modern European philosophy (Mills 1997), the numerous luminaries of the human sciences whose insights were filtered through a racial lens are scattered throughout various disciplines. Robert Knox's (1996) ethnological account of the degenerative effects of miscegenation; Hume's (1987) philosophical sketch of a hierarchical racial polygenesis; Kant's (1997) anthropological explanation of the moral and behavioural significance of human species racial variation; and Hegel's (1975) assertion of the geographical (read racial) sites of World History provide an indicative sample of the orthodox racial epistemology of the modern human sciences.

Within this orthodoxy the racial basis of human species differentiation is frequently imagined through a reworking of Cartesian dualism. The speculative racial taxonomies of the human species that understood and explained physical, moral and intellectual characteristics as hereditary racial attributes are directly informed by the analytical distinction between mind and body. Where environment, for Descartes, evinced alternative expressions of reason, Kant's understanding of the impact of climatic conditions on phenotypical variation informs the moral and intellectual characteristics of particular races: 'in short, the Negro is produced, well suited to his climate; that is, strong fleshy, supple, but in the midst of the bountiful provision of his motherland lazy, soft and dawdling' (Kant 1997: 46). Kant's Negro demonstrates the instinctive corporeality and unreflexive sensuality of the naturalized human mired in the body as opposed to the expansive mind. And furthermore, this corporeality does not simply signify an alternative embodied human state but instead highlights, as Fanon (1967/1986) has argued, that the Negro *is* their body. Where Descartes (1998b) points to the distinction between the perceptions of the body and the soul as different orders of human experience, Kant recognizes the Negro's strong, supple flesh and lazy, dawdling demeanour as a pre-rational primitivism that illustrates an infantile dependency. This is a common theme in the racialization of the Cartesian distinction where the rational capacity to develop the natural environment typically found in northern European races is countered by its absence in those Others who are provided for by the benevolence of nature (Locke 1960; Hegel 1975).

Mind/body dualism and the racial 'law of compensation'

The enduring salience of these philosophical speculations – even if as crude stereotypes as opposed to acceptable philosophical discourse – is due to their commonsense force as popular sentiments that can be reinforced in different social and cultural arenas. It is important to note that this commonsense corresponds to intellectual methods and resources as well as specific ideas (St Louis 2004) which means that certain media and contexts are more effective than others at communicating racial ideas. Given that sport is often regarded as providing a literal reflection of intrinsic physical (and intellectual) capacities, it is an especially useful popular medium for demonstrating the distinction between the mind and the body, and its racial character.

In *On the Origin of the Species*, Charles Darwin draws on the 'law of compensation or balancement of growth' advanced by St Hilaire and Goethe to observe the development of organisms by natural selection (1866: 174). Goethe's understanding that 'in order to spend on one side, nature is forced to economise on the other side' (cited in ibid.: 174) informed Darwin's hypothesis that natural selection is driven by a utilitarian dynamic that channels resources towards the areas of the organism where they are most profitable and useful. Therefore, for Darwin, natural selection reduces and eradicates parts of an organism that become superfluous to its operation and concentrates on allocating nutrients where they are most needed. However, as with many of his ideas, Darwin's notion of the 'economy and compensation of growth' has been greatly misunderstood and distorted. Despite his claims that natural selection *reduces* redundant parts of the organism 'without by any means causing some other part to be largely developed in a corresponding degree' and *develops* a given organ 'without requiring as a necessary compensation the reduction of some adjoining part' (ibid.: 176), the law of compensation, in its racial guise and related to sport, has often been rendered as precisely the zero-sum proposition that Darwin rejected.

This distortion is evident in John Hoberman's (1997) example of the work of psychologist R. Meade Bache who, writing at the end of the nineteenth century, recognized an 'inverse relationship' between physical and intellectual capacities observable within the disparate boxing ability of different racial groups. The key suggestion here was that the athletic performance of blacks was characterised by their reflex actions that marked them as instinctive creatures of an intellectually inferior and primitive race. Similarly, Scott Fleming (2001) outlines the emergence of a racial hierarchy in relation to athletic ability that categorises 'black physiques' as *the* appropriate type for physical activity. And, crucially, these understandings of physical suitability are dependent on the logical opposition between the 'apparent physical superiority' of the black race with its 'intellectual inferiority'. However, it must be noted that the description and explanation of physical racial characteristics within this racial law of compensation are subject to a conceptual conflation. The application of the racial law of compensation combines the description of racial characteristics – the physical and physiological specificities of racial groups – with an explanation of their practical function as the result of instinctive and reflex actions. While Darwin, as outlined above, *quantitatively described* the economy and compensation of growth within an organism as a utilitarian dynamic of natural selection, he did not *qualitatively explain* the resulting effects as a zero-sum proposition. However, this methodological separation is less clear within his conceptualization of race and his utilitarian theoretical framework leads to, or at least implies, a similar conflation of empirical description and evaluative explanation in the attempt to understand the differential status of racial groups. In other words, the zero-sum relationship between intelligence and physicality that Darwin strongly refutes within his theory of natural selection is implicit in his understanding of race, and mirrors a racial law of compensation that is enduring for understanding racial characteristics (Hoberman 1997).

This is evident in *The Descent of Man* where Darwin's evolutionist account of human development specifically refutes monogenesis and polygenesis explanatory accounts of racial groups derived from creationist doctrine.[7] His recognition of a single human species that is subject to (racial) variation is based on the notion of broad anatomical and behavioural consistencies across human populations. Indeed, Darwin asserts that 'the great variability of all the external differences between the races of man ... indicates that they cannot be of much importance; for if important, they would long ago have been either fixed and preserved or eliminated' (1901: 307). This frames racial differences as 'protean or polymorphic' forms that have not been eradicated through natural selection because of their 'indifferent nature' (ibid.: 307). However, Darwin identifies key differences in social organisation, environmental development, and cultural disposition that transform the *insignificant nature* of racial differences into *significant social* practices and effects. Put simply, the survival or extinction of human groups that results from the competition between races and tribes demonstrates the eradication of weak populations by natural selection: this is evinced in a range of objective factors such as natural disasters and (reproductive) health problems. In the struggle for survival between 'civilized' and 'savage' or 'native' populations, the former will triumph as a result of their ability to develop their physical environment and create social rituals in accordance with the interests of their self-preservation. The implication here is that Darwin's comparison of the human characteristics of civilized contemplation and primitive physicality are placed in opposition where the former enjoyed significant advantages over the latter. This distinction between the intellectual and the physical arguably informed portrayals of black people as ill-disciplined savages, as evinced by their primitivism and Darwin's equation of muscularity with 'the lower races' that marked them as inferior to the civilized whites within modern developed society (Hoberman 1997: 209).

This is not to re-enter familiar debates on whether or not Darwin exhibited racist attitudes or to re-establish an inevitable logical thread from his theory of natural selection to Social Darwinism that concludes with Nazi eugenics and the Final Solution. Rather, my point here is twofold. First, it is important to consider how this *description* of racial differences as insignificant – remember they are differences that are, in themselves, 'indifferent' – is problematized by attempts at *explaining* them. Darwin's foundational notion that there are no significant or meaningful differences between races relies on a description of race as mundane variation within the human species. However, by accepting the considerable *formative interaction* between the human species and its physical environment, the differences between racial varieties becomes significant given the profound constitutive effect that the environment has on the biological human as a tabula rasa. This is borne out by the concept of phenotype which refers to the meaningful external physical (racial) differences that emerge as a result of the interaction between the biological human organism and its physical environment. Therefore, even though the *natural differences* are insignificant in themselves, the *social differences* resulting from their articulation with the physical environment are tangible and meaningful. The social difference associated with racial varieties is deeply important inasmuch as it is neither incidental nor relativistic but surreptitiously attaches hierarchical judgements to the sociality of civilization in contrast to primitivism as a presocial state. And, given that 'Every one will admit that man is a social being' (Darwin 1901: 166), the relation of racial groups to the social (civilization) or the presocial (primitive) is significant in its power to ascribe them given positions within a human hierarchy.

Second, it is important to illustrate how an ostensibly benign description of the marginal biological significance of race, as mundane phenotypical superficiality, can – when articulated with an almost imperceptible Cartesianism – lead to hierarchical explanations of racial physical and intellectual propensities. It is also particularly worth considering how these pathologies are manifest within and disseminated through popular understandings of sport. To this end some sports scientists and writers understand sport as a 'natural laboratory' that isolates the physical propensities of individual athletes which can then be extrapolated as inductive observations into general laws about the athletic capacities of different racial groups (Burfoot 1999; Entine 2000). However, the resulting general law is racial and not human and makes good use of the Darwinian understanding of significant racial differences as biological mutations and dispositions that emerge within the social. (This reference to the social is especially rhetorically and politically effective: it provides a biocultural argument that appears entirely reasonable and is significantly distanced from the specious biologism of scientific racism.) The implication is that sport provides a social space for the isolation of the physical and intellectual capacities and deficiencies of certain racial groups and can illustrate the racially specific dialectic between them. For example, the 'natural advantage' of black athletes in sports that demand the sheer physical propensities for explosive power or endurance is eroded with the requirement of technical and skill development (Burfoot 1999). Therefore, even if not explicitly advanced as a zero-sum proposition, the racial law of compensation carries an implicit and strategic Cartesianism that recognizes the racialized polarity of brute physicality and reasoned cognition.

The education of anti-intellectualism
and the 'sports fixation'

The abstract racial law of compensation is further reinforced by its practical dissemination within and pervasive influence on the structural organisation of sports. For example, the US sports media customarily uses classic stereotypes in reference to the primal physicality of black athletes and their pathological indolent, aggressive, naturalistic, exuberant and deviant character (Davis and Harris 1998). The focus on the physicality of black athletes contrasts with the frequent reference to the intellectual capacities of white athletes and coaches (ibid.) which has serious repercussions in terms of the structural positions of black former athletes within American sports. Arthur Evans (1997) argues that despite the wide access to sporting participation enjoyed by black athletes in the post-segregation era, they have been unable to gain access to roles as 'key functionaries'. Black athletes are regarded primarily in terms of their bodies and physical abilities which limits their access to responsible and leadership roles during and after their playing careers. Therefore, the lack of black coaches, broadcasters and sporting executives primarily positions blacks within sports as performers instead of decision makers and illustrates the convergence of the racial law of compensation as an enduring historical discourse, which is a significant contribution towards explanations of the social reproduction of racial stratification.

These classic stereotypes of black physicality and the absence of black athletes and administrators from roles as key functionaries also serve an educative function in the reinforcement of hegemonic racial ideas and stratification. Some critiques of the potentially deleterious effects of sport on life chances do not simply suggest that sport acts as a distraction from academic and professional pursuits, but that the hegemonic position of sport actively challenges and erodes the intrinsic value and social utility of intellectual life. Indeed, considering that the NCAA Division IA universities and colleges are, to all intents and purposes, training and recruitment agencies for the professional leagues of the major sports – principally baseball, basketball and football – they are arguably less oriented towards academic achievement and their student-athletes demonstrate lower levels of academic motivation. And, as the disproportionate recipients of athletic scholarships,[8] it has been argued that black student-athletes' academic performance and achievement is particularly affected by the demands of sporting preparation and competition (Snyder 1996; Coakley 1998). However, even though there is a racial pattern of academic motivation and achievement, it is somewhat uneven. For example, Snyder's (1996) comparative study suggests that even though black student athletes demonstrated a greater preparedness to study for final examinations than their white counterparts, they exhibited a significantly different level of overall academic commitment and focus. Snyder also found that black student-athletes had far higher expectations of entering the professional leagues and, if offered (perhaps professional) athletic employment, they were less likely than their white counterparts to return to university to complete the academic requirements for graduation. Perhaps the most damning indictment of the collegiate sports system is the myopic emphasis that it places on sport: of those who make it through college – or leave early – and enter professional leagues, the high rates of injury or failure to make the required grade mean that a long and financially rewarding career is not a certainty.

The education of sporting ambition and academic miseducation is a fractious issue, at least partly because it raises the issue of the extent to which black student-athletes (and by extension a broader black social grouping)[9] are implicated in their own miseducation and unrealistic ambition (Cashmore 1982; Hayes and Sugden 1999). This line of argument has been forcefully advanced by John Hoberman in his book *Darwin's Athletes* (1997) and his recognition of an African American 'sports fixation'. Hoberman argues that the social production and proliferation of stereotypes of black athleticism and sporting prowess has become so dominant that a significant section of black youth and community have voluntarily subscribed to the idea of their athletic omnipotence. As a result, Hoberman identifies sport as a diversionary form that steered African Americans away from intellectual and academic pursuits throughout the twentieth century. This is seen to have had a series of profound effects including the rejection of academic ambition; the athleticization of (idealized) black identity; and the reinforcement of pathologies of physical supremacy to the extent that it has become a source of black pride. However, this argument has been criticized in that it fails to account for the crucial effect of the pervasive structural racism within society that informs and shapes the miseducation and unrealistic ambition of black athletes (Carrington and McDonald 2001). It has also been suggested that the attitudes of some physical education teachers, and their adherence to stereotypes of racial characteristics, educate black youth into accepting and adopting ideas of their innate athletic ability which detract from their academic and social development (Hayes and Sugden 1999).[10]

Nevertheless, Hoberman's argument is important. It usefully challenges structural deterministic positions that simplistically portray black people as the passive marionettes of a racist society and undermines the assumed innocence and guilt of certain racial groups. It also raises the question of the extent to which black people might accept some responsibility for subscribing to ideas of racial athleticism as well as pointing to the deleterious effect of the reification of racial sporting ability on the development of black political interests (Gilroy 2000). Indeed, Hoberman details the black middle-class adoption of the 'sports fixation' as implicating them in their public invisibility and the marginalization of their own professional achievement. The positive images and significance of black doctors, lawyers and business people are replaced by vacuous and nihilistic representatives, principally athletes and entertainers, which thus reduces social status to the accumulation of material wealth that is either achieved through or/and displayed on the (athleticized) body. This also implies a strict material objection to the systematic education of black athletic identification instead of academic ambition in that it challenges and undermines the core value of literacy and formal education within what has been understood as the African American cultural value system (Franklin 2002). Given African Americans' social history of enslavement and legalized subjugation, education and educational institutions have played an important historical role in advancing their collective interests, and the current financial crisis facing already underresourced urban public school systems characterized by high levels of academic failure and dropout rates (Franklin 2002) frames the (mis)education and unrealistic ambitions of black student athletes as especially ironic.

There is, however, a key problem with the notion of the sports fixation and its role in cultivating the public marginalization of the black middle class. Hoberman's assumption that the primacy of athleticism and invisibility of middle-class black professionalism leads black youth to disassociate success and achievement from intellectual and academic work has been criticised as based on anecdotal impressions instead of empirical evidence (Carrington and McDonald 2001). While this critique is problematic in its own suggestion of the superior veracity of empirical evidence against subjective impressions, the issue of the invisibility of the black middle class is an important one. Again, just as the life of the mind is presented as inherently superior to physical activity, the significance of black professionals is posited as intrinsically greater and more valuable than that of athletes (and entertainers). Half of the argument necessary to sustain this point is made in Hoberman's critique of the veneration of an athleticized black identity that defers to pathologies of black hypermasculinity and aggression and is increasingly oriented towards a narcissistic glamorous style with no or negligible progressive political and/or social content. This establishes an argument *against* the social and political desirability of a particular masculinist representation of athleticized identity but, however, does not build the opposite argument *for* the social and political desirability of middle-class black professionals. This oversight tacitly accepts the existence of black middle-class lawyers, doctors and business people as a good thing *in itself* rather than as a result of the specific social functions and benefits that they fulfil and provide. Therefore various questions of value are left unstated: for example, is a black business person a valuable role model if their business practice is harmful to others? Is a negligent black doctor an asset to society? Is an incompetent black lawyer an asset to the clients that they represent and the legal system?

Of course, part of the problem here is that this issue is overdetermined by the burden of racial representation and begs the question of whether (within a racist or just society with (un)equal opportunities and outcomes) a black person or black politics *necessarily* must be socially responsible and progressive as opposed to reactionary and conservative. This point has been made in a wider context of the internal conceptual contradictions of anti-racist politics (Gilroy 1992) and is perfectly valid; nevertheless if it is to be acceptable here then it ought to be broadly applicable. Therefore, if in a society characterized by racism and racialized inequalities of access and opportunity the very existence of a black professional inevitably constitutes a good thing – without needing to be associated with the social good – then there is no acceptable reason why the same ought not to be true of a black athlete. However, at least for a critical intelligentsia – personified here by Hoberman – this is patently not the case. The different values ascribed to intellectual and physical capacities are not based on objective differences but reflect a Cartesian hierarchy. As the mind houses the higher faculties of reason and intellect, the life of the mind is a higher vocation while the body as the site of base appetites and instincts relegates sports and athleticism to a trivial form of play that distracts individuals from rational, contemplative, and cultured activity.

Beyond a dualist critique of sport

The (even implicit) Cartesian framework that is assiduously applied within a materialist-structural approach to sport limits the range of its critical imagination and analytical and evaluative efficacy. For example, Evans's (1997) critique of the contemporary manifestation of a Calvinist ideology of living according to Protestant moral principles and ascetic discipline that regards blacks as undeserving of social and sporting roles as key functionaries and reproduces their social exclusion is descriptively satisfactory but prescriptively weak. His argument suggests that the benefits of rationalization and the general expansion of the black middle class will, in time, create increased professional mobility for 'upwardly mobile' blacks within professional sports. Therefore, the colour line that has historically impeded black people's social and professional progress will disintegrate and their career opportunities will expand. However, it is notable that 'only the better trained, talented, and educated segments of this group will be able to attain authoritative positions' allowing them to profit 'disproportionately from the process of rationalization, by removing artificial barriers to ... key functionary roles in professional sports' (ibid.: 57).

But this model of social change is unable to rationally map and predict the abstract and imperceptible ideals that affect material structures and circumstances. The expansion of the black middle class and its increased professional opportunities might point to the erosion of the colour line, but the pervasiveness of Cartesianism and the racial law of compensation as presented within this chapter points to the strategic discursive formation and social invisibility of that line. Therefore, Evans's faith in rationalization as a motor of social progress is only useful inasmuch as racial discrimination and exclusion are produced through explicit and material forms; the more subtle and idealist expressions of racialization are not so easily recognized and eradicated. Also, accepting that IQ-and-athleticism debates represent key underlying impressionistic principles informing contemporary discriminatory racialization, it is worth considering the way in which they both work to *describe* the Cartesian mind/body polarities of human species racial variation, that is then *explained* through the (racial) law of compensation. This is to say that these idealist forms of racialization are deeply embedded within society and are popularly accessible and reproduced as intuitive racialized understandings of intelligence and physicality: this knowledge is in turn widely disseminated as folklore, as science, and as commonsense. The combination of Cartesianism and the racial law of compensation is a powerful form of ideational racialization in its capacity to address an expansive range of human social identity, interaction and structure that we understand as sentient *and* rational selves.

In addition, by placing an emphasis on training, talent and education, Evans conceptualizes the amelioration of US racial stratification and black social immobility as a rational social process that will be achieved through objective capacities and strategies allied with the correct forms of opportunity and access, without realising the extent to which such a project of social change is also informed by abstractions and ideals. For example, the very establishment and assessment of standards of quality and potential, even when objectively measured, are themselves subject to partial judgements of value. Therefore, given the connection between black social mobility and the targeted social reproduction of its middle class in Evans's thesis, the intellectual and cerebral characterization of that group invites the continued use of a racialized Cartesianism for the further subjugation of working-class and socially and professionally non-mobile blacks. The substitution of a social class for a racialized group, in this case the middle class as *the* authentic exemplars of black identity, might easily turn the essential (intellectual) characteristics of the class into those of the group. As such, if its professionally mobile middle class suffices as *the* representative standard of blacks en masse, then the colour-blind, anti-affirmative action arguments asserting that a lack of effort and not racism is to blame for racial stratification becomes harder to displace. Furthermore, just as the racial law of compensation reifies the physical propensities and intellectual deficiencies of blackness, Evans's thesis may simply attempt to substitute one reified group identity with its converse, instead of trying to conceptualize a dialectic of mind *and* body.

The representative role of the black middle class and veneration of the intellectual and professional elicits a form of Cartesianism that ironically reinforces the enduring essential bases of racial weaknesses (such as hyperphysicality) and strengths (such as cognitive capacity and accomplishment). By privileging the intellectual over the physical and, by extension, the white-collar professional over the athletic, sporting interest and participation are overdetermined as problematic and detrimental to professional aspiration and success. This is especially evident within Hoberman's notion of the black American 'sports fixation' and transparent in his categorical statement that interest in athletes and sports (as well as entertainment) 'obscures *more important* stories of black professional achievement' (1997: 7, emphasis added). The *basis* of the relative importance of professional and athletic activities is left unstated which suggests that their disparate value is the result of their essential properties instead of *interpreted* as such. It implies that the life of the mind is *inherently superior* to physical activity without either specifying the precise terms of this distinction or providing the ethical arguments that may sustain it. This also presents the issue of the privileging of structural concerns that frame the body as inert matter that only becomes meaningful through the disembodied understanding of social action and discourse (Shilling 1993; Crossley 1995; Turner 1996) which, in turn, serves to marginalize the integrity and existential significance of bodily and athletic pursuits. In response, I would argue that the attempt to uncover the intrinsic character of sport as ideal and practice – whether that be progressive, regressive, or some formulation of structuration – should be abandoned in favour of making a critical distinction between the various social functions of athletic pursuits and their social potentiality.

A problematic spectre lurks behind this implicit appeal to a notion of embodied activity as meaningful in-itself instead of only meaningful when interpreted as such in relation to intellectually defined standards.

For example, identifying the inherent aesthetic properties of the body as lying outside of an interpretive process conjures the negative association with fascist politics that Walter Benjamin characterized as the 'introduction of aesthetics into political life' (1999: 234). Within this scenario, the democratic dialogue central to political activity is bypassed by the monological eloquence of the body that conveys ideas that are persuasive as an embodied form that is familiar and compelling to us. As such, a politics can be articulated through the body without being subject to discussion and dissent; and given the popularity and cultural currency of sport, the sporting body is especially eloquent here. In perhaps its most extreme manifestation, the potency of unspoken, implicit, and yet self-evident, racial meanings expressed within and communicated through the sporting body is transparent in the mobilization of fascist body culture to express the ideals of Nazi racial hygiene during the 1936 Olympics in Berlin (Sontag 1980; Mandell 1998; McFee and Tomlinson 1999). Such a concern leads Hoberman (1997) to rightly question those who regard sport as offering a site for the recovery of the 'well-balanced man' who combines intellect and muscularity as an enduring 'noble rhetoric' that has 'produced so little of permanent value for most black Americans' (1997: 10). Fascistic connotations aside, in its racialized guise this 'well-balanced man' is of course qualitatively different to 'his' inspirational descendant, the 'Renaissance man' of early-modern Europe, and Hoberman is correct to ask whether, given the social context of racism, 'he' would not just simply contribute towards the 'athleticization of black life'. An important and remarkably obvious principle is lost here however. The routine association of sport with regressive effects conveniently forgets that social groups and individuals can be disciplined within intellectual and academic spheres as well as the physical and sporting. For example, Hoberman's understanding of a 'policy of stylistic abstinence' in a Chicago school for black boys as a significant counter to the black American sports fixation and its 'intense peer pressure that equates academic excellence with effeminacy and racial disloyalty and identifies "blackness" with physical prowess' (1997: 8) is indicative of the fundamental flaws of the a priori deleterious character of athleticism. His argument fails to recognize that the 'stylistic abstinence' from chewing gum, sagging pants, sunglasses, biker pants, tank tops, earrings or designs shaved into hair substitutes the vacuous regimen of 'the showy male style flaunted by many black stars' (ibid.: 8) with a rigidly administered non-stylistic orthodoxy that promotes a group conformism based on obedience and compliance. Indeed given its martial order, the extent to which the regime of 'stylistic abstinence' can produce a motivational pedagogic experience that promotes truly voluntary academic commitment and autonomous thought that enables intellectual and academic advancement is arguable.

This fundamental aversion to the pursuit of physical activities as compromising the development of the intellect articulated within Hoberman's argument is indicative of the crucial fault line running through Cartesian-influenced analyses which understand sport as alienating work that subjects the bodies of selective social groups to disciplinary regimes (Brohm 1978; Gruneau 1983; Bourdieu 1992). However, while such Marxist (-influenced) critiques have (largely) passed out of season, acceptable less deterministic alternatives demonstrate their Cartesian stain by drawing attention to the unreflexive practical character of sport: as such sport is a meaningful practice in terms of what it signifies socially rather than any relatively autonomous properties that it might possess in-itself (cf. Morgan 1993).[11] However, accepting that the primacy of Cartesianism is not inviolable, a salient response must discard its normative dualism and begin again from the point of recognizing the complexities of sport as demonstrated within the dialogical relationship between its internal logic and social space (Bourdieu 1990; Morgan 1993).

Finally, as regards the racialization of athletic ability there is a simple point to be made. The athleticization of black life is not the single logical outcome of recognizing the corporeality and physicality of black people; it is a possibility, and maybe even a strong one given its social context, but it is neither a logical outcome nor a practical necessity. This indeterminacy suggests that a critical space for the conceptual (re)interpretation of physicality, its social significance and meaning exists, and ought to be opened up. The customary polarized approaches to sport through disdainful denigration and naïve celebration are profoundly limited. They lack the capacity to evaluate the extent to which the social and cultural meaning of sport is not arbitrary but emergent and contested. And they are also unable to theorize arguments in response that acknowledge and value the combination of physical *and* intellectual resources within sporting performance (Inglis and Hughson 2000; St Louis 2000). Furthermore, the dogmatic denial of corporeality found within orthodox social constructionist critiques fuels the descriptive and explanatory antagonism between the social and the biological which, without the support of intuitive sentiment, may even fortify the commonsense veracity of arguments for biological racial characteristics (St Louis 2004). Therefore, the sheer incongruity of attempts to deny the significance of something as fundamental and immediate to being as the body invites responses that crudely reassert its existence in the most commonsensical and impressionistic manner. And, by refusing to enter the social terrain that perceives and understands the body, the denial of corporeality is also culpable in the reproduction of racial myths by surrendering the critical space wherein these issues are interpreted and eschewing the political work of argument and debate.

Notes

1. Harry Edwards has calculated that the probability of black American student football and basketball players becoming professional athletes in the NFL and NBA is 1 in 6,318 and 1 in 10,345 respectively (cited in Snyder 1996: 655).
2. For the seminal discussion of the definitive formal-structural characteristics of modern sport as based on principles of secularism, egalitarianism, specialization, rationalization, bureaucracy, quantification, and the compilation of records, see Guttmann (1978: 15–55).
3. For a useful discussion of the qualitative and class-stratified distinctions attached to sports according to their cultural status as contemplative and health-related enterprises (such as golf, riding and skiing), or mired in base physicality and explicit displays of bodily power (such as weightlifting and boxing) see Bourdieu (1992). Similarly, Elias (1986) notes 'sportization' as a significant constituent of the 'civilizing process' where sport provides a social space for the release of 'stress tensions' and sublimation of violence (such as the use of hounds that allows English fox hunters to 'kill by proxy').
4. Cartesianism is a path-breaking approach to physical science which is usually associated with Descartes' understanding of the mind. Although his feted theory of 'dualism', maintaining that the *mind* is an entirely separate substance from the *body*, has been subject to intense and ongoing debate, for the purposes of our discussion Cartesian dualism is suggestive of a critical distinction between mind and body that relates to the mental and physical: as fleshy, corporeal matter the body is opposed to the conscious, purposive and active mind – our bodies are, therefore, a physical vessel but our meaningful selves, our souls, our human essence is our capacity for conscious contemplation and understanding.
5. In this chapter I refer to 'racial' as a normative term that is taken to denote a salient category either in relation to an individual or group – while accepting its problematical conceptual and objective status. I use the term 'racialization' to signify a productive process through which the racial is constructed.
6. Of course, in referring to '*ardent* Cartesians' as rejecting the significance of race within understanding the human, Eze acknowledges the existence of alternative interpretations by the less ardent or non-Cartesians. For example, he cites John Searle's critique of the central Cartesian assertion of the capacity for thought as *the* essential human characteristic as susceptible to the notion that this capacity is itself subject to racial differentiation (Eze 2001: 56–7). This possibility of the *racialized application and extension* of Cartesian distinctions is central to the argument in this chapter in terms of understandings of sport as indicative of the physical and intellectual capacities of racialized groups.

7. Taken from the notion of Genesis central to Creationist thought, monogenesis identifies all humans as descended from Adam and Eve and understands racial differences as incidental while polygenesis recognizes racial groups as having different ancestral origins (see Banton 1998: 17–18).

8. A 1996 survey commissioned by the NCAA found that black people comprised only 9.8 per cent of the student population of the 305 NCAA Division I institutions. However, they accounted for 25 per cent of all athletic aid which translated into 63 per cent of male basketball players; 52 per cent of football players; and 36 per cent of female basketball players (Coakley 1998: 469).

9. I use the term black 'social grouping' intending a more fluid category for an ethnic collective, in recognition of the problem of identifying a notion of community that exists with full physical coherence and ideational consistency. For a useful discussion see Alleyne (2002).

10. The findings of Hayes and Sugden's (1999) survey of physical education teachers in the north Midlands region of England is interesting here. The teachers believed that black students were disproportionately successful at sports they were particularly advantaged in. The respondents also reported that this 'advantage' of black students was due to naturally endowed physical capacities, including speed and power, and that their sporting success was primarily due to their physiological characteristics (74 per cent) over social factors (23 per cent). Psychological reasons (3 per cent) were understood as the least influential contributory factor in the sporting success of black students.

11. The voluminous social scientific literature on sport in relation to social travails bears testament to this. Sport is often employed to document and analyse explicit and tacit forms of oppression such as racism, sexism and homophobia and its critical value is read through its representational capacity to inform a cultural politics conversant with accepted communities and frameworks of resistance such as anti-racist and feminist struggles.

Chapter 7

Remembering Bodies, Healing Histories: the Emotional Politics of Everyday Freedom

DENISE NOBLE

> But I who am bound by my mirror as well as my bed
> see causes in colour as well as sex and sit here wondering
> which me will survive all these liberations
> > Audre Lorde (1974/1994) 'Who said it was simple?'

> The Negro suffers in his body quite differently than the white man
> > Franz Fanon (1967/1986: 138)

Introduction: Black cultural politics – contesting Black identities

This chapter asks whether transcending the racialised body is an ethical requirement of anti-racism. In order to answer this it is necessary to recognise the imbrication of Black subjectivities and embodiment in modern theories of the self. The philosophical dualism of René Descartes in the seventeenth century helped to establish the modern Western understanding of what it means to be human. The rational mind was the basis of being human whilst the body was merely the material addendum to the mind of reason (see St Louis, Chapter 6, this volume for a fuller discussion). Enlightenment racial biology legitimised the idea that the capacity for reason was the natural attribute of the white European 'man of reason' and that non-Europeans, being defined by their bodies, were not capable of achieving full personhood.[1] Fanon rejects this vision of the ideal self that makes a disembodied (therefore invisibly white) European mind the subject of humanism and freedom and erases Black human-ness by reducing Blackness to an objectified embodiment. Fanon does not reject embodiment but rather asserts the embodiedness of existence. The 'fact of blackness' (Fanon 1967/1986) for Fanon lies not in

132

the body as biological point of closure and permanence but as a productive and reactive existence in time and space.

Isn't it ironic then that official recognition of institutionalised racism as a condition of Asian and Black existence in Britain, confirms and reproduces the embodied epidermal identity that Franz Fanon first named in *Black Skin, White Mask* (Fanon 1967/1986: 112), whilst apparently detaching its visibility from any references to 'race'? The Macpherson Inquiry[2] institutionalised and disseminated the phrase 'visible minorities' as the latest euphemism for people who are not white. It confirmed the privileged place of *seeing difference, marking* it on the body. Overlooking momentarily the masculine bias, Fanon wrote that the moment a black man is 'seen' by the colonising European gaze, he becomes objectified; he no longer has control over his own bodily integrity in which ego and body are united. He ceases to exist for himself, but instead he becomes objectified as 'a Black man': no longer a unified subject, merely a representational iconic body – that can be read in a transparent chain of signification; the Black body reduced to stereotype and metaphor signifying drugs, guns, sexual hedonism and so on, depending on the time and place.

The perniciousness of this racial 'epidermal schema' for Fanon (Fanon 1967/1986: 111) is its power to penetrate the self-consciousness of the Black-African, to alienate the Black subject from his own experience of his body so that he comes see himself through the dominant perspective of the legislative gaze of the Other; he learns to objectify himself (see Stuart, Chapter 9, this volume). What else is implied by thinking of oneself as the 'visible minority' to an invisible majority? Yet the category 'visible minority' suggests this alienated corporeality is not merely reducible to skin colour as a surface inscription of physiognomic difference. Skin colour is the paramount sign of this visible Otherness in which body and subjectivity, visibility and invisibility are fused in a kind of permanent state of embattlement: however, being also an 'historical racial schema' (Mohanram 1999: 26) it is cultural and performative, revealed through clothing, speech, experience, culture, accents – all of which can function as secondary markers of a visible subordinate status as Citizen-Other. Visible minorities are not recognisable merely through racialisation as an epidermal schema constituted through skin colour, texture of hair or other physiognomic markers, but also embodied a second time over through hair styles, clothing, comportment, movement of the body, hijabs, beards and *salwaar-kameez* (see Alexander, Chapter 11, this volume). In other words, *racialisation* is not simply the 'representational process whereby social significance and therefore social relations are attached to biological (usually phenotypic) human features' (Miles 1989: 75).[3] Styles, cultural practices metonymically linked to racialised bodies can become objectified and alienated from the selves that are lived through them and the bodies that animate them. By detaching 'race' from biological markers and reworking it through the cultural, the aesthetic and through the body's performativity, Black bodies can be simultaneously visible as citizens and objectified as Others. In this way, racism (as discredited false biology) is transcended, 'thus distancing cultural essentialism from many of the social and political criticisms that biological essentialism has received' (Lury 2002: 158).

This works both ways, making the moment of coming into view as a Black person potentially inherently risky, for one risks becoming simultaneously 'hypervisible yet invisible' (Mohanram 1999: 26) always trapped by an identity, *whether self-defined or not, anti-racist or racist*, that threatens to reduce you to an essence or caricature of your own or someone else's making. The struggle to transcend this contradiction has defined the history of Black cultural politics in Britain in the 20th century. Stuart Hall has summarised this as the struggle of two sequential but overlapping moments. The first Hall defines as the struggle over *the relations of representation* (Hall 1996: 442), which seeks initially for *recognition of the presence* of Black people within the nation. This is resistance against the *invisibility* that comes when Britishness signifies only whiteness. So the struggle over *the relations of representation* also seeks *recognition of one's value and dignity* and opposes the pathological *hypervisibility* of racist stereotypes. This moment particularly characterises the cultural politics of the postwar settlement of Blacks in Britain up to the early 1980s. The second phase in Black cultural politics is exemplified by struggles over *the politics of representation* (ibid.), which emerge when internal differences around gender, sexuality, and class begin to weaken or unsettle 'Black' as a composite racial category.

Academic and political debates have increasingly focused upon this second moment and the kinds of cultural and political implications that flow from it. This has tended to shift analyses and discussions away from merely or primarily how Black cultural and political practices contest racism, to how they deal with the internal politics of Black identity. Black identities, practices, and discourses are increasingly framed within a dominant critical paradigm, which sets the terms upon which politics of Black representation and criticism can be discussed. The extent to which Black cultural practices and representations offer new emancipatory possibilities 'beyond race' (Gilroy 2000) becomes a primary criterion for assessing their political and ethical merits. Black cultures and practices that can transcend racial categorisations, by valorising syncretism and hybridity are typically celebrated as making possible new anti-racist futures beyond the confines of 'race'. Cultural expressions that emphasise cultural or biological sameness, which can be shown to deny or suppress internal differences within, and external similarities across, racial categories are dismissed as essentialist. The extent to which the former is effective in producing new postracial/non-racist or anti-racist futures is read off from their capacity to transcend fixed certainties around race, ethnicity, nation and so on, whilst the extent to which the latter reproduce racism can similarly be deduced from their essentialism. What is less certain, however, is how effective this division is in understanding what such practices mean for those who deploy them and the material and social conditions of racism to which they may be a response, or how such formations and practices maybe internally differentiated and contested.

In this chapter I want to use the example of the Sacred Woman African-centred women's healing and personal development programme to think through the complexities of the politics of representation, the politics of Blackness. I set out, through close textual analysis as well as interviews, to understand the formal discourse of the programme and then how it is interpreted by women who use it. The chapter will examine how Black identity as a racialised embodiment is deployed – strategically[4] and non-strategically – in the untidy everyday tactics that some Black women deploy to empower themselves in struggles against the various individuals, groups, institutions and systems that they understand as blocking their path to autonomy, self-determination or freedom. These 'new' liberation struggles take place largely outside of the old forms and arenas of politics, increasingly emerging at the level of the individual and acted out in the contours of the everyday, the personal, and on the body, producing a poetics and aesthetics of the self.

The Sacred Woman programme is one of many life-coaching and self-development programmes specifically targeted at Black women that have appeared in recent years. From the popularity of books by Iyanla Vanzant (1993, 1998, 1999, 2001) to workshops run by a variety of Black trainers in the UK, many Black women have been embracing these programmes as a vital resource of self-development and social empowerment. In the analysis[5] that follows, I suggest that the programme is concerned with the aesthetics of Black existence and freedom, and the states of mind, health, body and social relationships that ought be considered as adequate signs of freedom for Black women. In order to introduce the programme I shall first outline its general philosophical and ethical base before discussing the structure of the programme and some of its key techniques.

Afrocentrism and the Khamitic Nu(bian) woman

The Sacred Woman programme, devised and written by Queen Afua – herbalist, holistic health specialist and lay midwife – is based primarily on

Khamitic-Nubian African-centred philosophy, which provides its core historical, religious, biomedical and philosophical knowledge base. In addition to this, it relies heavily on a variety of alternative therapies such as yoga, numerology and herbalism. These are brought together to produce an educational, therapeutic, and spiritual self-development programme. In this analysis I shall concentrate on the overall philosophy of the programme and how it is developed and deployed in the construction of what I call a Khamitic-melanin discourse of the body and history.

The stated core knowledge base of the programme is Khamitic-Nubian cosmology and philosophy. Although the training manual makes no direct reference to Molefi Kente Asante, its philosophy is clearly that of Afrocentrism as developed in his work (1990, 2001), which in turn relies heavily on the ideas of Chiek Anta Diop (1963, 1974), and Maulenga Karenga (1984, 1989). However, the main Afrocentric sources cited in the manual are Wallace Budge's (1895) translation of the *Egyptian Book of The Dead* and Karenga's translation of *Selections from the Husia: Sacred Wisdom of Ancient Egypt* (1984). The Afrocentric interpretation of ancient Egyptian cosmology expounds a philosophy of human existence and the body that regards the human body as a miniature universe, in which each part of the body is linked to one of the Egyptian deities or divine principles. Each principle governs a part of the body and its influence can be brought to bear on it, through rituals of supplication and homage. It is grounded in a homology in which all parts of the body are joined to each other and to the particular divine principles, associated with particular parts of the body in a spiritual exchange. In addition one's lifestyle is regarded as a manifestation of the psychological, physiological and metaphysical processes of the body, which are themselves manifestations of cosmic spiritual processes (Gadalla 2003). Consequently, how one looks, behaves, thinks and so on are all expressions of one's level of spiritual development and Khamitic consciousness.

Afrocentrism conjoins this Egyptian cosmology to an African-centred histography offering an alternative theory of history and knowledge about Black people, culture, and Black reality to the one that dominates within Eurocentric and Western epistemologies. The primary preoccupation of Afrocentric philosophy then is to challenge Eurocentric accounts of the world, and specifically the status of Western modernity, as the hegemonic time/space of normative reality (Asante 1990: 5), through the elaboration of an alternative theory of African history, existence and historical consciousness, in which a Black-African Egypt is the centre and standpoint of knowledge.

Reassigning Egypt's place in human history is a fundamental tenet of Afrocentrism. In this the work of Chiek Anta Diop is central. The main thesis of Diop's work is a redefinition of the place of Egypt – or Khamit (a pre-Grecian name for Egypt) – in African history in particular, and in world history in general. Diop lays out extensive historical, archaeological, and anthropological evidence to support the argument that the civilization of Egypt is Black African, is inseparable from a unified continental African culture (rather than classical Greek culture) and is the real origin of Western civilization. Diop argues that a redefinition of history is a prerequisite for the empowerment of an oppressed people's capacity to know themselves and to resist external aggression (Diop 1974: 214). In other words, rediscovery of self involves developing an African historical consciousness. This requires the recovering and recentring of the true African Personality through a process of moral, historical and psychic re-education and transformation in which the African rejects the impositions of Western 'Black' subjectifications and identities (ibid.). In Afrocentrism, this involves the rejection of modern Black identities such as 'Black' and especially 'Negro', which are viewed as Western impositions that obfuscate African reality (Asante 1990: 134). Instead, as seen in the Sacred Woman programme, an African-centred approach reclaims African terms such as 'Khamit' for Egypt and 'Nubian' or 'Afrakan' for Africans.

The debates concerning the origins and status of Egyptian civilisation have been exhaustively addressed elsewhere (Bernal 1987; Lefkowitz 1996; Appiah 1997; Howe 1998; van Binsbergen 1999) and the veracity or otherwise of the philosophy upon which the Sacred Woman programme is built is not my primary concern here. What is of interest is how an African-centred philosophy is applied within the Sacred Woman manual to: (i) produce an ethical and aesthetic programme of self-transformation and creativity in which biology and history are fused in a poetics of African-Diaspora femininity and subjectivity; (ii) reject the Cartesian dualism of Western modern subjectivity; at the same time as inscribing an alternative *biohistory* (Foucault 1978/1990; Burkitt 1999) of modernity; (iii) show how the formal discourse of the programme, that by any reckoning would fail the 'hybridity – good, essentialism – bad' test, is disrupted and adapted through the processes of cultural translation that occur as it flows through the African Diaspora.

The Sacred Woman programme: liberating the Black woman

The structure of the Sacred Woman programme is a nine-stage developmental programme for 'healing the feminine mind, body and spirit'. The nine stages or *gateways* that one must pass through to reach true womanhood all involve a range of techniques aimed at healing and liberating women of African descent through a programme of education, consciousness raising, self-healing and spiritual development. In fact there are ten gateways. There is a prerequisite 'Gateway 0' that one must pass through in order to gain access to the others. The purpose of liberation is to empower each participant to be healthier, more effective in her role as partner, mother and healer of the African family and community, and ultimately of all of humanity, 'This book is a reminder from the universe that you possess the innate power to create transformation and change – personally, communally and globally' (Queen Afua 2000: 3). It targets women of African descent in the Diaspora, especially African-American women, and aims to connect them to what Queen Afua says is the ancestral philosophy and way of life in ancient Egypt from which Black people have become forcibly alienated through the effects of racism – that is, Nubian-Khamitic philosophy.

Liberation of one's authentic Khamitic feminine selfhood involves becoming conscious of oneself as a spiritual African woman, and how to care for the particular needs of the African body. Freedom is constituted in rediscovering and re-entering the 'spiritual traditions of ancient Khamit – the Mother of Northern Egyptian culture' (Queen Afua 2000: 5) through overcoming ignorance (ibid.: 7) and thereby achieving Nubian Afrakan-Khamitic consciousness and harmony – *Ma'at*. The gateway to Khamitic consciousness and *Ma'at* is through both knowledge of the body and embodied knowledge of an 'ancestral memory' (ibid.: 14) written in and on the body.

The sacred gateways to self-knowledge

Each of the gateways offers a set of regimes which Queen Afua calls 'spiritual exercises' (Queen Afua 2000: 28). Each represents a complex care regime, targeting different aspects of the self, the body and one's family and social relationships. These include bathing, altar and libation rituals, prayers, chanting, affirmations, breathing and meditation exercises, dietary observances, and daily journal writing. The most intensive and detailed is the *Sacred Womb Gateway*, which is the introductory gateway numbered 0, that must be passed through in order to proceed onto the programme. It targets the whole body in a holistic programme of self-awareness in which the body, spirit, and consciousness are ministered to. Other gateways are the *Sacred Word*, which focuses on speech, communication, and cognitive awareness; *Sacred Foods*, which deals with eating and weight disorders, nutrition, and the social aspects of food preparation and consumption, together with the rights and responsibilities of women as feeders of other people. The *Sacred Movement* gateway acts directly on the body in terms of posture and movement, including dance, in order to harmonise body, mind and spirit. The *Sacred Beauty* gateway addresses skin and hair care, cosmetic procedures, dress, etiquette and sexuality and aims to harmonise the inner and outer body and release spiritual energy. *Sacred Space* focuses on the aesthetic and physical aspects of the home, domestic hygiene, the use of colour, aromas and positioning of objects to bring 'your home and work space into divine clean order that will create balance and harmony within and throughout your life' (ibid.: 248). The *Sacred Healing* gateway teaches women how to use intuitive knowledge and natural healing methods, together with herbal remedies. The *Sacred Relationships* gateway is where women can explore their inner relationship with themselves and with others, especially other women. This work 'eliminates toxic, dysfunctional relationships that destroy life and creates and supports cleansed, honest and harmonious relationships that energize one's life' (ibid.: 322). The *Sacred Union* gateway builds on the previous one and focuses on inti-mate heterosexual relationships, marriage, and sexuality. It is the only gateway that includes exercises for men. Finally and always last of all, is the *Sacred Initiation*, when the successful adherent of the programme passes into the Khamitic community, marked by adopting a new African name.

Each gateway represents a spiritual path but they are not sequential. Gateway 0 establishes the primary importance of the womb as the centre of the Sacred Woman's consciousness and agency. Thereafter, subsequent gateways can be followed in any order. Each largely repeats and consoli-dates the same rituals and regimes laid out in Gateway O. Additional techniques target the particular focal point of that gateway and the divine principle or deity associated with that part of the body. Through this vast array of practices one is invited to transform oneself from a Negro to an Afrakan, from a pathological identity and way of life to a free person. Freedom is achieved and maintained through the work one does on one-self, for 'If one expects to sort out freedom and move from a dead to an alive existence, one must have the courage and be willing to sacrifice one's old worn out non-effective self' (Queen Afua 2000: 3).

Bearing slavery, feminising freedom

The Sacred Woman programme provides health education through the provision of diagrams and information regarding the structures and processes of the human body and psyche. The programme offers a diag-nostic and therapeutic discourse of the Afrakan body, which produces novel explanations for the causes and appropriate cures for a variety of physical and emotional ailments. The Sacred Woman programme sets out to correct and manage what it regards as the pathological inauthen-tic identities, bodies and modes of existence of Black people within Western modernity. Queen Afua asserts that 'Afrakan people in America and the Caribbean and various parts of the world' are in a state of physical, cultural, and social pathology. This pathological identity and lifestyle is the result of Diaspora Afrakans' enforced separation from Africa and from their traditional culture and religion. Slavery, racism and imperialism have produced 'incomprehensible trauma, carried through our blood into the present day …' (Queen Afua 2000: 126).

Therefore the aim of the Sacred Woman programme is the recuperation of what it regards as the authentic premodern Afrakan consciousness and personhood. Transformation and liberation involve an ontological recovery of self through care of the body. Failure to follow the programme's prescriptions for liberation and health leaves you in a 'toxic' state of existential, spiritual and physical pathology, chained to a 'non-effective self'[6] and suffering all manner of somatic symptoms of your soul's distress.

Queen Afua deploys melanin to establish her authority to guide and instruct initiates when she states 'I have been blessed to pick up where I left off thousands of years ago, because knowledge of self is in my DNA, in my melanin' (Queen Afua 2000: 14). Just as melanin is posited as the essence of the Afrakan body and emotionality within the ethical regime of Queen Afua, so the womb is the centre of the Afrakan woman's being and virtue. In numbering the Sacred Womb Gateway 0, the womb is represented as the zero-sum of Afrakan woman's being. Gateway 0 aims to raise Black women's consciousness through 'womb enlightenment' (ibid.: 33). Womb enlightenment '[p]romotes the ability to contact true femininity through grounding in the female organs; the integration of the feminine with the female sexual and biological self' (ibid.: 31). The womb secures the Afrakan woman to her symbolic value and social identity – creator/mother. This also affects her biological, emotional and social functioning. Although the womb physically and symbolically is the centre of an Afrakan woman's power, it is also the site where the emotionality produced by melanin makes her most vulnerable. Queen Afua says that since opening her Heal Thyself Centre in New York in the early 1980s, she has discovered first hand that African women 'are holding 400 years of pain, abuse, secrets, rape, incest, anger and resentment in our wombs'.[7] The impact of this for Black communities is potentially catastrophic, she says, because the Black woman is the Mother of the nation and ultimately humanity, and is responsible for its well-being (ibid.: 75). Therefore care of self is a prerequisite for care for others and for exercising personal agency and social power. This requires bringing to the surface the deep embodied memory of these womb traumas.

Two important exercises in Gateway 0 involve journal recordings and confession. Women are asked to produce a Womb Work Journal in which participants are to record reflections on their wombs and the histories and stories of their wombs; the pleasures, the abuses, the sexual relationships, miscarriages and abortions, and so on (Queen Afua 2000: 44).

In producing this journal Queen Afua counsels women to avoid putting their minds above their bodies (ibid.: 43) and instead let their wombs speak to them. 'As we enter into the depths of our wombs, we will discover that our womb remembers and is prepared to speak to us of every fear and joy' (ibid.: 44).

The second exercise involves forming a Sacred Circle with other women in which each woman shares with the group the insights she has gained through their Womb Work Journal work. As each woman takes turns to tell her womb story, the rest of the group recite a chant called 'I Cry A River of Tears That Heal'. One verse of this chant is

I am an Afrakan Woman, crying out my pain, screaming and retching Rivers of Tears from generation to generation. My tears boil up from the bile of plantation slave life here in America the Beautiful. Here, where institutionalised sex factories were brutally imposed upon a stolen people. (Queen Afua 2000: 57)

The prevalence of fibroids, menstrual problems and hysterectomies amongst Black women in America are explained by Queen Afua as the scar tissues left by slavery and racism. However, by practising the techniques and regimes laid out in the Sacred Womb Gateway, Queen Afua assures Black women that we can rediscover the natural state of our wombs that our ancestors once possessed in Africa, when Africa first gave birth to humanity. It is this DNA-melanin encoded memory of Africa that must be discovered and released through exercises that attempt to fuse contemporary experience and historical memory. It is through such acts of performative remembering that the programme sets out to facilitate the internalisation of Afrakan-Nubian consciousness in which 'mind, body and spirit' are unified in *Ma'at* harmony.

African-American women's wombs have indeed been a site of intense social and political struggle concerning the right of African Diaspora women since enslavement to control their bodies and their reproductive capacities. Loretta Ross (1993) in an analysis of African-American women's experience of abortion and reproductive rights from 1800 to 1970 offers a harrowing account of African-American women's health experiences. In the slave economy, the Black woman's womb was a source of profit and labour for the slave owner. Ross outlines the practices by which enslaved women would seek to both control their own fertility and also resist the alienation of their sexual bodies by the economic system of slavery, in which a prime value of a Black woman was as a 'breeder woman'. This included various means of preventing pregnancy and inducing abortions as pragmatic acts of resistance to slavery (ibid.: 144). Even more compelling and tragically, infanticide was one way that an enslaved woman could refuse to pass on the 'uterine legacy' (Bush 1990: 137) by which the slave status was passed on through the maternal line.[8] Infanticide and abortions in this context became practices in which the enslaved African woman could seek to liberate her hyphenated subjectivity as *'slave'-'woman'*, shackled to an alienated and objectified body, in which her own womb and its creative potential was itself the source of her inherently feminised and racialised dishonouring.

In post-emancipation America, Black women's procreativity has been no less the target of white racist and Black sexist power. African-American women's activism around reproductive and women's rights in the twentieth century has contended with issues such as forced sterilisation under the influence of the eugenics movement prior to the Second World War; the anti-birth-control lobby within masculinist Black nationalist discourses since the 1960s; contemporary public policy initiatives which target, pathologise and then penalise Black women's reproductivity through the stereotype of the 'welfare mother'; inadequate public health provision for uninsured poor people, and the misogyny and violence that can be found in conditions of urban disadvantage and expressed in some forms of Black popular music (Ross 1993).

In targeting the womb as the centre of Black women's subjectivity we can see an attempt to address the situated historical and contemporary experiences of Black women within the USA. However, whilst Queen Afua acknowledges the statistical evidence regarding the health outcomes for African-American women, her explanation and remedy lies not in society but in contemporary Black women's relationships to their bodies and to history. In an interview in London with the Black-British comedienne and radio presenter Angie La Mar, Queen Afua was asked to explain what 'womb wellness' means. She responded:

> I have seen thousands of women over the years who have come to see me for different health-related problems. What they all have in common, approximately ninety per cent of them, is some kind of womb affliction, whether it was incest, or rape or they were in a relationship which was sexually abusive, whether they did not take good care of themselves or they went from one relationship to the next trying to find a blessing but instead received hurt and pain, so they ended up having some form of womb trauma.[9]

In a disturbing conflation of rape, bad relationship choices and 'not taking care of oneself' Queen Afua seems to make individual Black women solely responsible for overcoming the effects of poverty, racism, sexism and male violence. Yet it is important to recognise that the Sacred Woman programme is acknowledging and responding to the situation of many women of African descent across the African Diaspora, where female-headed households are prevalent (Senior 1991) and women have accepted the responsibility of earning, rearing children, maintaining the home as well as taking care of the general well-being of the community. In many African Diaspora cultures, as in most others, motherhood is a paradoxical condition; for it is the 'gateway' to honour and adulthood, *but simultaneously* to an increased vulnerability to poverty, sexism and racism (Noble 2000: 161). In this regard, it could be argued that the programme seeks to revalorise Black women's reproductive and caring labour, which structures and governs the lived experience of so many Black women, in order to transform it into a source of power rather than victimisation.

So in the powerful Womb Circle exercise we see firstly the naming of the historical trauma of rape, sexual exploitation and the specifically feminised forms of dishonouring that racism and sexism inflict upon Black women's bodies. Secondly, Queen Afua locates the scars of this experience deep in the wombs of contemporary African-Diaspora women 'that damaged them down to their DNA' (Queen Afua 2000: 57). The Sacred Woman programme tells us that this embodied memory of contemporary and historical trauma is brought on by the sensitivity and vulnerability produced by the effects of melanin, that we all, regardless of where in the Diaspora we might be, share in and are at risk from. However, through the painful and moving Womb Circle exercise this history of Black women's suffering is reified, and thereby rendered accessible to Black women's personal agency. It becomes personal, manageable, and available to therapeutic intervention creating the possibility of not just health but also self-empowerment.

Khamitic ethnobiology: melanin, trauma and the biopolitics of remembering bodies

In the Sacred Woman programme, melanin is cited as the primary ontological and biological mechanism within the Afrakan body, its defining and master DNA marker. Beyond this no explanation is offered of what DNA or melanin are. Instead we are only told of the effects of melanin on the African body and consciousness. It is beyond the scope of this chapter to discuss the biological evidence for the properties and importance of melanin. However, the uncontroversial properties of melanin are that it the biochemical mechanism and substance that gives the colour to the skin as well other organs of the body – both visible and non-visible (Nicolaus 2003). Melanin is also a substance impacting on a number of important biochemical functions within the body. As we shall see many of the claims made about melanin in the programme reflect a growing melanin discourse within Afrocentrism, that has been widely disseminated within the USA and is being globally disseminated across the technologically advanced locations of the African Diaspora through the many Black and African-centred websites accessible on the Internet.

Within the Sacred Woman programme, melanin is conceived as being at the interface of the inner body (soul/spirit) and the outer body (skin colour/social identity). Queen Afua says that melanin is the transmitter of the 'natural' emotionality of the Afrakan, which in its damaged state of unconsciousness is at risk of a terrifying assortment of somatic responses to the pain of racism and existence within the West.

> Melanin plays a contributing factor to our ill health ... The stronger your melanin, the more you will hold emotions and chemical toxins. When it is time to let go other races with less melanin can release these things more easily, but our melanin holds on to all that.
> (Queen Afua, interview with Angie La Mar on *The Women's Room*)

This implies that being Black is inherently risky, for in the absence of a proper awareness of this relationship of self to the body, the 'Afrakan' subject is in a state of unconsciousness leaving one vulnerable to a variety of dangers. By these mechanisms the programme establishes a relation between self and the body that is racialised. It also feminises this racialised subjectivity through particular practices of the self, which seek to naturalise and authorise a particular construction of 'true Afrakan womanhood'. It does this by asserting that the Afrakan woman's body 'naturally' produces particular needs, which if left unattended (due to ignorance or indiscipline), produce psychological, emotional and physical ailments. In short, lack of self-knowledge makes you sick and keeps you oppressed. The programme advances a model of Black subjectivity that is grounded in a dialectical relationship between the racialised body and an embodied memory or history. In so doing it establishes a continuity between these two aspects of the self as the ontological truth of Black existence. Thereby it denounces the racial bodily schema of modern/ westernised Black identities as being damaged by fissures and discontinuities in the 'proper' or 'truthful' relationship between the body, memory and the self. In this fractured state of disembodied and self-alienated consciousness the African descendant in the West cannot experience real and effective freedom. Therefore, liberation requires knowledge of the body. In this regard, the programme offers an alternative biopolitics of the Black body to the hedonism found in some elements of contemporary Hip-hop and R'n'B music (Gilroy 1994). Through an African-centred axiological reinscription, it disinvests from those pervasive commodified representations and reinvests the Black body with more spiritual and historically accountable meanings.

The kinds of knowledge or remembering being articulated through the role assigned to melanin can be explored through the literature on trauma and post-traumatic shock syndrome. Allen Young (1996) describes the processes by which a relationship is established between physical trauma and mental trauma in post-traumatic stress disorder. A transferral circuitry is set up between physical trauma and the mental and emotional memory of trauma. This circuit is established by analogy and genealogy. *Analogy* establishes a psychological connection by transferring images, emotions and words located in one space (the body/the world) into another (the interior processes of the body/the psyche). *Genealogy* establishes an historical connection where the memory of an event triggers neurological reactions in the body that become unconsciously learned automatic triggers producing instinctive fears (ibid: 89–91). Applying this model to the Sacred Woman programme, we can see how harmful and painful experiences in the world (racism and sexism) are transferred to the inner space of the body. Secondly, the *collective* memory of slavery and the *personal* memory of past individual experiences of racism and sexism are explained as the 'triggers', which instigate the instinctive reactions of melanin, producing particular pathological effects on the body, mind and spirit. 'Memories are acquired ontogenetically, through the organism's own experience of pain and they are acquired phylogenetically through inherited fears' (ibid.: 91). This insight is helpful, for it enables a way of understanding how the *memoropolitics* of the Sacred Woman's ethical regime invests in melanin as the master gene structuring Afrakan ontology. *Ontogenetically*, melanin is the mechanism and substance by which the Black female body, mind and spirit are rendered vulnerable to the traumatising effects of contemporary racism and sexism. *Phylogenetically*, melanin is the transmitter of the traumatic as well as redemptive legacy of African history. In this way the programme establishes a psychogenetic model of both cultural transmission and racial memory. It is melanin that connects the diverse ontogenetic experiences of contemporary racist-sexist abuse to the phylogenetically embodied racialised memories of the historical trauma of slavery and colonialism that unites Africans in the Diaspora within a single structure of being.

In articulating this performative, embodied 'memory-politics' (Young 1996: 89) the Sacred Woman programme constructs a theory of a universal Afrakan subjectivity in which melanin is the transcendental marker of Afrakan being and identity. The Khamitic-melanin discourse of the Sacred Woman programme both *uses* and *refuses* old and new forms of racial science and racial discourse. In this regard, it appears to offer an African-centred counternarrative or complement to new scientific uses of racial and ethnic categories emerging through the new life sciences (Kohn 1996). It is as though in the face of the new geneticism of the life sciences, it becomes necessary for Queen Afua to seize some control over this new science and find a way of making it work in the service of Khamitic femininity. In this sense it directly engages the biopolitics[10] of modernity.

Biohistory and the racial ecology of modernity

Biopower refers to the rationalisation and mechanisation of life and the body that emerges within modernity. It is a modern mode of governance, which deploys technologies for disciplining the body and securing the docility and integration of citizens into the efficient social and economic running of society (Foucault 1978/1990: 141). Biopower can be contrasted with biohistory, which describes the interaction between life and the processes of history (Foucault cited in Burkitt 1999: 15). In *Bodies of Thought – Embodiment, Identity, and Modernity*, Ian Burkitt (1999), in challenging the splitting off of the body and subjectivity within modern humanism, argues for the mutual interdependence of mind and body in human nature (ibid.: 17). Not only are mind and body in mutual interaction and therefore both responsive to changes in either, the body also exists in time and space. Thus the human body develops in relation to environmental conditions which are also constituted in historical and cultural processes (ibid.: 16). He calls this interaction *biohistory* and the body is the very axis upon which biohistory turns (ibid.: 16). Thus Burkitt argues that 'life is a relation that can only be sustained as an ecology, as a series of interrelationships between different life forms and between these life forms and the environment,' in interaction with the relations of social history (ibid.: 16).

If we understand biohistory then as referring to the matrix of combined biological, social and cultural processes, relations and discourses historically produced over time and space, we can suggest that the Sacred Woman programme engages the biopolitics of modernity as a deeply racialised ecology. In this the Sacred Woman programme deploys melanin as a paradoxical substance. The mutual interdependency of mind and body within the programme's philosophy means that working on the body can harness melanin's potency in the service of self-care and self-determination. Yet the body's malleability is not infinite (Burkitt 1999: 17), for the capacity of biohistory to shape the body through cultural processes (biopower) is limited by the materiality of bodies. For just as a 'body can be worked too hard, placed under too much stress' (ibid.: 17), likewise according to Queen Afua melanin both enables and limits the capacities of Africans in the Diaspora to deal with the racial trauma of modernity. Yet the programme's attempts to secure an authentic unchanging African identity is constantly being undermined and unravelled by the ethnobiology of the programme, which insists on the body's biohistorical formation, and the interactivity of melanin, environment and experience. For of course this also means that the capacity of an homogenous melanin-fixed Black identity to provide the basis of liberation is also limited by the differential biohistorical formations of African identities across the Diaspora. This can be illustrated by looking at how the formal discourse of the programme is translated by Black women in different places as they adapt it to fit their specific and local experiences.

Colonial biohistories and transnational landscapes of memory

Despite the African-centred assurances of the Sacred Woman programme, it highlights the complexities of Black identity at the beginning of the twenty-first century, and reminds us that the politics of identity and racialised embodiment have never been identical across the global landscape of either colonial or postcolonial Black modernity (Gilroy 1994). Almost all of the women I have interviewed in London who use spiritual development and life-coaching resources turned out to be middle-class university-educated professional women. All of them expressed a strong commitment to personal success and social advancement, as well as to ideals of social justice and anti-racism. The ways in which these women spoke about themselves as Black women explicitly fused embodied sensibilities that drew on transnational networks of experiences (their own or other women's) in the Caribbean, Africa, the USA, and Europe as well as representations of Black women in local British and global media. All of the women interviewed considered appearance and comportment as potent symbols and elements in embodied aesthetics and poetics of identity, which could elicit both potentially racist reactions from white people and negative political or personal judgements from other Black people. For women who had used the Sacred Woman programme, comportment and style were regarded as significant markers of one's political and social identification with Blackness and/or anti-racism and needed to be consciously managed and manipulated. This was also shared by many of the women who were not familiar with Afrocentrism. However, some of these other women saw freedom in terms of liberation from the assumption that their political consciousness and social identifications could be simply read off from racially encoded modes of dress and self-presentation. Style and disposition were also used actively and unpredictably to contest a variety of Black identifications and as well as discrimination and racism. Being Black and *staying Black* was central to their attempts to shape their own identities and advance in British society. Staying Black was viewed by the women interviewed as an important mechanism for resisting hegemonic white/ middle-class incorporation. In this situation staying Black was often closely associated with refusing the invitation to collude with a symbolically 'white' middle-class establishment considered racist, and to disidentify with the Black working class.

Where aspects of the Sacred Woman programme could be useful for the personal agendas of individual women, they adopted and adapted them; where they did not, they were totally discarded. One participant in a Sacred Woman workshop in London told me of her experiences when she attended some workshops in the USA. She said she became aware that the women amongst whom the programme was popular in the USA seemed very different from its constituency in the UK. She reported that many of the women in the US workshop were from very educationally and economically disadvantaged situations, having experienced extreme levels of poverty within segregated American ghettos, high levels of domestic violence and sexual abuse. She contrasted this with the higher class and educational background of women she knew to participate in African-centred movements in the UK and Jamaica. These women she described as women who were politically engaged, and often with present or past links with Rastafari, who were attracted by the pan-Africanist and African-centred base of the Sacred Woman and other similar workshops. They did not necessarily accept all aspects of the programme's philosophy, but took the elements that were useful and relevant to them personally and politically and ignored those that were not. Her account of the differences she encountered between London and New York illustrates what can happen when transnational configurations are translated into and by new contexts.

Despite the surface appearances of similarities and equivalences between Black urban experiences in the USA and the UK, there are significant differences between specific locations of the African Diaspora. Black cultural practices have similarities and differences as they circulate through the global networks of the African Diaspora. To understand the different contexts in which the Sacred Woman programme is translated and localised within the experiences of being a Black woman in the UK it is helpful to reflect on the different *colonial biohistories* of people of African descent in the USA and Britain. Britain's relationship with its colonised labour force took place at a distance, at the other end of the world, whereas America's took place on its own soil; in other words, external colonialism and internal colonialism (Lemelle 1997: 142). The effects of these two colonial experiences on the contemporary positioning of each nation's racialised ethnic minority populations within the nation and national imaginary are rarely foregrounded. Racial segregation as an element of colonial governance occurred culturally, socially and psychically *inside* the American nation. It was tangible, visible, and routinely reinforced through brute acts of segregation and violence. Certainly until the mid-twentieth century, African-American experience and identity was fairly stable with very limited degrees of diversity due to the forms of structural and social separation and legal segregation that pertained there. Sidney Lemelle takes the view that this structural marginality informs the persistence of a unified culture of resistance across all classes of African-Americans (ibid.: 142). Consequently, a popular view amongst many people on both sides of the Atlantic is that 'race' and racism persist as the defining marker of difference in the USA.

On the other hand Britain, despite its imperial history, has managed to hold on to an innocent sense of itself as a self-contained 'island nation'. This, in part due to sheer distance, enabled indigenous British people to largely remain sealed off from the day-to-day brutish realities of colonial rule. Within Britain, it was decolonisation and the postwar mass migration of people from the new Commonwealth that brought the majority of white British people finally into close proximity to their erstwhile colonial subjects. Unlike the USA, the image of a racialised segregated black substratum across all levels of society is not so smoothly accomplished in Britain, where Black Britishness is more visibly and audibly hybridised and differentiated by intersections of country of origin, culture, language, patterns of settlement and religion. Moreover, in Britain 'race' is strongly articulated through class in such a way as to throw Britain's racialised ethnic minorities and the white urban working classes together in complex networks of social and institutional proximity. These have produced antagonistic as well as ecstatic encounters and relationships, which have evolved a specifically working-class 'urban' culture of multiculturalism that is simultaneously celebrated and fretted over. The underside of this urban multiculturalism is the uncomfortable reality that the British class structure also bears the traces of the colonial caste systems in which social advancement was often predicated on assimilation to delicately racially encoded class distinctions.

In the context of Britain, for some women oppositional Black-self assertiveness, *as the day-to-day re-enactment and re-creation of Black identities*, can involve the capacity to hold your ground against *coercive racialisation's* seductive liberal manifestations, and so avoid being alienated from one's embodied experiences and knowledge. This means refusing the invitation to enter into an invisibly racialised (therefore white) gendered, and classed middle-class[11] conformity as the condition of being recognised and accepted. On the other hand, for many of the women interviewed, Black embodiment (as an ethical or aesthetic performativity) was often strategically deployed in refusing or even mocking hegemonic assumptions by other Black people of what Black Britishness could signify.

Conclusion

By paying attention to what is presented as the specific (though not necessarily always unique) needs of Black women the Sacred Woman programme articulates *and* responds to the question that Fanon in *Black Skin, White Mask* (1967/1986) failed to consider when he wrote that 'the Negro suffers in his body quite differently than the white man' (ibid.: 138). That of course is how the Black *woman* might suffer quite differently in her body. The programme draws on an African-centred ethnobiology to produce a countermodern philosophy of the self, that rejects the mind/body dualism of liberal humanism and insists on modernity's accountability to the traumatic biohistorical formation of African-Diaspora identity and selfhood. Yet the programme's attempts to secure an authentic African identity are continually undermined by its diasporic circulation. Despite its own best efforts, the Sacred Woman is unable to finally hold at bay the deconstructive and reconstructive force of differential vectors of gender, class, and location within African Diaspora identities. No doubt there are women who hold rigidly to the programme's model of Black femininity, but what I found were more contradictory and diverse responses. The Sacred Woman's essentialism is revised and creolised through the processes of cultural translation that occur in different localities of Black identity. Translations of the Sacred Woman programme in London adapted much of its core ideas of Black homogeneity whilst also holding onto a strong sense of the continuity of Black embodiment across time and space. In my research I found that the Black body was brought in as a witness to the materiality of Black existence in Britain, whilst also being a supplement to other multiply hyphenated self-identifications (such as French-Haitian-American, Grenadian-Black Londoner, African-Jamaican, Black British from Manchester). From this perspective, Black embodiment appears as an organising biocultural nexus through which diasporic circuits of personal and shared experiences, histories and narratives of the self converge, in ways that deny the possibility of final closure but insist on the body's complex biodiscursive ecology in space and time.

Reclaiming the importance of Black embodiment is risky but does invite attention to the conditions in which emancipatory visions cannot afford to collude with an idea of freedom that assumes that the aesthetic erasure of bodies can be achieved 'without damaging the overall integrity of a person, his status as a unitary whole' (Gardiner 1979: 31), and that liberty can be detached from the structuring effects of one's embodied social experiences. In such a circumstance, deracination may simply catapult you to a kind of default human position – *white and male*. These are not irrelevant concerns, at a time when we again find politicians committing armies to war to in the name of advancing universal freedom and the values of Western civilisation. Or when Black women's social and sexual freedoms are celebrated and defended in the lyrics of Dancehall[12] DJs by condemning the freedoms and existence of other Black people whose forms of sexual liberty are regarded as 'foreign/ white/unnatural corruptions of "true" Black values and identities' (Noble 2000: 164).

In circumstances where being a 'visible minority' produces specific environmental and social risks that must be managed and overcome, critiques of essentialism must be historicised and contextualised, for there are no identities devoid of essentialist elements and moments. Historicising essentialisms means going beyond identifying their construction or mythical status to analyse the material, embodied and cultural ecologies and biohistories in which they emerge. This may help avoid the arrogance of simple dismissal or the romanticism of excessive relativism. Engaged cultural criticism involves a critical reflexivity on the conditions of possibility in which some essentialisms are rendered visible and others invisible and their rejection possible or impossible. It also seems important to take the time to find out whether there may paradoxically be emancipatory elements in moments of essentialism, which can be brought to give voice to criticism from within.

Notes

1. Cf. Eze (1997).
2. The Macpherson Report (1999) of the inquiry into the racist murder in south London in 1993 of Black teenager Stephen Lawrence at the hands of a group of white youths.
3. *Racialisation* denotes any circumstance where the idea of 'race' is employed in discourse. Robert Miles defines racialisation as the representational process in which social significance is assigned to biological human differences and used to group people together into social groups (Miles 1989: 75). Barker (1981) introduces the concept of 'new racism' to describe the processes by which racialisation works through cultural rather than biological differences.
4. Gayatri Spivak (1990) introduces the concept of 'strategic essentialism' to argue that there are moments when it might be necessary for members of oppressed groups to essentialise themselves, in order to resist forms of oppression.

5. My research and analysis have so far been limited to studying the very detailed and extensive manual for the programme *Sacred Woman – A Guide to Healing The Feminine Body, Mind and Spirit* by Queen Afua (2000). In addition I have interviewed users of this programme and other life-coaching self-development programmes designed for Black women.

6. Queen Afua, *Mission Statement*: www.blacknet.co.uk/sacredwoman/mission.htm (visited 20 July 2002).

7. Queen Afua, interview with Angie La Mar on *The Women's Room* (2000).

8. The slave status was legally passed on through the mother, as the law governing slave societies did not allow slaves to marry or recognise paternity in slaves as a significant social or legal status (cf. Guttman 1978).

9. Queen Afua, interview with Angie La Mar: 2.

10. Biopower also relates more closely to the actual biological efficiency of bodies. It deals with the regulation of biological processes to do with reproduction, health, death and so on. In contemporary society this takes the form of systems of health and social care, which invest in the body as the object of systems and procedures for the care ands welfare of the population. 'Their supervision [is] effected through an entire series of interventions and *regulatory controls: a bio-politics of the* population' (Foucault 1978/1990: 262).

11. Such concerns are often entwined with the desire to be regarded as respectable, which for women of all identities is often bound up with interconnected themes of gender, class, sexuality and 'race'. See Patricia Hill-Collins (2004); Beverly Skeggs (1997); Denise Noble (2000).

12. Dancehall is the name of a genre of reggae music that is characterised by the celebration of Black hypersexual femininity and masculinity, compulsory heterosexuality, and gun violence. Cf. Noble (2000).

Chapter 8

Uses of the Exotic: Body, Narrative, Mixedness

SUKI ALI

> When we live outside of ourselves, and by that I mean on external directives only rather than from our internal knowledge and needs, when we live away from those erotic guides from within ourselves, then our lives are limited by external and alien forms, and we conform to the needs of a structure that is not based on human need, let alone an individual's.
>
> Audre Lorde (1984: 58)

Biology for brown folk

At secondary school, we learnt about melanin. It was, we were told, the reason that black people were black. All it took was enough melanin to cover a sixpence to make a black person. In this biological model, the black person is clearly a deviation from the white norm, with a known and identifiable 'substance' – something to be studied in isolation – making 'the difference'. I imagined this melanin to be some kind of sticky stuff like treacle or tar, indeed I had heard on many occasions that people of colour were those who had 'a touch of the tar brush', another saying of the time. Melanin provides a link between the interior mysteries of the body and the surface recognition of 'race'. In the 'melanin class', I was told to stand up so everyone could get a good look at me and the teacher then suggested very cheerily that *I* probably had enough melanin 'in me' to 'cover half a sixpence'. This allusion to the cheeky Cockney chappie, Tommy Steele, who was a famous entertainer of the 1960s and early 1970s (when I was being used as an example for the class) still strikes me as ironic in the extreme. Less 'funny' was the lesson that there was a good, scientific reason for me to be brown, not quite white and surely not dark enough to be black. The one 'Asian' girl in the class was not singled out in this way, which I now find significant. It was my mixedness, arising from the sexual liaison of a white woman (my mother) with

153

a man from the Caribbean (my father), who must by default have been black, which entitled me to become this object of amused scrutiny.[1] Scientifically, socially and psychically I became an anomaly amongst my peers. I had to use this discourse of biological difference for many years to try to explain my raciality to myself (never to others), and yet I always knew that in fact, things were rather more complicated. It was a method of unsatisfactory simplification, which neither assuaged my own curiosity about the complexity of mixedness (and resulting inauthenticity as not 'properly' Black, white nor Asian), nor foreclosed the endless questions about my 'background' that dogged my own and my siblings' early lives, and continued into adulthood.

This story is not unique and is undoubtedly a story that comes from a particular time and location, and it is the possible changes to the ways in which we revisit such body narratives which provide the foundation for this chapter. The title is a rather impertinent borrowing from Audre Lorde's (1984) 'Uses of the erotic: the erotic as power'. I use it with all due respect for the profundity of her intellectual insights into the sexualised sensuality of her own body and the potential empowerment it afforded her once she accepted it. This story of my embodied difference, its visuality, its emotional depth, and its undeniable sensuality (eroticism?) is one which Lorde's work helps me to revise. Her work on the *liberatory* potential of eroticism is the inspiration for this chapter. The specific argument about embodied experience is not followed through to the exclusion of a social dimension, and is considered in relation to Foucault's work on the 'technologies of the self'. These two might appear to stand in opposition to each other at first glance; the one expounding the power of corporeal knowledge, the other with the ways in which external regimes of truth impact upon our own corporeal work, but I believe that insights from both can be usefully engaged in ways that are not necessarily incompatible. The shifts in the ways in which we imagine 'race' form the basis for a dialogue with narratives and memories of embodied raciality.

The development of the racial economy in the 'Western imagination' has a long and varied history. The ways in which 'race' developed as an idea has always been worked through in a variety of distinct yet interdependent disciplines. The 'natural sciences' emerged as particular forms of investigation into 'nature' but nonetheless have a clear relationship to the social sciences as we understand them today (Foucault 1970, 1975). In addition, we know that visual technologies, art and representation have played a key role in the development of scientific categorisations of social differences (Gilman 1992; Mirzoeff 1998; Sturken and Cartwright 2001). 'Race' was initially founded upon visible bodily differences such as skin colour, hair texture, facial features and so on. It is still the case that visual images play an important part in the dissemination of scientific developments and in gauging and informing broad and 'popular' understandings of scientific and social change (Crary 1990; Cartwright 1998). In addition, the ways in which we come to understand our own positionality, our sense of who we and others think we are, are in constant negotiation with the visual.[2] As Stuart Hall explains, '... seeing is regarded as a social practice' and 'social and psychic positions and related practices not only influence "readings" of popular culture (especially images), but are also "used" and "lived" subjectively, influencing from the inside out – not always in manifest or conscious ways – both what and how meaning is taken' (Hall 1999: 310).

In this chapter I will draw upon one aspect of the racial economy, the meanings and values attached to 'race', as represented within particular forms of popular culture and thus the popular imagination. I discuss the way in which 'the exotic' functions as a mediator of racialised (hetero)sexualities both in the popular and in the lived experience of those who occupy the discursive and experiential spaces of mixedness. If we understand the ways in which selves are subjectified as occurring within complex relations of power/knowledge we can ask how we might think of embodied experiences of mixedness, often perceived as undesirable and impossible positions as sources of strength and potential, as spaces to challenge, rather than of political evasion (Foucault 1982, 1984, 1994). Foucault's account of subjectivation suggests that although we are always constrained by the discursive regimes in which we are induced to become (racialised, gendered) subjects, the instability of the field of power, the interaction between techniques of domination and techniques of the self, allows potential for resistance and subversion (Foucault 1994). This means that although our 'choices' about who we might become are to some extent limited by the discourses available to us, we still have the possibility of subverting or resisting these, and thus challenging dominant ideals of, for example, 'race' and gender.

Below, I will begin by reviewing some of the writing on the historical relationships between racialised bodies, science and visuality, and how these inform discussions of 'stereotypes'. The idea of 'race' as visible difference has long been circulated into the public domain through the use of mass culture. Although this is crucial to the development of 'visible' identifications, the chapter does not engage with in-depth readings of the exotic in contemporary (mass) popular culture. I look at 'popular blackness' which is often, 'in fact', 'mixedness', and use the recent images of the 'new global beauty' to provide a brief situation of the kinds of issues at stake in appearances of the exotic. Next, I will discuss the way some 'mixed-race' adults narrate their own memories of embodied difference and multiplicity and recoup them into a coherent form of non-specific exoticism. The exotic in the collective cultural imagination is, of course, contextualised and may stand at odds with experiences of exoticness, and in concluding I will look at how the memories of embodied encounters are profoundly revealing of the impossibility of fixity in racial stereotypes of all kinds.

Exotic bodies – knowing others

The ways in which raciality is currently sustained follows well-established patterns and has been discussed at length elsewhere. It has been well documented how Enlightenment science was tied in to colonial enterprises, providing scientific evidence of the hierarchy of 'racial types' which was used to subjugate Other peoples (for example Goldberg 1990; Back and Solomos 2000; Gilroy 2000). It is also well documented that the fear and desire for Other bodies informed the building of Empire both in terms of creating national and racial identities and in managing these in ways that disciplined gendered and classed bodies (McClintock 1995; Stoler 1995; Young 1995). Importantly, the ways in which science classified Other inferior races was inextricably linked to the development of visual technologies and particular kinds of representation. Timothy Mitchell argues that in the nineteenth century the 'new apparatus of representation, particularly the world exhibitions, gave a central place to the non-Western world' and were an important method of constructing Otherness (Mitchell 1998: 294). Museum displays exhibited a wide array of artefacts and images from Other cultures and in so doing 'fixed' whole groups of people as savage primitives (Hallam and Street 2000). Victorian advertising took an explicit shape in constructing racial differences using images of black people to circulate stereotypical views of 'natives' in the 'homeland' that were then fed back to those in the colonies. McClintock (1995) discusses in detail how 'dirty' and 'uncultured' black people were used as a counterpoint to 'clean', culturally sophisticated white people in ways that established particular modes of heteronormative, classed whiteness as well as crude homogenising of black peoples. The relationship between art and science formed a link between sexually deviant working-class women and black women, linking in the imagination the rapacious (exotic) female body with the dangers attached to sexual excess such as disease and moral decrepitude of the white working-class female body (Gilman 1992). Particular 'racial' types became associated with certain kinds of sexuality, and these stereotypes inhere in many contemporary forms of representation. The list is immediately recognisable and is highly gendered: the black male as sexual predator; the insatiable, again animalistic, black woman; the sexually expert South Asian woman; the feminised South Asian man; the submissive Pacific Rim Asian woman; the sexually mysterious and cruel Pacific Rim Asian man; the lascivious and dangerous Arab (man) and so on (for example Doy 1996, Alloula 1998). These stereotypes are constructed through colonial discourse that required its relation to the colonising peoples of the West; such as the 'proper' and asexual, white woman who is of course middle-class (Hall 1992; Ware 1992), and the middle-class, white man, master of all, including his own sexuality and that of others (Davis 1990; Mohanram 1999). Working classes as mentioned above come much closer to the ethnic model of the excessive racialised Others and both were caught in chains of signification:

> The stereotype, which is its [colonial discourse's] major discursive strategy, is a form of knowledge and identification that vacillates between what is always 'in place', already known, and something that must be anxiously repeated – as if the essential duplicity of the Asiatic or the bestial sexual license of the African that needs no proof, can never really, in discourse, be proved. (Bhabha 1994: 66)

What these stereotypes have in common is an effect of corralling heterogeneous ethnic and/or 'racial' groups into fixed 'types'. Bhabha's point is that these supposedly obvious and natural 'types' are in fact constructed and highly unstable. They are also always incomplete, as they are impossible to achieve, which is why the processes through which they are produced, discourse in all its forms, have to be repeated. The discourse of 'the exotic' has similar problems and potentials to those of the 'types' outlined above and it functions in a similar way. It becomes a catch-all category of uncertain 'racialisation' and enables an erotic frisson that comes from confronting the relationship between something desirable, out of the ordinary and potentially dangerous. It is a vague, unstable yet useful category that can be reiterated in diverse forms. As such it is possible for travel agencies to discuss exotic locations, such as the Far East, for foods to be exotic, and, of course, for bodies to be exotic. Exotic bodies are though always sexualised and gendered, so whilst Edward Said quite clearly states the case for the West having been constituted in relation to the Oriental rest, he has been criticised for not considering in what ways such discursive strategies are gendered (Said 1978 and critiques, for example, Lewis 1995) The 'Oriental' is a gendered concept, Oriental subjects gendered. It is notable that 'Oriental' women occupy centre stage in the repertoire of the exotic. Pacific Rim Asian women have come to represent a particular kind of sexually desirable beauty in the Western imagination with the spread of global (sexual) tourism (see for example Jolly 1997).

Exotic and exciting: the popular face of Blackness

So far the racialised types I have discussed, which form the basis for thinking about the exotic, are considered to be clearly defined and known types, and all of these are based on an intersection of 'race' with 'colour'. The simple workings of 'commonsense', the myth of race, argues that the Negro is black, South Asian is brown, East Asian is yellow and so on. What is also clear is that much of the contemporary writing about 'Other' bodies falls into similar traps. Bhabha's African is undoubtedly a Black person. Said's Oriental is 'yellow' or brown. They come from a bounded ethnic group, recognise themselves as belonging to that group and are identified monoethnically and racially. They fall into a neat area of difference that is already binaried. This is white against Other/non-white and offers little in the analysis of the relations between the other Others, especially those who cross neatly defined boundaries of 'Asianness' for example (see Song, Chapter 3, this volume).

Racism takes many forms and those are indeed often based upon the centrality and hegemony of valuing whiteness. However, the relationship between and across 'non-white' Others is complicated and 'colourism' or 'shadism' is depressingly commonplace. The range of skin tones that encompasses the full spectrum of racialised ethnicities has huge amounts of overlaps. Despite this, hierarchies of colour operate in places that have highly multiracial populations such as Brazil, Mexico, the Caribbean as well as, arguably, the whole of the overdeveloped (white?) world.[3] Within these formations of difference, 'blackness' as 'colour' becomes a complicated and non-homogenous form of exoticism. Images of blackness are important to both challenging and maintaining the relationship between blackness, other 'non-white' identifications and uncertain exoticism as mixedness.

In an earlier piece of research I used auto/biographical memory work with my own family to explore the meanings of mixedness we held. The 'exotic' was a theme that appeared at an early stage and has been a feature of much of the research that has followed. Here, the role of mass media and public consumption of images of difference, including representations of blackness, were key to understanding how my mother 'learnt' about 'race' and racism. She revealed a fascination with exoticism that emerged as a young woman. Her girlish opinions were tempered by her growing understanding of racism as she became an adult who engaged in an interracial relationship in 1950s London, and was subject with her partner to racist abuse and violence. In the interview, she talked of being taken as a teenager to see the *Ballet Negre* in London.

She described the attractiveness of the dancers in a quite sexual way, as 'different ... exotic ... the ultimate brunette ... out of this world'. These people were highly desirable to her, yet at the same time totally 'alien'. The articulation of gendered discourses of 'race' and sexuality available to her at that time inevitably contributed to my mother's responses to these Others. The types of entertainment she was exposed to were limited and she quite openly, though with embarrassment, reported her entrancement at the sight of the people on the stage who were so different from any she had seen or even encountered in other forms of visual culture. Black, Asian and 'Oriental' performers were few and far between, and her politicisation around issues of 'race' was unformed.

A more ready source of images in popular culture at that time came from Hollywood films, and still provides a powerful supply of racialised images in contemporary popular culture. The Hollywood star system throughout my mother's childhood and young adulthood was famous for its inherent racism and its manipulation of acceptable forms of exoticism. The tradition of white artists performing blackness was well-known and accepted, as witnessed by minstrelsy and black-face, but also in less obvious ways. This was in part due social and legal conventions which forbade the interaction and sexual liaisons of white with black. A powerful example comes in the film 1951 film *Showboat*. Screen goddess Ava Gardner took the role of Julie La Verne, variously described as a 'mulatto' or 'half-caste', who passes as a white woman and is married to a white man. African American actress and singer, Lena Horne had already played the role in a 1947 biopic about Jerome Kerne, but was passed over for the Hollywood movie version. Horne, although pale-skinned, could not be allowed to be seen on screen in a sexual relationship with a white man, despite the fact that this was indeed the whole point of the storyline. In this case the representation and cooption of blackness work together. The black body is 'in fact' the white body in masquerade. Thus the exotic Other here is a whitewash. By removing both 'real' and 'imaginary' black women from interacting with 'white' men this very widespread and popular image of blackness is 'sanitised' through the workings of hegemonic whitenesses. The Hollywood system effectively reflected the way fear and desire for the Other is controlled, and the fiction of racial purity is maintained both on screen and off, by having a well-known 'white' woman play the role of an exotic 'black' woman.

Contemporary exoticisms

Despite the continued prevalence of whiteness in all forms of visual popular culture, particularly film and television, hegemonic beauty standards are changing and the ways in which whiteness has been the measure of beauty is shifting.[4] Halle Berry was recently voted 'the most beautiful woman in the world' in a readers' poll of a popular magazine.[5] Berry was the first black woman in the history of the US Academy Awards for Screen Acting (Oscars) to win the award for 'Best Actress'. Berry has discussed her mixedness openly and, as with many others, identifies as both black *and* mixed, a position that has been difficult for her. As bell hooks has noted, darker-skinned women are often seen as less sexually desirable than those whose blackness is 'tempered' by whiteness; the pale-skinned are desirable because they are less extreme and therefore less 'dangerous' (hooks 1992: 72). Certainly, gendered discourses of beauty are enmeshed with the eroticisation of 'colour' and ambiguous raciality. In Judith Butler's discussion of Nella Larsen's work on 'passing' she argues of a male character that '... it appears that the uncertain border between black and white is precisely what he eroticises, what he needs in order to make the exotic object to be dominated' (Butler 1993: 172). The mixedness is what makes the 'black' woman desirable to the white man. In similar vein we might argue that it is no accident that a woman like Berry becomes an icon of black femininity, appearing on the cover of magazines for both black and white women, desired and feted by white and black alike. She is both beautiful and black, exotic but not too dangerous, milk chocolate rather than dark. In common with other discussions about 'authentic' black beauty, this Berry falls foul of the old adage, 'the blacker the berry, the sweeter the fruit'. So for her this is the space-of-in-betweenness, not of her own understanding, but in the discourses of white vs black.

I agree that obviously Halle Berry's beauty does not intrinsically challenge hegemonic standards. But if meanings are produced discursively and through contestation I would argue that Berry has challenged some standards with her presence in film and print media. However, if she is to disavow her own mixedness, she becomes a body which is all surface, one which has no depth, no history. She is denied her own subjective positionality and becomes a sign to be read. Her own narratives of family and belonging challenge the surface reading of her body as unproblematically 'black' or 'mixed'. In hooks' analysis, representation of the exotic (mixed) female body is always consumed through the gaze of white males and is always and only ever repressive. This seems equally restrictive as it is a heterosexist reading and does not engage with discussion of black female desire, or range outside of the black/white binary.

Bhabha argues that a key feature of racial stereotypes in colonial discourse is fetishism and the disavowal of difference. The fetish, as above, comes to stand in for all that is not the same as oneself. The disavowal of difference requires a desire for 'originality', an originality in terms of 'purity' and certainty of belonging and type, which is inevitably always false. It is because of this falsity that there are possibilities for disruption (Bhabha 1994: 74–5). It is therefore essential that we acknowledge Berry's mixedness as well as her blackness in order to challenge the fiction of 'purity' in all racial types, and in relation to the exotic, popular blackness in particular. We should not assume that there are any 'true' originaries for those who claim to be either 'mono' *or* 'multi' racial. *All* narratives of 'race' are complex and constructed and this example is more graphic than most. Berry's mixedness is not literal or real any more than her monoracial blackness, it is the relationship between the 'blackness' and 'mixedness' as verbal and visual narratives that reveals the instability of the stereotype. Berry is both like and not like 'us', whatever our own 'racial' identification.

Global beauty

So far I have discussed the dominant discourse of mixedness, that of black and white, but another face has appeared on the global stage – making it as far as the cover of *Newsweek*. The new global beauty is the exotic par excellence – she is of 'mixed heritage', not Chinese, not Black African, not Indian, but mixed. Further her heritage is Indian, Irish and Canadian. Perhaps here is some potential for further disruptions of 'exotic' black/white, binaried stereotypes. The global beauty is, as with beauty more generally, female and feminine. She is a woman of 'mixed race' who is neither too dangerous nor too safe as she transgresses the simplistic limits to the racial imaginary of bounded raciality. She becomes everywoman.

> The 5 ft 11 inches sinuous beauty has cosmopolitan looks – a chiselled, sensitive face and a dusky complexion that is not too Asian for Western sensibilities. On a given day, Saira can transform into a girl of Indian or Spanish descent, a Moorish girl in gypsy skirts, an elite Italian socialite, or an all-American girl with a winsome smile, lounging in beachwear. She recently told a newspaper: 'I capitalise on all the angles. I am what I am, and if they want to pay me for being Punjabi, great. If they want to pay me for looking Spanish or Italian, wonderful.'
> (*Newsweek*, 6 November 2003)

This global beauty, Saira Mohan, is not only the embodiment of all things exotic, but also lives the cosmopolitan capitalist dream to the full. She is a highly paid model, but in addition to her life as a jet setter, Saira is a painter whose work has been exhibited in quality outlets

(*Newsweek*, 6 November 2003). She is no 'tragic mulatto' nor supposed rich man's plaything like the earlier 'exotic' women. Like Berry the narrative of her fame is that of a woman who has it all, and is in control of her globally spread, bourgeois life. So famous is she, she has been added to the pages of IncredibleIndia.org as something of a tourist attraction. Her beauty is of the type to entice visitors to the country of origin. Here she again perhaps becomes a commodity of raced gender when the sale of her image as the 'new spirit of India' echoes the old-style sexism and sexualisation of the Singapore Airlines 'air hostesses' of the past[6]. How are we to read the success of Saira Mohan and Halle Berry? As ciphers for the white man's fetishistic desire, or as women who reflect a shifting understanding of 'race' and ethnicity as unstable categories? Is their desirability just a new form of 'colonial' commodity spectacle – with the USA fulfilling the role of cultural imperial power – or could it be their success is in some part due to wider changes in thinking about 'mixed-race' bodies? Clearly there are competing ways of understanding these phenomena, and positioning them as a Manichaean puzzle, in which they have to be either white or black, serves no real purpose other than to tie us in to the tired old debates. What is interesting to me is that these women whether, 'black mixed', or 'Asian mixed', openly eschew the dominant model of monoraciality. They are part of a move to thinking across racial boundaries through narratives of genealogy – using 'private' and personal stories of family, heritage and blood to position themselves in the public domain.

Subjectivation: narratives of memory

The implications of the acceptance of the exotic into the mainstream of the popular imagination may be multiple but are often interpreted in two ways. One – this is progress; women of colour are beauties. Two – this is typical, the only way for blackness to be accepted is when it is diluted (sic) with whiteness.[7] This is less problematic than having a 'fully' South Asian or Black model of beauty in place. My argument is that something of both has to be true at the same time. Just as Halle Berry may be ambivalent about the way her mixedness has 'worked' for her, so many of us who are positioned as mixed are ambivalent about the rejection and the potential that comes from acknowledging our embodied multiplicity. The difficulties are fundamental to one's own subjectivation. For Foucault, the question is not how to theorise the subject, subjectivity itself, it is to ask how the subject constitutes himself (sic) through technologies such as the search for truth and self-knowledge. This is what he terms as the processes of subjectivation. He describes his position in the following way:

> ... I wanted to try and show how the subject constituted itself, in one specific form or another, as a mad or healthy subject, as a delinquent or non-delinquent subject, through certain practices that were also games of truth, practices of power and so on. I had to reject a priori theories of the subject in order to analyse the relationships that may exist between the constitution of the subject or different forms of the subject and games of truth, practices of power and so on. (Foucault 1994: 290)

This concern with methods and practices – what he calls techniques – by which a self becomes a subject is one that is open to shifts and contradictions. Lack of certainty is a fundamental part of the means by which we seek ethical freedoms to become selves, a process which is never complete. Who we might become is constrained by what we understand is available for our becoming and whether it is acceptable to us – morally, ethically, politically and so on. Whilst Foucault is notoriously unconcerned with issues such as gender and 'race' in his work, it is nonetheless fruitfully explored in relation to these issues in the work by a range of authors (McNay 1992; Ramazanoglu 1993). In looking specifically at the experiences of gendered, racialised 'exotics' it is the struggles with the games of truth, with the discursive regimes by which we come to explore our own selves, and thus constitute them, which we can understand as the 'mode of subjectivation'. In revisiting some of the practices with which my family and myself made sense of our own positionality, the ways in which discursive regimes work on issues such as sexuality, gender and 'race' are rendered explicit.

As a child, I was aware of being different. My siblings and I attended a small primary school in which the vast majority of pupils were 'white'. We were not; nor were we black in the way in which we had learnt. That we were Other went without saying. I recall knowing that I was not white but not really knowing what it meant. I was a brown child living with a brown brother and sister, and with a white mother. This was even more strange than had I lived with a brown mother, given that this was my 'birth mother', not adoptive. Once having revealed this fact to smiling strangers, she was immediately shifted from being an object of approval to one of disgust and shame. We children were the living proof of my mother's sexual liaisons with a black man, a man who did not live with us. I could make no sense of these things as a young child, and they continue to inform my own questioning of the way in which we have to negotiate our 'place' in racist, sexist societies. Clearly being 'seen' to be 'raced' in one form or another, being visibly different from our mother and the white majority, made us think about how we could both belong and not belong, were both similar and different to all kinds of 'others'.

Unknown others – ambiguity and the unknown self

I have already shown how the ambiguous and stereotypical exotic mediates black/white binaries in popular culture. In our everyday encounters the ways in which we have to engage with the stereotyping of exoticism often take the starting point as misrecognition. Drawing upon the limited understandings of 'race' and visible difference, encounters with strangers require them to position the unidentifiable 'mixed', non-white person into an identifiable category. In such cases we find ourselves in the situation of being positioned by others in ways that are counter to our own sense of identity. Sara Ahmed (1997, 1999, 2000) has written about this happening to her and her own discomfort about her responses. In her accounts she is passed as 'white with a sun tan', and she explores how her refusal to disabuse her interlocutors renders her complicit with dominant models of hegemonic whiteness. She argues that the politics of 'race' need to be reconsidered in relation to the ways in which all of us are at all times passing as something, and how particular antagonistic contexts invoke strategic responses.

My sister recounted to me that she vividly remembers her difference at primary school being mutable and unstable. She was always playing 'the gypsy or the Chinese girl or something' in the end-of-year plays. As she grew older she has also been passed as Turkish, Greek, French to name but a few, by people who originate from those countries themselves, while white English people were more likely to be uncertain and liked to ask for explanations of her appearance. In such cases we are all being asked to narrate a plausible account of our embodied presence. Although those who claim so-called monoracial backgrounds are likely to have to do this in any number of encounters, they do show that in addition to the conditions of hostility that Ahmed describes, we are often 'claimed' by ethnic collectivities, and then rejected from most as the 'truth' is told. My sister still experiences this to this day, and has 'learned to live with it'. It is she says, simply inevitable that people will not be able to recognise her 'correctly' in spite of her perception that the context in which this happens is less hostile to 'multiraciality'.

My brother also recorded feelings of great ambivalence about his appearance as a young man and the potential advantages and pitfalls attached to its reading by others:

> That was the first time really at school, at secondary school when I was first really aware of race I think ... or understood that I was, well – I never thought of myself as different, but I don't know how to put it really. But it was the way I was, not the same as, that's essentially different really, isn't it – well yeah – I suppose that my skin colour was slightly different, it was only slightly really.

The constraints of language are evident as my brother tried to verbalize his subjective experience of self; yet he continued to actively negotiate his own identity. He says that he does not remember being upset by racism, that he laughed off name calling and that 'acceptance' was most important to him:

> ... it's all just about being accepted really, you know, establishing pecking orders and all that sort of thing ... I sort of knew my place really, if you like in the ... in the social structure. Knew how to get on really, who not to piss off ... (pause) but whether actually I would've been higher in the social structure if I hadn't been tinted I don't know.

My brother used the word 'tinted' a lot as a way of describing his 'colour difference'. It has many overtones, not least of which, for me, is its proximity to 'tainted'. I also see his concern over hierarchy and achievement, acceptability and pecking orders as a 'gendered' concept. For him acceptability and achievement, some measure of dominance over others is crucial and it is only how 'race' impinges on this that bothers him. This theme is repeated when he talked of racism in the work place and the fact that he has encountered little of it and used 'diplomacy' and 'humour' to defuse any difficult situations he encountered.

My sister also said that she had racist name calling throughout primary and secondary school, though not a great deal, and her way of dealing with it was to administer humiliating verbal put-downs, or use humour. My own temper resulted in me physically attacking a girl who called me a 'nigger', and as I grew older I became incoherent with anger at the subject and found it difficult to respond to. I lacked the verbal and conceptual resources by which to make sense of my own position. I 'knew' difference was embodied, but not how that could be made sensible in other ways.

Enactments of self

My sister's accounts of her exoticism are all highly gendered. Her developing raciality was enmeshed in her understandings of herself as a young woman, who was an object of fascination and desire in a small town dominated by whiteness. She knew that both these aspects of her public presentation of self were crucial. She talked about how it was she knew herself to be sexualised by others in her daily interactions. She said that when she hit teenage, her anxieties about 'being different' shifted as she began to know that she was 'attractive to men'. Her understanding of her attractiveness was less focussed explicitly on her exotic appearance, although her positioning by others remained a source of comment. Her sexualisation continued to be a source of difficulty within her work environments where she felt particularly acute heterosexed gender relations were always racialised. Her friendships were characterised by a disavowal of difference, with her friends claiming they saw none, she was 'just Lisa'. This colour-blindness is typical of that era of assimilationist models of multicultural politics. It was exacerbated/enhanced by her upbringing by a white mother, with the major cultural influences in her life coming from hegemonic British (ipso facto 'white') culture.

The kind of sexed race my sister talks of is not confined to a singular notion of 'race'. The truly exotic in these terms gets stripped of authenticating culture or ethnicity and embodied signifiers become the most important aspects of the analysis. One does not have to have 'proper' credentials to claim belonging to a group or 'type'; that work is done by simply looking 'not-white'. The perplexity for myself and my siblings was such that this is somewhat of a relief in the face of the constant demand for the 'truth' of the self, an authentication of 'race', but left us in the superficial realm of visibility, a very unstable location. This instability could be a source of pleasure as well as difficulty.

My brother clearly remembers 'playing' his appearance as a teenager and remembers having a choice in this. He too reported feeling uncomfortable about reference to his 'exotic' appearance (his own word) and was explicit about this. His experience of being male and exotic took a particular form which was a type of sexual innuendo which he said was sometimes hard to decipher. He said that it had been very difficult to tell whether young women 'really fancied you or really loathed you'. Clearly this fits well with Bhabha's discussion of the fetishised stereotype, the object of fear and desire. But, the notion of choice is problematic here. It reinforces hierarchies of difference between black and mixed. It assumes a fluidity of possibilities, despite the skin being dark, that are less likely for others of more clearly monoracial backgrounds. It is also less clear how, for example, Said's exotic Oriental would function in this space.

As we can see from comments above, we have all at times also been misrecognised; in my sister's case as Chinese, in my own, Japanese. On the personal level it confused us, yet we used the same useless methods to make sense of our family.

Cohering narratives of uncertainty

One of the most striking features of the work done with my family is the variety of narratives that we drew upon to make sense of our situations. Not only had we (reportedly) differing experiences of our racialised embodiment, but our ways of working with these differed, and our memory work had utilised a range of meanings changing over time. The context in which we struggled to find a place in a small town in the 1960s and the ways in which we think through these issues in the new era of interracial exploration are the source of new positionalities. As Antze and Lambek note – we need to attend to the cultural shaping of memory:

> ... to the roles of trope, idiom, narrative, ritual, discipline, power, and social context in production and reproduction. Beyond the insistent metaphorisation of memory, we have been struck by the spread of talk about memory and especially by the interpenetration of individual and collective discourse: both how history borrows from psychotherapy and vice versa in their respective construals of their subjects, and how the memory of the individual – precisely that which is often taken to epitomise individuality – draws upon collective idioms and mechanisms. (Antze and Lambek 1996: xiii)

The process of narration acts as a technique of the self, similar to the writing of the self, but in much more fluid ways. The narrative process involves remembrance as a means of working from the surface of the body to the internal workings of the psyche and emotions which are felt as corporeal and sensual. Just as memories fall foul of archaeological metaphors of 'digging down' to 'uncover' an already existing memory-truth, so do the emotional selves narrated into place within the constraints of political raciology, which constantly reinvokes the body whilst disavowing its primacy. In this chapter it is not memory itself that is under investigation, but the broader cultural politics within which subjects are induced to think themselves as 'exotic', and the way these politics change over time. How do memory narratives of change operate in the contemporary moment of intense concern about interracial issues and the increasing numbers of people claiming 'mixedness'?

'Memories' of embodied encounters need narration and renarration in the changing relation of self and identity to the collective cultural discourses of 'race' and mixedness. As Audre Lorde argues, our most powerful encounters with the social are felt as erotically charged. '[For] the erotic is not a question of only what we do; it is a question of how acutely we can feel the doing' (Lorde 1984: 54). Thus this erotic sense of bodily rightness and joy (ideally) permeates our whole lives, especially our relationships with others, our work – everything. For Lorde then the erotic is an essential part of the politics of gender and race. In looking at how the exotic is felt, and then recuperated into the ordinary repertoire of selves we see how important it is to acknowledge the difficult uncertainties. From the early days of cinema, the visit of the *Ballet Negre*, my mother's generation saw exoticism as the acceptable and desirable form of 'racial' difference. In the 1960s and 70s, as we saw the technologies of home entertainment expand, the racial lines were still clearly drawn. It has taken until the last ten years in the UK, and the last five in the USA, to see the seismic shift in acceptance of interraciality on screen and in mainstream popular culture. With it, of necessity, the acceptance of the exotic has increased, but this is arguably still a 'safe' form of exoticism, the stereotype that Bhabha reviles.

The discussion here has shown how it is necessary to utilise certain methods of avoidance and management in the face of a remarkably adaptable form of Othering. The way in which Othering of an 'exotic mixed' position works is by maintaining the illusion that bodies can be read as 'racialised'. Over time the form that this takes may change, and also the ways in which this is used. The links between the personal and public culture of raciality are processed through the memory work of the subject of uncertainty. This results in a form of narrative dexterity that manages to hold together a thread of identity that is both sexualised and raced in ways that are constantly changing.

Searching for origins

During the past ten years one aspect of the narrative of racial heritage has grown enormously and that is the explosion of interest in family genealogies. There are numerous websites dedicated to the search for ancestry which claim to be able to trace the 'family tree' back across the generations. The systematic investigation of heritage is mirrored by the rise and rise of interest in 'race' in the life sciences. This is developing in relation to biomedical attempts to recognise how 'populations' may be differently susceptible to disease, and how they may also respond differently to drugs and treatment (Duster 2003). In addition, the Human Genome Diversity Project has also worked on the basis of mapping 'racial' and ethnic diversity (see Haraway 1997 for a critique of this work). Now, we are told, we can use DNA databases to search for our ancestral roots.[8] In a recent BBC programme, 'Motherland', several Caribbean British people did just this with the express desire to find their origins in Africa.[9] Predictably and movingly, they did not all find what they hoped for. Setting aside the one man whose ancestry included a white German in the not-too-distant past, those who visited the 'motherland' found for them were both uplifted by the sense of connection and rightness, and unnerved by their disconnection and difference from the 'indigenous' populations who embraced them with differing levels of enthusiasm. In a climate in which nationality, community and belonging are such centres of racial tension, in a world in which slavery is still a powerful and defining memory for many, it is no wonder so many turn to this kind of search in the desire for 'answers'. The search for 'roots' in these cases is not just idle vanity, but a political statement. Avtar Brah (1996) suggests the desire for homeland is a powerful force in diaspora identities, and in the examples here we see that this is true even when it holds potential for huge disappointment. What is relevant to this discussion is the centrality of the body, in this case the interior, hidden aspects of bodily inheritance. Now it is not just blood that gives us 'race', not just melanin that gives us our skin colour (see Noble, Chapter 7, this volume), but DNA that is carried in the blood and facilitates transmission of melanin. It is this that gives us histories and our narratives of identity.

In his late teens, my brother took an extended holiday during which he undertook a limited 'search for roots'. As part of his travels he visited Kashmir which is where my father's family had come from before 'ending up' in Trinidad.[10] He found the experience very emotionally powerful. He was strongly impressed by the appearance of the Kashmiri people whom he described as very striking-looking; 'very tall ... pale skin and green eyes ... not terribly "Indiany" looking'. He said in the interviews that to him this meant that our father was not purely Indian or certainly not purely Kashmiri, as he had dark skin and very dark eyes and hair and just did not 'look the part'. In other words, somewhere down the line there had been even more blood mixing with the African. In one of the more interesting memory quirks, my sister told me that she thought that my father had very pale skin, and hardly looked Indian at all. My brother's assessment accords more with my own, I always remembered my father as 'black', but most importantly these accounts reveal the ways in which our memory processes are capable of completely revisioning our memories – what we saw and how we interpret that. These memoropolitics are operating at the micro-level of the family in similar ways in which they operate at the cultural. We all used our own narrative forms to make a 'rational account' of various discrepancies and inconsistencies in the production of 'family stories' and a collective familial memory of raciality.

Conclusions

The 'changing face of race' remains a favourite theme of journalists and others in popular media. Despite a dominant politics of singularity in 'race thinking' the need to think outside black/white binaries is acute. Not least as we see important writing about Chinese diasporic identities (Parker 1995; Song 1999), ongoing work with the heterogeneous South Asian diaspora raising questions about identities (Alexander 2000a, 2000b), concerns with the demonisation of Arabs and Jews in British society (Silverman and Yuval-Davis 1998) and finally the work of those specifically engaged with 'mixedness' (although much of that is founded on black/white oppositions, for example, Ifwekunigwe 2000). What this work points to is the complexity of those who fall within the 'exotic' catchment of appearance and representation. Representation here inevitably incorporates the ethnic and cultural markers of difference including language, clothing, religious practice etc. These kinds of multiplicities require us to rethink the potential of postcolonial theory such as Bhabha's for those who occupy the interstitial. Crucially, these are not the margins or the borderlands any more, they are now part of the central zone of representation and more importantly of lived experience and the narration of self. In addition, claims to multiple ethnic or 'racial' affiliations go a long way to mitigating against the discursive anomalies of racialised stereotypes. Opening up spaces for discussions of multiplicity is important for the way they can be used to as challenges to the dangerous fixity of racial stereotypes, including that of the 'exotic'.

Notes

1. My mother is white, English, my father Caribbean Asian. My father was absent from the family from an early age and we were raised in a small town on the South Coast of England by my mother.
2. As I write this I am aware that this is a particularly 'ablist' version of the identification which relies upon vision as central to the 'successful' formation of an individual. This is an indefensible and problematic part of the writing on visual culture and subjectivity which if taken literally would exclude partially and unsighted subjects from being fully cognisant. This is not my intention, but I am working with materials here from three sighted adults for whom vision has been a central part of their racialised development.

3. See for example, Twine (1998) on Brazil, Sheller (2003) on the Caribbean, Yelvington (1993) on Trinidad, Hill-Collins (1990/1993) and hooks (1992) on the USA, Tate (2003) and Weekes (1997) on Britain.
4. There is a range of writings on racialised beauty and black anti-racist aesthetics, for example, Jones (1995), Hill-Collins (1990/1993), Weekes (1997) Tate (2003). I have written about this in more detail elsewhere Ali (2003) and Ali (2004).
5. *Eve* Magazine is published by BBC Magazines Worldwide.
6. See Puwar (2000) for a discussion of South Asian women, fashion and the commodification of 'Asian Cool'.
7. See for example a recent article celebrating the 'ethnically ambiguous' (Alridge 2004). In it a range of celebrities are feted for their ambiguous racial and ethnic style. It appears under the heading 'The New Melting Pot' and shows commodity exoticism at its worst.
8. A quick search on the internet reveals this to be a growth area of business. Many of the websites dedicated to searching for ancestry state that it 'doesn't matter which "race" you are', which is a clear indication that this service has been targeted at people for whom 'race' does matter – such as Black British.
9. This programme won the 'One World Media Prize' for 2003. For details see www.bbc.co.uk/science/genes/dna_detectives/african_roots/index.shtml
10. Some of my father's family are still based there, others are spread through the USA and Canada.

Chapter 9

Fear and Loathing in Front of a Mirror

OSSIE STUART

> For almost as long as I can remember I have loathed myself. It was a loathing that was renewed every time I looked into a mirror. For too long I have wished I was somebody else.

Reading these words still unnerves me. However, writing them is to remove a burden from my insubstantial shoulders. I have finally confessed my dirty little secret.

If I were to tell you that I am a disabled person would this self-loathing appear more rational? After all, who would not feel the same if they too had been struck down at the tender age of 18 by an accident and confined to a wheelchair? Even now, many years later, any dream of being treated equally in adulthood has slowly slipped away. Instead, I write these words with a kind of fatalism. Surely I am a victim of misfortune? Yet, my disability is not the sole reason for my self-loathing. No, my little secret is far worse. I am also of African Caribbean descent. I had been born and raised in the UK in the 1960s and 1970s. It was a time when you quickly learnt that your skin colour was a liability. Because of my black skin I found it impossible to obtain equal treatment from my peers or teachers. Indeed, by the age of four I had already learnt what Fanon had discovered decades earlier, that it was only though the gaze of others that I existed. The 'others' are white men (Fanon 1967/1986). What they chose to see – a nigger – I hated. That was, of course, until I became a disabled person.

When the editors of this volume asked me to write this chapter I knew it was an opportunity to bare my soul. My dirty little secret had to be told. For all those who surreptitiously share my secret, see this as a liberating act. Far from being a cathartic self-indulgence, this 'confession' might tell us a little a bit about what the black male body means in the UK at this moment. It has long been apparent to me that the experience of disability and 'blackness', though closely linked together, are mutually exclusive experiences. I simply cannot be both a disabled man and a black man. I was surprised to learn that Fanon too saw this in his disabled war veteran, who had a 'stump' where his leg used to be. Disability was a mirror image of Fanon's own futile rage against his own objectified 'blackness'. As Fanon's disabled man said, 'Resign yourself to your colour the way I got used to my stump; we're both victims' (Fanon 1967/1986). Fanon recognized that both disabled and black men were allocated a space not because of who they were, but because of what they look like. British society is obsessed with body image; I can either be a black man or a disabled man. I cannot be both.

In the space I have been given I want to say just three things. First, that the black disabled male is a challenge to social theories of disability as created by disabled writers. The black presence makes sayable those things which have long been avoided by disabled writers (mainly male) as a threat to their particular orthodoxy. Second that, as Fanon had already recognized, the black disabled man can only exist in opposition to an objectified black non-disabled male body. In a perverse way, the representation of the oversexualized and the overtly physical black male body has its converse in the desexualized and near invisible reality of the black disabled male body. Yes, you have got it; I do not exist. Yet, you cannot have one without the other. They are polar opposites and intrinsically linked together, yet each denying the other's existence. The third and final thing I want to say is this obsession with the body has at its core an invisible tragedy. The marginalization of any other possible representation of the black male body has its consequences. Every black man fears the void into which I have fallen. In a world where the sexualized body is everything, this is the kind of fear that can rapidly turn into loathing.

Am I a black or disabled man?

Despite the obvious similarity between experience of black people and disabled people, the literature fails to represent this. I have contributed to the discussion on 'race' and disability and the odd thing is that although many writers on disability acknowledge that disability is a social construction, that disability is 'created' by society; there is a great deal of reluctance to discuss 'race' fully within the context of disability. Likewise with writers on 'race', there has been no discussion of the impact of disability on black and minority ethnic communities, Frantz Fanon notwithstanding. The only exception has been in the case of mental health (Lloyd & Moodley 1992; Cochrane & Sashidharan 1996; Browne 1997) and what can be described as 'race-specific' impairments, such as Sickle Cell Anaemia (Anionwu & Atkin 2001).

Rather than talk about specific impairments, I am far more interested in the social production of 'disability'. By disability I mean its social meaning; the way in which society reacts to disabled people, where they are placed in social hierarchies and the extent to which they are allowed to participate in society (Oliver 1990). This is called the Social Model of Disability. The economic and social barriers that disabled people face are so pervasive that they are prevented from ensuring for themselves a reasonable quality of life by their own efforts.

The Social Model of Disability shifts the focus away from the impaired individual and on to restrictive environments and disabling social attitudes. Proposed by Disabled People's International in 1981, it adopts a twofold classification of 'handicap' and 'disability'. Most British disabled people substitute the word 'impairment' for 'handicap', although the latter term still has wide currency and acceptance internationally (Barnes 1991).

> '*Impairment*' is described as lacking part of or all of a limb, or having a defective limb, organism or mechanism of the body.
> '*Disability*' is the disadvantage or restriction of activity caused by a contemporary social organisation that takes little account of people who have physical impairments and thus excludes them from the mainstream of social activities. (Oliver 1990)

The Social Model of Disability is important because it allows us to talk about the structures and forces that produce disadvantage rather than focus on physical impairment an individual might have. We all have impairments. It might be ingrown toenails, HIV or a spinal injury. These impairments only become a 'disability' if society places a meaning or barriers that prevent an impaired individual from participating in society. In other words my impairment is not the cause of my 'disability', society is. Disability in this model means social disadvantage or discrimination.

This scheme is a simple yet effective way of looking at the social processes that create disability. Its importance to social policy should not be underestimated. Unfortunately, it has become the dogma of the Disability Movement. Like certain anti-racist or radical feminist ideas, the belief in the Model has become the touchstone of credibility. The result is that the Social Model has begun to define disabled people and their experience (Barnes & Mercer 2004). One consequence has been the near impossibility of talking about disabled people in any other way.

For me, the dominance of the Social Model has had two consequences. First, it has been complicit in the removal or erasure of masculinity. While the disabled figure is implicitly male, it is maleness without sexuality. The image we are presented with is an invisible actor who can never truly act out a sexual role as a lived experience. While this has serious implications for all disabled men, this very fact is catastrophic for black disabled men. Performance and sexual prowess are central inventions of the 'black' man. As Brett St Louis points out in Chapter 6 of this book, the body's significance takes a whole new meaning when placed within a racialized meaning. So, when thinking about black men we immediately come to physical prowess and sexual ability, all of which are constructs invented by white men (Fanon 1967/1986). Strip my disabled body of these constructs; far from giving me a disabled identity, I become invisible.

For me this has long been a daily reality; one example will do. While at Oxford, a close female friend often accompanied me on trips around the city. She is also of Asian descent, the significance of which will become apparent in a moment. The friend was initially surprised by what happened to her on these trips. I was not. People interacted with her frequently, smiling sympathetically or moving to assist her when she held a door open for me or another such similar task. The shop checkout was the key point. Here my companion would frequently be thanked for her kindness in taking me out for the day! It had never occurred to anyone that it was *I* who was taking *her* out. Nor did anyone assume that, rather than a mere carer, she might actually have been my girlfriend. That she was of Asian descent distanced further the possibility of a sexual agenda. Instead, the racial/gendered stereotype available to her was that of caregiver in this context. Mine was complete anonymity.

Let us change the context. Now imagine that same day as if I was not a disabled person. Over six foot four inches tall and naturally athletic, I would have, as you would expect, a very physical presence. The happy couple wandering through a sunny City of Oxford could not be constructed in any way other than an overtly sexual one and, in my case, possibly dangerous (I think I could live with that!). In both cases it is not my actions or even my mind that tell this story. All that is required is our racialized bodies.

Within disability discourse there is nowhere to discuss this or the other consequences of the black male body. The Social Model has become the dominant political discourse within disability. This has meant that disability as a lived experience can only be talked about in positive terms. We can talk about the physical segregation of disabled people by society. We can talk about legislative injustice done to disabled people. We can also talk about rights for disabled people. What we cannot acknowledge is that being a disabled person is about the kind of body you inhabit. What is unsayable is that many disabled people think it might be better if they were not in so much pain or, worse, that they might prefer to walk and run rather than rumble around in a wheelchair. The social model discourse has helped to render the disabled body invisible at the very time when the body and, in my case the black body, is at the very centre of contemporary political and social construction. My black body is, instead, silenced and invisible.

The attempts to include black disabled people when discussing disability have missed this point. Instead these discussions have become a 'badge' to be pinned on to disability social theory by contemporary disabled writers to bolster their credibility. We read the oft-repeated confession that any information or research on black disabled people is sorely lacking. Which means we continue to ignore black disabled people and their experience. In a significant contemporary social introduction to disability, black disabled people receive barely two pages of considered analysis (Barnes, Mercer and Shakespeare 1999). However, in those two pages we do learn quite a lot.

In the late 1980s the view of the black disabled person's experience was a binary one. He or she had to be either black or disabled. As such they had a 'double disadvantage' or a 'double disability' (Barnes et al. 1999). However, starting in 1992, there was a real effort to move to a more sophisticated idea of what it meant to be a disabled person and from the ethnic minority communities in contemporary Britain. As a consequence, writers (well, me actually) borrowed heavily from feminism and adopted the phrase, 'simultaneous oppression' to describe disability within an ethnic minority context. At the time I wrote:

> So I reject the notion that black disabled people experience a kind of double oppression. The oppression black disabled people endure is, in my opinion, a special situation. It is one, however, which is closely related to the atmosphere of intolerance in Britain. Thus, on the contrary, I suggest that racism within disability is part of a process of simultaneous oppression which black people experience daily in Western society. It is also an experience that divides disabled people from their black able-bodied peers. (Stuart 1992: 179)

I did see 'simultaneous oppression', as meant by Hazel Carby (1982) and other black feminist writers, as a way of invigorating the debate about race within the disability movement. One cannot overemphasize the importance of her central argument. It was a powerful corrective to the Eurocentric feminism of the 1970s. Here is what Carby meant by 'simultaneous oppression' with reference to women:

> The fact that black women are subject to simultaneous oppression [her emphasis] of patriarchy, class and 'race' is the prime reason for not employing parallels that render their position and experience not only marginal but invisible. (Carby 1982: 214)

From this bit of borrowing came a brief flowering of writing about 'race' and disability, by black disabled women, I would like to point out, in the mid-1990s. Nasa Begum (Begum et al. 1994) extended my analysis to include disabled lesbian and disabled gay men and the fact that black disabled people face complex oppression that requires alliances to be made with other groups. Millie Hill (1994) talked about how disability was mediated through the experience of being black. She argued that black disabled women cannot compartmentalize their experiences; rather, 'race', disability and gender shape and inform their lives. It was gratifying to see these and others followed my lead. It was not so pleasing that they also repeated my obvious mistakes. They were not the only ones.

The most obvious mistake I made was the uncritical approach I adopted regarding disabled people from ethnic minority communities. Very unwisely, I wrote about them as if they were a single undifferentiated group. Implicit in the use of 'simultaneous oppression' is that members of this group can only be 'black' disabled people if they had been exposed to a certain set of oppressive experiences. Membership, in theory at least, would be reserved for those deserving disabled people only if they experienced racism. Those that do not fit this criterion would be excluded regardless of whether they were also from ethnic minority communities and disabled people. The more you boasted of your own oppression the more 'black' and disabled you became. Yes, it is as illogical as that! This is obviously makes the notion of a 'simultaneous oppression' seem ridiculous. Indeed it was the evolution of these debates within black feminism that first alerted me to the absurd nature of my argument.

As Knowles and Mercer (1999) point out, the consequence of this approach is that the experience becomes the demarcation point for membership of this particular group (in this case black women). To qualify for membership black people are expected to experience racism. Those who deny its existence are accused of false consciousness and denied membership. Yet 'racism' and 'sexism' are social and political constructs. The experience of each differs for different people. There are no end of dramatic divisions and distinctions within an apparently unified constituency. It is very unlikely that black women in Britain will experience racism and sexism in a uniform manner. This makes the task of the spokesperson very difficult. It is important to understand that writers such as Carby were reacting to a certain feminist school of thought. Even so, they did claim to speak on behalf of 'black women' irrespective of country of origin and differing sociopolitical circumstances; we need to be mindful of the nature of the social construction the concept 'black women' implies. Indeed, they might be just as vulnerable to the same criticism that they have levelled at white feminists. Namely, they too seek a unitary nature of black feminism and fail to recognize the great diversity such a term implies (ibid.).

The fear of disabled writers concerning 'race' has always been that it might point up divisions within and among disabled people. That limited resources would be wasted pursuing a 'side issue' when compared to the 'more significant' problem of the unequal treatment of all disabled people. In response, disabled writers from black minority communities have accused those who concur with this view as being 'racists'. This polarized argument misses the point. Both disability and 'race' are social and political constructs. There is nothing absolute about either. Each can be changed or be reinvented at any given time. Indeed, we know that 'race' was very different for most of the twentieth century to what it is today.

Yet this discussion is a million miles from the real significance that the body has for me as a black disabled man. To put it frankly, does the value of understanding where the social barriers are remain purely academic while I still remain impotent and invisible in the eyes of the white man? This goes to the very heart of disabled social theory, as created by white disabled men. Laws removing physical barriers might get me into buildings but once inside I still will remain invisible. For me, nothing changes.

So, we are still stuck with Fanon's black or disabled reality, no more so than in the supersexualized black male image of contemporary Britain. Perhaps what I am loathing is not actually my impaired body, but that the myth of the black man has been made real by my disability. Fanon helps further when he points out that the black man only becomes black in the white man's gaze, or in relation to the white man (Fanon 1967/1986). In this context, the disabled black man is a significant challenge to the ongoing ontology of black maleness. Yet there are huge differences between the ways we construct black physical and mental disability. The former is rendered impotent and invisible while the latter is demonized and criminalized. Each construct is neither natural nor inevitable. Yet both rely for their construction on the naturalized black male body.

Envy of blackness

I have loathed my body. When I look at the idea of 'the black man' I know I do not measure up. I envy black men. I am forced to accept that I am not a black man because I cannot be or choose those spaces available to be black. Not even in the eyes of other black men do I become 'black'.

This was brought home to me in a crushing way two or three years after the accident that left me a wheelchair user. Part of my family still live in the Caribbean and there was talk of me visiting in the very near future. That was until I heard what the topic of conversation among my uncles and other male relatives was. Their chief concern was to discover whether I was still a 'man'? Maleness to them was quite simple. It was the ability to engage in sexual activity and to father a child. If I could not do that then I was at best a child or, worse, 'dead'. Luckily for me, they meant socially dead (I think!) and they feared my visit. As a non-male there would be the difficulty of communicating with me. For them it was best that on any visit I should remain with the women.

I was not alone with this problem. Sharing the same ward in hospital immediately after my accident was a Zimbabwean fighter pilot. He was as impaired as I was but never spoke to anyone, save me on one occasion. He asked what I intended to do once I left the hospital. I told him some inspiring rubbish that I had learnt non-disabled people liked to hear. I said I intended to overcome my impairment and go to university to become an academic (you may laugh at this point). Feeling quite pleased with myself, I asked him if he had considered a similar path. He just shook his head and said that he would take his own life at the first possible opportunity he got once he had left the hospital. I was shocked by his reply to my question 'why?'. 'I am no longer a man', he said, 'I have no life in front of me. And you should consider the same thing.' In my arrogant youth I thought I knew best and argued to the contrary. I did so because I did not understand what he meant at that time. He did kill himself, as he had planned, no more than two years after our conversation. I do not relate this story to make the case for suicide. Nor do I believe disability means social impotence. Nevertheless they do demonstrate that in a racialized West I am no longer a man.

Yet what these two stories also show is the tragically tiny spaces black males are allowed live in. Claire Alexander in two books on, first, boys of African-Caribbean descent (1996) and, second, boys of Bengali descent (2000a), demonstrated clearly how these boys manipulated their social space to play with the range of identities available to them. From sexual stud to teenage gang members, Claire presented them all to us. Likewise, Brett St Louis, in Chapter 6 in this book, discusses black male sports participation and its impact on the regressive racialization of black physicality. What is interesting in both works is the way in which black men use the social faculties available to them to 'buy' into a position of status. In other words they collaborate with and reinforce these racialized spaces to such an extent it becomes impossible to exist in other spaces. Is my exclusion from even these spaces the reason why I loathe myself? Or should it be? I must admit to wishing for the body perfect. Yes, I am as vulnerable to notions of 'normality' and perfection as the next person. Yet my envy takes on a dangerous edge when I feel excluded and locked out of the social spaces available to black males.

I had begun by saying I hated being a black boy growing up in provincial England in the 1960s and 70s. Black maleness at that time was very different to the dangerous, sexual and marketable kind of the 1980s and 1990s. Suddenly everybody wanted to be 'black', including white Essex boys who play football for Real Madrid and captain England. By then it was too late for me. I had broken my neck and I was forced to watch the reinvention of black men from the touchline, wrapped in a blanket to keep me warm. This is when I began to despise my disability (my social disability). I despised it not because I thought being a disabled person was to be an object of pity or patronage. No, I despised my new body. This body has no meaning except in what I am not. I am not sexually dangerous (darn it), I am not physically dangerous and I am no danger to the opposite team on the sports field. I know you will think that very few black males are any of these ideas either. Few could aspire to them too. That misses the point. It is true few black males are as they are racialized to be. Yet most, like Claire's boys, manipulate these constructs and exploit the empowerment these ideas give them. In other words black men try and occupy the space assigned to them. I am, like the poor 'lame' boy in the Pied Piper story, left behind.

So where does this leave me? I began this chapter in fear and loathing of myself because I did not like what I saw in the mirror. Do I end it in the same predicament? The simple answer is no! If I look beyond the symbolism my body represents, what I actually see in the mirror everyday is a slim, tall, intelligent early-forties guy, greying at the edges in that devastatingly handsome way. More to the point, I see an image that is at the completely opposite extreme of the black male idea. Yet, as long as black males are produced this way in Western society we will be forever bound together at each extreme of a taut rope, aware of each other but never able to meet.

Which end of the rope do I prefer? I would say my end, of course! Black men in the UK are only offered stilted, limited and claustrophobic spaces to inhabit. Gangster, sportsman, supersexual stud are some of a poor choice in the sweetshop. I have noticed that the black men I know find it almost impossible to even communicate with me. This is because I do not inhabit the spaces they do. I do not need nor share the language of their experience. This is significant because it demonstrates that my choices in the sweetshop are very different. I can inhabit spaces not available to most black males. My interactions appear free of the baggage that every black man has to bear. I do not have to manipulate in a stultified arena. I do not need to live up to that impossible fantasy image that most black men are trapped in. My sexuality or sexual prowess, contrary to what black men think, is not in question.

Yet, this optimism should not mask the larger message within my essay. If Fanon's black man exists only through the gaze of white men, where is the black disabled man? Does that gaze and that of the black non-disabled man doubly erase him too? Is it really the case that these voids I inhabit really provide black disabled men with a kind of freedom or liberation? No of course it does not. The void remains, yet I have found a way to make anew my locale and create new spaces to find a degree of dignity. Others may not be able to follow. This does not make me a superman. It is simply that I have learned not to be so fearful of my reflection.

Chapter 10

Culture, Sexuality and Identity in an Ethnic Minority Community: the Case of Greek-Cypriot Gay Men in London

CONSTANTINOS N. PHELLAS

Introduction

Attitudes toward sexuality differ within the diverse ethnic and racial communities that exist in Great Britain and the cultural values and beliefs surrounding sexuality play a major role in determining how individuals behave within their sociological context. The family unit is a primary domain where such values and beliefs are nurtured and developed. An individual's value system is shaped and reinforced within the family context, which usually reflects the broader community norms. Disclosure of a gay sexual preference and lifestyle by a family member presents challenges to ethnic minority families, which tend not to discuss sexuality issues and presume a heterosexual orientation.

For ethnic minority gays the 'coming out' process presents challenges in their identity formation process and in their loyalties to one community over another. Often ethnic minority gay men tend to live within three defined and semi-independent communities: the gay community, the ethnic minority community, and the society at large. While each community provides fundamental needs, serious consequences and potential conflicts would emerge if these communities were to be visibly integrated or meet. It requires a constant effort to maintain oneself in three different worlds, each of which also fails to support significant aspects of a person's life. The complications that arise may inhibit one's ability to adapt and to maximise personal potentials, and provide challenges to the creation of an individual's self-identity (Dyne 1980; Mays and Cochran 1988; Morales 1989; Garnets and Kimmel 1991; Chan 1992; Gutierrez and Dworkin 1992; Greene 1994).

It has to be emphasised that ethnic minority gay men comprise highly heterogeneous populations, with individuals who make diverse choices in coping, functioning, and empowering or disempowering themselves. For example, some ethnic minority gay men may not turn to their ethnic and cultural traditions for emotional support. However, many ethnic minority gay men will look at some level to a source of comfort and/or nurturing that only their community or family of origin can bring. Indeed, there is no monolithic concept of ethnic minority gay men. What applies to an Anglo-African man does not necessarily apply to a Greek-Cypriot. Furthermore, issues of homophobia vary from culture to culture and within the same ethnic group.

Theorists have conceptualised lesbian and gay communities as 'a bounded group possessing special norms and a particular argot' (Simon & Gagnon 1967), a 'psychological kinship system' (Barnhart 1975), a 'sociopsychological unity' (Wolf 1979), a 'satellite culture' (Humphries & Miller 1980), a 'communal sense' (Rainone 1987), and 'a range of social groups in which lesbian individuals may feel a sense of camaraderie with other lesbians' (Krieger 1982). Murray (1992) argues that lesbian and gay communities meet technical criteria for the term 'community' as do other social collectives, such as ethnic communities. He defines community as 'a concentration of interaction among those who identify themselves as gay into gay primary groups, concentration of space (of residence, but more important, of community institutions) in specifiable territory, learned (though not monolithic) norms, institutional complete- ness, collective action, and a sense of shared history' (ibid.: 113). In his view, territories with unusually large concentrations of lesbians, gay men, and bisexuals encourage the perception of community, but 'not all people engaging in same-sex sexual behaviour would share that perception or the need for social interaction' (D'Augelli & Garnets 1995: 294). As Sarason (1974: 131) argues:

> A community is more than a political or geographical area. It contains a variety of institutions which may be formally or informally related to each other – or not related. It is made up of myriads of groups, transient or permanent, which may have similar or different purposes and vary in size, power and composition. It possesses resources and vehicles for their disbursement. Its groups and institutions vary considerably in size, purposes, and the power they possess or seek. And a community has a distinctive history which, although it may no longer be relevant in the psychological sense, is crucial for understanding some of its present qualities and social, political, religious, and economic characteristics.

The 'coming out' process is defined as the experience of acknowledging a gay, lesbian, or bisexual sexual orientation to oneself and others – as joining this imagined community. In this paradigm, 'coming out' is characterised by a person's development and acceptance of her or his sexuality and of a homosexual identity. In the social discourse about 'coming out', there are many common assumptions that may be of questionable validity but often go unchallenged. One assumption is that the process of 'coming out' is a singular constellation and is dichotomous. That is, a person is either 'out' or not. It is also presumed that acknowledging a gay/lesbian or bisexual sexual orientation, especially to heterosexuals, can reduce the level of homophobia, as it provides others with positive role models of non-stereotypical gay, lesbian, and bisexual people. Disclosing one's sexual orientation is thought to be a ubiquitously positive experience that creates self-acceptance and confidence through repeated practice. Indeed, for gay men and lesbians, not making public pronouncements about their sexual orientation is presumed to be negative and less than healthy psychologically and is characterised by negative terms, such as living double lives, hiding, or being in the closet and is presumed to indicate shame, denial, and self-hatred (Carrier 1985; Morales 1989; Greene 1994; Phellas 2002).

In various forms, these assumptions have found their way into the conceptualisations of research on 'coming out', development of sexual identities, and homosexuality. Most of these assumptions, however, are based on clinical and empirical studies conducted with White lesbians and gay men from majority communities. Lesbians and gay men of ethnic minority backgrounds have received scant attention in the sociological and psychological literature on homosexuality and development of sexual identities. Very little work has been carried out on gay men who also belong to cultures that are less tolerant of homosexuality, for example, Greek-Cypriot, Jamaican or Somali, or those who are Asian, Russian and Serbian.

My focus is specifically on Anglo-Greek men resident in London (who have sex with men) because they have received very limited attention in the sociological and psychological literature (Phellas 2002). For the most part, empirical investigations and scholarly work on ethnic minority gay men devote little time or attention to the specific issues relevant to Anglo-Greek men and the ways that ethnicity and racism 'colour' the experience of heterosexism (Williams 1986). As Greene (1994: 392) argues:

An understanding of the meaning and the reality of being a man of colour who is also gay requires a careful exploration of several factors. These factors include the nature and importance of the culture's traditional gender role stereotypes and their relative fluidity or rigidity, the role and importance of the family and community, and the role of religion in the culture.

This chapter attempts to explore some issues and raise some questions about accepting one's homosexuality, and subsequently developing a sexual identity, as a process that is always embedded in a cultural context that can profoundly shape the experience of that process for individuals. It also examines some of the key cultural concepts and relevant historical factors that may shape the development of gay identity among Anglo-Greek men. Accounts of sexual identity experiences provided by a sample of homosexually/bisexually identified Anglo-Cypriot men (second-generation) resident in London are examined in the light of this analysis to explore how these men negotiate their Greek-Cypriot and gay identities.

Ethnicity and difference in gay and lesbian studies

For a century, research on the history of homosexuality has been constrained by the intolerance of governments and academics alike. However, over the last two decades one witnesses an unprecedented out-pouring of scholarship in lesbian and gay history pertaining to sexual orientation and about homosexual lives in general. More precisely, we now know more about the experiences of young gay men (Trenchard & Warren 1984), the old (Berger 1982), those in prison (Wildeblood 1957), those who offer sex in exchange for money (Reiss 1961), and those who lived during particular historical periods (Porter and Weeks 1990). However, whilst knowledge and awareness about what it means to be gay, lesbian or bisexual in terms of sexual orientation have increased considerably, there remains a deep-seated ignorance on a number of planes. Scientific knowledge about why sexual orientations differ is still scanty, and in a society that can still be overtly hostile towards 'deviant' sexual relationships there is still much to learn about the way being attracted to one's own sex, particularly in conjunction with various other factors, can affect self-esteem and the development of personal identity. In addition, the way that sexual identity can be cross-cut by other issues such as 'race' and ethnicity or religious belief has been underexplored, particularly where ethnic difference is subsumed, or rendered invisible, by an assumed hegemonic 'White' identity.

What does it mean to be an ethnic minority gay man? As I mentioned earlier, for ethnic minority gays, life is often lived in three different communities: the gay community, the ethnic minority community and the predominantly heterosexual White mainstream society (de Marco 1983; Loicano 1989; Greene 1994). Since these three social groups have their own norms, expectations, and styles, the minority gay man must balance a set of often-conflicting challenges and pressures. The multi-minority status makes it difficult for a person to become fully integrated and assimilated within any of these communities. Within the mainstream society, ethnic minority gays experience prejudice and discrimination for their ethnic identity, as well as for their sexual orientation. In the gay community, the social values mirror those of the mainstream society in relation to their perception of ethnic minorities, which includes negative stereotyping and prejudicial attitudes about ethnic and racial minorities. In some ethnic minority communities, the social norms and values concerning sexuality foster homophobic attitudes and consequently gays within these minority communities face disapproval and rejection, or even violence (Morales 1990).

Another way to view the lives of ethnic minority gays is to consider them as both a visible and an invisible minority. As a visible minority they have no choice but to cope with being the object of racist practices. As an invisible minority, they can be discrete about their sexual orientation and hope to minimise the homophobic reactions. Consequently, the communities' racist and homophobic attitudes compromise the potential support they can receive. In contrast, White majority gays do not experience racism in mainstream society. As an invisible minority they can choose to remain silent and not 'come out' or remain invisible. However, the homophobic attitudes of mainstream society and ethnic minority communities limit the support for gays. Thus, remaining invisible usually means suffering in silence.

The study of identity development among ethnic minority lesbians and gay men has tended to draw upon models of *either* ethnic minority identity *or* lesbian and gay identity (Wooden et al. 1983; Espin 1987) rather than as an intersection and translation of these two experiences. The question remains, how does an individual who is lesbian or gay *and* a member of an ethnic minority group come to terms with identity issues?

Sexual behaviour, its specific expression and the meanings attached to it, occur as a function of the culture of which that person is a member. This can be at the macrocosmic level: whether that depends on the culture of their country of origin, the response of their host society, or some new set of dynamics which have arisen in response to their adoptive culture. Or it may exist at the microcosmic level of the city in which they live or the particular locale visited.[1] What is also evident is that while *sexual acts* are very similar throughout the world, the *cultural meanings and responses* to these acts are not universal and can differ markedly (Whitehead and Ortner 1981; Caplan 1987).

However, at the same time, it is important to remember that while the traditional culture may form a template for a minority ethnic group, the beliefs, values and lifestyles of minority groups do not form a culture which is a microcosm of their traditional culture. Nor do they fully reflect the values of the dominant culture. Similarly, it is important to acknowledge the effect of minority ethnic groups' values and behaviours on the host culture. It is reasonable to expect that considerable sexual mixing between men of different ethnic groups will impact upon the dynamics of sexual behaviour and its expression among the various host cultures' subgroups. These interactions generate unique and constantly evolving and transient systems. At the psychosocial level of the individual, each person will have different ways and rates of assimilating into the host culture or remaining separate from it.

Morales (1983) proposed an identity-formation model for ethnic minority lesbians and gay men that incorporates the dual-minority status of this group. This process is postulated as five different states.[2] Each state is said to be accompanied by decreasing anxiety and tension through the management of the associated tensions and differences. As cognitive and lifestyle changes emerge, the multiple identities are said to become integrated, leading toward a greater sense of understanding of one's self and toward the development of a 'multicultural' perspective. Each community offers to ethnic minority lesbians and gay men important resources that support their lifestyles and identities. The lesbian or gay community can offer support in the expression of one's sexual identity: the ethnic community can offer emotional and familial bonding as well as cultural identity; and mainstream society can offer a national identity as well as a mainstream culture and multidimensional social system. Some individuals choose to keep each community separate using a strategy which Breakwell (1986) termed 'compartmentalism', while others vary the degree to which they integrate the communities and lifestyles in which they are involved. The advantage of this model is that it proposes different states rather than stages. Therefore, it is possible that persons may experience several states or parts of states at the same time, unlike a stage model in which resolution of one stage leads to another.

In the above paragraphs I tried to highlight the complexities of coming out in a multicultural context and attempted to highlight a number of issues that a gay ethnic minority man must resolve as part of the 'coming out' process. These include: (1) deciding whether or not to disclose to the family; (2) finding a niche among gay peers; and (3) reconciling sexual orientation with other aspects of identity. For the son of immigrants, the 'coming out' process takes place against the backdrop of ethnic traditions, values, and social networks. For some, this adds a dimension of complexity to the issues. Homosexuality, often in conflict with Western religious and cultural mores, seems even more incongruous and unacceptable in the context of conservative and traditional values. Furthermore, the rift that occurs between parent and child over sexual orientation is set in the context of an existing conflict, as the son is seen as pulling away from the traditional culture to espouse a Western way of life. These issues will be explored in relation to my own study of Greek-Cypriot gay men resident in England.

However, any analysis of Cypriot gay men's identities needs to be set against a broader understanding of traditional Greek-Cypriot cultural values around sexuality, religion and the role of the family. The following section explores some of these debates and provides the backdrop against which to place the conflicts and negotiations confronting Cypriot gay men in London.

Family, religion and sexuality in Greek-Cypriot culture

Some might argue that people of Greek-Cypriot background living in the UK present different social characteristics from those living in Cyprus. However, my own personal experience (as a Greek-Cypriot man born and raised in Cyprus) and the various conversations and meetings I have had with diaspora Cypriots show a lot of similarities in terms of cultural and ethnic dynamics. The same beliefs and values, traditions, motivations, religious practices, principles and moral codes and, to a large extent, psychosocial dynamics exist. Indeed, it is true to say that, if anything, the Greek-Cypriot communities living outside Cyprus tend to show greater conservatism and adherence to 'old-fashioned' ideas than those in Cyprus. However, the cultural construction of homosexuality is very much interwoven with two major social institutions that seem to dominate Greek-Cypriot society, namely the Greek-Cypriot family and the Church.

In Greek-Cypriot culture, the individual man is merged with the family and the community. It could be said that he does not have a discrete, individual identity as his private affairs are shared with the rest of the family. It can be very difficult for a man to develop his own personality and character, as he often stays with his family until he marries. Should he decide to break away from the family and set up his own home without getting married, he is seen as acting against the family. To a large extent, individuals are not allowed to have any secrets or to have private lives. If they do, this is seen as signifying that there is something wrong that ought to be shared and resolved within the family itself. Decisions regarding financial, emotional or business affairs are taken jointly with the rest of the family. From an early age, children learn that their actions reflect the whole family's social status. They cannot take any decisions without first considering the consequences that their actions would have for the rest of the family (Espin 1987; Greene 1994; Phellas 2002).

The concept of sexual behaviour in Greek-Cypriot culture is closely tied up with the 'honour and shame' value system. This system predetermines the way Greek-Cypriot women and men view themselves in relation to issues concerning sexual and moral codes, and the way they are viewed by others in relation to these matters. Women are seen as passive but also as a source of danger (Caplan 1989; Loizos & Papataxiarchis 1991). 'Their supposed capacity to control their sexual urges and, at the same time, the belief that men's sexual drive is "natural" but uncontrollable, renders women responsible for maintaining the moral code' (Lazarides 1994: 11). On the other hand, a husband's infidelity is more or less accepted amongst Greek-Cypriots. As long as he does not neglect his family duties and does not 'overdo' it, he is forgiven. He has to show the necessary respect to his wife and his family first and only if that is undermined by his extramarital affairs will he be criticised, by both men and women.

The second major influence on the construction of Cypriot sexuality is the Greek Orthodox Church. Georgiou's (1992) study (believed to be the first such study in the Orthodox world to date) which examined the sexual attitudes of Greek Orthodox priests living in Cyprus on topics such as adultery, premarital sex, abortion, contraception, masturbation, homosexuality and coital abstention, showed the following attitudes with regard to the subject of male homosexuality:

- That male homosexual practices (it was not made clear what type of practices) were unusual, perverse and a form of disease.
- That male homosexual practices were considered to be a cardinal sin.
- That homosexual acts could be discontinued by confession.
- That male homosexual intercourse degraded man into woman.
- That Sodom and Gomorrah were destroyed because their inhabitants had sinned by committing homosexual acts.

Even a brief consideration of religion and family in this context shows that although the main categories that have dominated Western literature on 'homosexualities' – that is, 'heterosexuality', 'homosexuality' and 'bisexuality' – are clearly present in Greek-Cypriot culture (Loizos & Papataxiarchis 1991; Phellas 2002), they are inflected differently through a religiocultural lens. Indeed, the notion of a single gay/homosexual identity or a distinct gay/homosexual community is one that is fairly new to the Cypriot community. The structure of sexual life in Cyprus – and, as a result, the way Cypriots perceive the concept of sexuality – has traditionally been conceived in terms of a model focused on the relationship between sexual practices and gender roles, with the distinction between masculine (activity) and feminine (passivity) being central to the order of the sexual universe.

As a result, the societal definition of male homosexuality in Cyprus originates around the schema of penetration and, in this conceptualisation, the 'homosexual' label is attributed to any individual who is being penetrated, or is thought to be penetrated. The penetrator remains free of this label, regardless of the fact that he is engaged in homosexual sex as well (see Tapinct (1992) for an analysis of a similar dynamic in a Turkish context). This argument highlights a major difference between the Western and Greek-Cypriot cultural settings for male bisexuality: the lack of stigmatisation amongst Greek-Cypriots of the active inserter participant in homosexual encounters. As a result of the above a lot of Greek-Cypriot men do not believe that 'one drop of homosexuality' makes a person totally homosexual as long as the appropriate sexual role is played (Carrier 1985).

It is along the lines of such perceptions that the distinctions between male and female, masculinity and femininity have traditionally been organised in Greek-Cypriot culture. A Greek-Cypriot male's gender identity is not threatened by homosexual acts provided that he plays the insertor role in sex. Men should always penetrate and should never allow themselves to be penetrated. Therefore, the 'active' homosexual is still entirely and unambiguously a 'man'. He may transgress against religious prohibitions but he does not place his masculinity in doubt. As long as he is a competent husband and householder, as long as he is manly and keeps his dalliances private, he is allowed by society to be a 'sinner'. On the other hand, the worst social stigma occurs when the effeminate man is also known to be a passive homosexual. He is regarded by society as the greatest subversive of all and he is widely seen to be not merely immoral, but mentally deficient as well.

Loizos & Papataxiarchis (1991: 227) write in relation to the passive homosexual man (called *poushtis*):

> ... he is strongly denigrated as someone who fundamentally lacks full humanity, and his moral weakness exposes him to all sorts of evil dispositions ... Poushtis comes to be a synonym for a liar or thief, a man without dignity, and it strongly contrasts with the characterisation of the man who adopts the 'male' role and who may claim a 'super male' reputation, much as he might if he consorted with a prostitute ...

As Campbell (1964) and others have remarked, the word *poushtis* in demotic Greek signifies a man who receives another man sexually, who solicits to be penetrated, or accepts and enjoys it. The *poushtis* in the Greek-Cypriot culture is the man who willingly gives up his sovereignty and power to control and to own. He relinquishes his masculine social being and also his claim to any social place of his own. He prefers to be identified with the passive and the submissive rather than exercising his power and energy.

Gay identity in diasporic Greek-Cypriot culture: negotiating and translating sexual and cultural identities

My earlier research (2002) examined the sexual, social and cultural lives of 25 self-identified second-generation Greek-Cypriot gay men living in London during the period 1994–97. These men were recruited by advertising in the gay press, by writing to community groups and organisations and by 'snowballing'. Semi-structured, face-to-face and telephone interviews were conducted with the men recruited through these channels. Due to the lack of research on Anglo-Cypriot men who have sex with men, the research parameters were set to explore the formation of Greek-Cypriot gay identities within a broad cultural framework, rather than focus on specific 'gay Cypriot' issues. The research explored the following areas:

- factors affecting the disclosure or nondisclosure of gay identity to their families;
- factors within Cypriot culture that impact on the acceptance of gay identities;
- ways in which gay Anglo-Cypriot men negotiate a path through their two worlds (Cypriot culture and homosexual orientation), particularly focusing on strategies employed to avoid these coming into conflict, and the implications when these two worlds collide.

In the following subsections, and drawing on fieldwork from the above study, I propose to look more closely at the these issues beginning first with the disclosure of gay identity.

Disclosure or non-disclosure of gay identity to their families

As has been discussed earlier, the tightly knit Greek-Cypriot social context carries many benefits that have been lost within more individualised, atomised, fragmented Western societies. However, for Greek-Cypriot men whose emotional and sexual investments are directed towards other men, their cultural context may well present them with significant difficulties. In specific terms, how can one talk about a 'gay identity' within a culture in which the Western concepts of individual identity and (homo)sexuality are problematic? How can Greek-Cypriot men (gay-identified or not) start addressing their sexual needs when they cannot even express their needs or voices as individuals? How can a man accept and act on his sexuality when the family and society denies him the right to be himself? Gay identity emerges when people are free to make choices and decisions about their lives and lifestyles. However, in a culture where the individual is firmly embedded within the community, such a definition becomes unrealistic.

As George (aged 31) said in my study:

> The main reason I haven't come out is my mother. I cannot do that to her. Even though we're not close, I do acknowledge the fact that she has sacrificed her life for me. She was the one who was getting beaten up by my dad, she was the one who had to go out to work to feed us. I find it hard for me to turn round and say to her 'Yes, I am gay.' That would totally destroy her. You see, she is homophobic – like most of Greek people. They're racist, you know. She is a typical Greek person. It's OK to be anything else, anything you want to be, as long as you don't bring it back to the family. That's their way of thinking and that's the way with my mum. As long as it's kept outside the family, it's fine. It's my duty now to look after her. They've looked after you for so many years, now it's my turn to look after her. That's the way I see it.

Coming out in the family and making one's sexuality public knowledge may be considered an act of treason against the family *and* the culture of the migrant community. It may be seen as a form of rejection and abandonment of all the things their parents and culture represent. As Espin (1984, 1987) and Hidalgo (1984) have noted, a gay or lesbian family member may maintain a place in the family and be quietly tolerated but this does not constitute acceptance of a gay or lesbian sexuality. Rather, it constitutes the denial of it. The gay son is very much welcomed within the family, as long as he does not disclose or declare his sexuality.

Cypriot cultural factors in acceptance of gayness

Furthermore, another element that contributes to the difficulty Greek gay men face in establishing a cohesive personal identity is the position the Greek Orthodox Church takes towards issues on sexuality. Often, there was a strong religious element attached to my respondents' upbringing where God represents the ultimate punishment. To fail the parents' expectations is one thing, but to fail God's wishes is seen as a sin. As a result, Greek-Cypriot gay men internalise negative attitudes that have been conveyed by loved and trusted figures, which has a detrimental effect on the possibility of developing self-acceptance and a positively evaluated perspective on one's sexuality.

One of my interviewees (Costas, aged 33) said the following when I asked him whether his religious upbringing had any effect upon his identity and personality development:

> In fact, I felt guilty from the very outset till I was mature and understood myself better. The society didn't recognise what I was up to. It wasn't normal to speak as a gay man. In addition to that, the biggest factor that induced guilt in me was the religious aspect that ran very strong in my family. While I was in Cyprus, I was quite a religious person. I used to go to church very frequently. As a matter of fact I used to be the priest's assistant. As a result of that I saw my sexual tendencies as being in disunity with the religious teachings I was brought up with. It did bother me a lot. It still does actually, but I have learnt to live with it now.
>
> I have now created a more positive image about myself in that I don't fight it anymore. I used to worry a lot about my own personal experiences and what the society and the church wanted me to experience. You know something, those people that obey the religious teachings and get married and have families do so many things that are much more hypocritical and morally wrong than me being gay.

For Constantinos (aged 36), the fact that the Orthodox Church cannot embrace his homosexuality made him abstain from any religious festivals and other relevant events:

> I am not participating in any organised religious festivals as I used to. I don't go to church on Sunday any more as I used to do. That doesn't mean I am not religious anymore. I am religious as much as before. It's just that I am much older now and I have my own concept of God and religion.

In some instances, guilt overshadowed any pleasure that might have arisen from any sexual activity:

> I thought God was going to punish me for being gay. I mean, the first time I masturbated, I thought it was really wrong. I took the Bible out and prayed hard. I held it and swore to God that I would never do it again. I prayed that I would be cured from any homosexual tendencies. Well, you know, it was all about my upbringing.

Negotiating cultural and sexual communities: the non-primacy of sexual identity

For the majority of my respondents, identity did not seem to have crystallised around their sexuality so as to render sexual identity *the* primary identity dimension. They appeared to have accepted that constructing an all-embracing gay lifestyle might not be feasible for them without abandoning, or at least challenging and unsettling, their family and family contexts. It was clear from the interviews that, despite the anti-gay sentiments embodied and expressed in the Greek-Cypriot community and in their families, the men retained a deep attachment to their Greek culture, and inhabited a frame of reference that most frequently claimed ethnic identity and community as more primary concerns than sexual identity. Rather than defining themselves primarily in terms of sexual identity, they chose to see themselves in terms of other personal relationships with their families, their peers at work and with other members of their community. What came across clearly in the interviews was the men's fears of becoming outcasts in their own cultural community. The ways of coping and dealing with their sexuality varied from person to person. Many had tried to incorporate their sexuality into their everyday lives, sometimes by juxtaposing it with other aspects of their lives and sense of self. The main aim in all the coping mechanisms was to minimise psychological and social strain by finding a happy and workable balance between their sexuality and their familial and social lives.

Ioannis (aged 29) spoke for a lot of the interviewees when he pointed to the difficulties of integrating (rather than simply juxtaposing) aspects of his different worlds:

> The thing that I dislike most is not being able to come out to my family – that's what stopping me from being a really fulfilled person. Once you've come out to the family and they accept it, then you are free. I think that's the only annoyance that I've got – not to be able to share my sexuality and my partner with my parents. The issues I've got have to do with my own culture and Greek community and not the gay community.

As a result, a lot of interviewees had expended considerable energy in devising ways of balancing the two worlds. These men existed as minorities within minorities, with the multiple oppression and discrimination that accompanies such status.

Tasos (aged 42) spoke frankly about this struggle:

> I was an emotional mess when I discovered my sexuality. It was all the guilt I was feeling about my homosexuality. When I was 24 I tried to

kill myself. I overdosed myself. I had just about enough with all the mental stress and trying to live a double life. I was torn between my Greek upbringing, my religious background and my homosexuality. Luckily, my mother found me unconscious on time and I was rushed to the hospital. I nearly died. Since, that incident I have become more tolerant about myself and who I really am.

Georgios (aged 43) spoke frankly of the imbalance between the worlds of his culture and sexuality, and the difficulty he experienced in finding a place for himself:

The time I missed more my Greek connection was last year when I went to a Jewish Bar Mitzvah. I went away feeling extremely sad. I often get this sense of deep sadness because there isn't a community that I belong to. There's the gay community but it doesn't fulfil me. It's a sense, yes, it's a sense of belonging. When I hear Greek music being played, it triggers off a sense of loss or a sense of not belonging. I felt it most strongly when I went to this Jewish gathering. If I go to a Greek gathering, I tend to link up with my brother and his family and I feel ill at ease because they're being very intrusive. They keep asking me a lot of questions. I'll answer them and if they ask me if I'm ever going to get married then I'll turn round and tell them the truth. Really, it's up to them whether they want to accept that or not.

Kenan (aged 26) told me that as he grows older his family does matter to him and he tries very hard to keep a balance between the two worlds. He said:

The older I get I've started to become more aware of my family and I've just told my sisters that I'm gay and that didn't go down too well. I used to think what I'll do as a young person I would run away from my family, never see them again and get on with my life. The older I get I realise I don't want to do that because I actually love my family. I'm considering coming out to my whole family although it scares me a lot. If they don't know that I'm gay there is a lot of me they don't know.

In some instances, the outcome of the 'coming out process' to the family was successful. The following two examples show that the parents did not reject the respondent but on the contrary the parent–child relationship remained intact. At the very least, the parents reached a personal understanding of their son's sexual orientation that, distorted or not, enabled them to come to terms with it. Although a complete understanding and a positive feeling may not exist, sexual orientation was no longer a constant focus of attention and conflict.

> On the positive side, I think the closeness that I feel with my mother, the fact that I can laugh with her and that she can laugh with me makes the whole thing worthwhile. If a mother was going shopping with her son, let's say, and she would pick up a bra, would she say 'What do you think of this colour?' to a straight son? She wouldn't, would she? We connect and that's very beautiful. I know my mother doesn't have this connection with my brothers. I think if it wasn't for my mother, I wouldn't be happy as a gay man. The fact that there's someone that close to you, who acknowledges that you are gay, but doesn't talk about it, I think it helps and makes you feel good about it. (Dinos, aged 31)

Oz's mother, although from a working-class background and of little education, has been understanding and supportive. He said:

> When I came out to my mum I must have been about mid-twenties. It was very difficult. I was surprised because she was very calm and emotionless because by this time she had worked herself up that something was very wrong. Therefore when I told her about me being gay, it wasn't what she expected. It wasn't as bad as I thought it was going to be. I could see she was a bit confused but she was glad it wasn't something like death or a major illness. She hugged me and reassured me that she still loves me. (Oz, aged 29)

Conclusion

The personal accounts that arose from this research reinforce the notion that identity is multiple, contested and contextual. Sexual identity is not an essential fixed given for any individual, nor is it developed within a vacuum. Concepts of lesbian and gay identity have evolved over a two-hundred-year span in the West, heavily influenced by social and political conditions, from the initial sexual categories in sexology, to a male homosexual identity, to the New Woman, to lesbians, gays, bisexuals, and most recently 'queer' identity (McIntosh 1968; Plummer 1975; Trumbach 1977; Foucault 1978/1990; Herdt 1981; Weeks 1986; Seidman 1995). The modern homosexual identity remains a Western construct. There is no comparable sexual identity in the Cypriot culture.

For a Cypriot man in Cyprus to have a gay identity, he has to define himself through Western cultural concepts. For an Anglo-Cypriot who is defining a sexual identity, he or she must also adapt Western codes of sexuality and sexual expression to meet his/her own needs. At the same time, this individual will have to respond to Cypriot cultural influences, which require a different set of demands on family responsibilities, privacy, and the forms of sexual expression that are considered to be acceptable. Weighing the Western pressure to 'come out' and be openly gay against the Cypriot cultural demand for privacy requires a balance of opposing forces. While some individuals may never openly admit or act on their homosexuality, others will embrace the Western model enthusiastically; still others will be openly gay/lesbian only in safe (generally non-Cypriot) environments. However, the Cypriot cultural restrictions on open expression of sexuality may create a diminished dichotomisation of heterosexual versus homosexual behaviour. Given the importance of the concept of having only a private expression of sexuality, there could actually be more allowance of fluidity within a sexual continuum.

Social science research on gay and lesbian issues has focused on the evolution of people whose primary political and ethnic identification is a gay or lesbian, and who have been able to organise a multidimensional way of life on the basis of their sexual orientation. But we need to focus on other forms of homosexuality – other ways in which homosexual desire and behaviour have been organised, understood, named, or left deliberately unnamed (Chauncey 1989). We need to be careful not to view the evolution of a homosexual identity only through a Western lens, expecting that non-Western cultures, with modernisation, will eventually follow the same course in achieving greater openness with homosexual behaviour. Cultural differences in the construction of identity and in the expression of sexuality have to be taken into account. We are just beginning to know which questions to ask.

From this study, it was clear that any attempt to globalise all gay men into a homogeneous group based on a 'Western' model of homosexualities can be misleading and inappropriate. Not only can important differences between gay men be hidden but local and national differences of culture, traditions and political strategies will not be properly addressed.

For a lot of the Greek-Cypriot men in this study, the translation of their sexual desires and behaviours into a political statement of gay identity was not only difficult but was also resisted. Sexual identity – although relevant – was not a primary identity dimension to them. Many men have developed more or less effective coping mechanisms to manage the conflicts they face. Most importantly, though, the men I spoke to were united in their struggle for acceptance by the Greek-Cypriot community.

There is still little empirical information about sexuality, sexual identity, and sexual expression for Anglo-Cypriots and other non-Western ethnic minority groups. Future research questions will address important factors, specific to each cultural group, examining: (1) modes of sexual expression; (2) constructions of sexual identity; (3) attitudes toward sexuality in the context of cultural values and generational differences; (4) assimilation to the values of the host community; (5) gender roles; (6) expectations of one's family of origin; (7) the economic role of the family, particularly for women and immigrants; (8) the importance of procreation; (9) ties to the ethnic community; (10) assimilation and acculturation, and (11) the history of discrimination and oppression specific to that cultural group. By exploring sexuality in the context of these factors, the discourses are broadened for all individuals, as silences are broken and the range of sexual expression is more carefully articulated.

It is my hope that this chapter has contributed towards a better understanding of the complexities involved for men who identify as Anglo-Greek gay men. As Fygetakis (1997: 188) poignantly remarks, 'If there is a main point to be made, it is that these men should not be discounted as simply not brave enough, not proud enough, or not having enough of a positive gay identity. On the contrary, they are on a personal journey of discovery where they try to embrace both worlds with dignity, self-acceptance and compassion.'

Notes

1. See Back, Chapter 1, this volume for a discussion of the role of urban space in the formation of ethnic minority identities, and their intersection with ideas of safety and danger.
2. *State 1: denial of conflicts*: during this state the person tends to minimise the validity and reality of the discrimination they experience as an ethnic person, and to believe that they are being treated the same as others.
   State 2: bisexual versus gay: this state argues that there is a preference for some ethnic minority gays to identify themselves as bisexual rather than gay.
   State 3: conflicts in allegiance: during this state the member of an ethnic minority becomes uneasy and uncomfortable as he becomes aware of both his ethnic minority status and his homosexuality.
   State 4: establishing priorities in allegiance: a primary identification with the ethnic community prevails in this state and feelings of resentment concerning the lack of integration among the communities, becomes a central issue.
   State 5: integrating the various communities: as a gay person of colour the need to integrate his lifestyle and develop a multicultural perspective becomes a major concern.

Chapter 11

Embodying Violence: 'Riots', Dis/order and the Private Lives of 'the Asian Gang'

CLAIRE ALEXANDER

Details have emerged this week about a recent flare up between black and Asian youths at the Thomas More School ...

Police had to call on support from the Territorial Support Group to deal with the tension that erupted last month.

Police patrols were stepped up and were called to deal with several stand offs between youths on the nearby Stoneleigh Estate.

Things came to a head when officers patrolling Abbey Street came across youths making petrol bombs – with six already prepared.

Police called in the TSG to ensure a large presence to deter any more trouble, particularly when large groups of youths were seen roaming the Estate.

Superintendent Hirons told the SPCGG: 'We must get the message across to young people that they should not be taking the law into their own hands. They risk damaging the quality of life for everyone where they live if they continue to behave in this way.'

Local press report, Summer 1996[1]

Introduction

One weekend towards the end of May 2001, the streets of Glodwick, Oldham erupted into violence. In what were proclaimed as the first 'race riots' in Britain since the 1980s, the Asian young men of Oldham confronted police and National Front demonstrators in two nights of angry protest that were to presage similar clashes across England – in Aylesbury the following week, in Leeds and Burnley in June and, most dramatically, in Bradford in July. In the weeks and months that followed, the unrest was interpreted as the inevitable result of a clash of cultures, which gave a renewed urgency to the debates around race, multiculturalism and citizenship and which placed Britain's Asian-Muslim communities squarely in the firing line. This unenviable position worsened in the aftermath of the New York attacks on September 11th that year and the subsequent 'War on Terror', which has increasingly defined Britain's Muslim communities through images of danger, violence and anger. These images have been particularly focused on the threat posed by Muslim young men, who fuse ideas of racial, religious and cultural difference with the spectres of social marginalisation and urban deprivation – a layering of racial, religiocultural, classed, gendered and generational dysfunction and alienation. Post 2001, photos of swaggering masked young men with petrol bombs merge with the image of young British Muslims kneeling, heads and faces swathed in black hoods, on the floors of the compounds of Guantanamo Bay, to define this new enemy within and abroad.

This chapter aims to explore the reimagination of Asian-Muslim youth in Britain in the wake of these shifting images, and particularly in relation to the construction of Asian-Muslim youth violence. It falls into three sections, exploring the intersection of race/ethnicity and masculinity with the interpretation and performance of violence. The first section focuses on the 'riots' of 2001, and particularly the state responses to the outbreak of urban violence. Second, the chapter explores the interpretation of this violence. It argues that the violence has been largely portrayed as an irrational, abnormal rupture in social organisation, and that the attribution of irrationality is legitimated in the appeal to racialised ideas of premodern cultures and uncivilised bodies. The responses of the Home Office and the criminal justice system to the disturbances can be seen, in turn, to reflect the attempt to legislate and control cultural bodies through the inscription of highly racialised institutional violence. The third part of the chapter draws on an example from my empirical work with Asian-Muslim young men in London (Alexander 2000a). Through an account of our very own 'riot', described in the press report at the beginning of this chapter, I argue that, far from constituting an expression of momentary or irrational disruption of the social order, much violence in urban contexts has to be understood as instrumental, rational and everyday. This is not to excuse or naturalise such encounters, but is to insist on the need to place violence both in context (Keith 1993, 1995) and as part of a performance of masculine power and resistance that carries with it its own set of rules and expectations.

Re-constructing the Barbarian at home: the 2001 'riots' and the legislation of urban violence

Although urban violence and protest amongst Britain's Asian communities is not a new phenomenon – for example, Southall in 1979 and 1981, or

Bradford in 1995 – the events of 2001 are marked by their scale and ferocity, and by the moral panic generated in their wake. In Oldham, 500 individuals were involved in clashes with the police, causing estimated damage of £1.4 million; in Burnley, 400 white and Asian young men were involved in fighting between themselves and with the police. In the biggest disturbances, in Bradford, up to 500 Muslim youths fought running battles with more than 1000 riot police and support staff, 455 counts of criminal damage, arson, assault, robbery and violence were recorded, and an estimated £11 million worth of damage was caused (Allen 2003).

The location, size and intensity of the violence and anger seem to have caught everyone by surprise. Although the tensions had been clearly signalled in the very fraught racialised atmosphere that accompanied the runup to the General Election that year; in the anger and anxiety caused by the Greater Manchester Police claims that the majority (60 per cent) of racial attacks in Oldham were Asian on White and that areas of the town had become 'no-go' areas for whites; and in the weekly presence of the National Front and British National Party jumping on the resurgent anti-immigration/anti-asylum bandwagon; the notion that the violence came out of nowhere laid the foundation for the portrayal of the 'riots' as spontaneous and irrational acts of destruction. This image was clearly apparent in the immediate aftermath of the events in Bradford: thus Chief Superintendent Phil Read, of West Yorkshire Police, described the disturbances as '*wanton* violence' continuing 'there can be *no excuse* for this *criminal* behaviour' (cited in Allen 2003: 23, my emphasis). The notion of excess, of irrationality and the links to criminality are recurrent themes; the Home Secretary, David Blunkett, dismissed the events as '*wanton* violence and destruction' and 'sheer, *mindless violence* – people behaving in a totally *anti-social and thuggish* fashion' (ibid., my emphasis), while a spokesperson for Tony Blair similarly decried the unrest as '*simply* thuggery' (ibid.: 24, my emphasis).

The dismissal of the events in Bradford and elsewhere as mindless criminality was reflected in the refusal of the Home Secretary to investigate the underlying causes of the disturbances.[2] This in turn is reflected in the very particular view taken in the slew of reports that were commissioned in the wake of the violence. These eschewed explanations that sought to place the 'riots' in the historical context of longstanding structural inequalities, deindustrialisation and racial discrimination, or within the immediate local concerns over Far Right activism, racist attacks and police harassment (Amin 2002; Webster 2002; Allen 2003). Taking their cue from Herman Ouseley's earlier report on Bradford (2001), the reports[3] placed the origin of the disturbances in ethnic and racial segregation and cultural difference – in what the Cantle Report (2001) captioned as 'parallel lives'. The Denham Report thus points to 'the fragmentation and polarisation of communities – on economic, geographical, racial and cultural lines – on a scale which amounts to segregation, albeit to an extent by choice' (2002: 11).[4]

The reports' primary focus serves ultimately to reduce the very complex processes of social marginalisation, exclusion and tension to a simple paradigm of cultural difference and antipathy. The reports thus reinscribe a version of 'culture' that naturalises and reifies ethnic boundaries as impermeable and unassailable, and their content as homogeneous and unchanging – what might be referred to as an 'ethnic bubble' approach (Gates 1992). Cultural identity thereby becomes the privileged ontological site, transcending and erasing any alternative identifications – gender, class, age, location – that cut within and across 'community' boundaries (Amin 2002). Poverty, unemployment, educational underachievement, poor housing, crime and violence are then seen as the consequences of a failing culture, rather than as the result of wider social and structural disadvantage and discrimination (Webster 2002) – an underscoring of pseudo-sociobiological/ecological notions of 'cultures of poverty' (Lewis 1966). This works in turn to naturalise the violence of the 'riots' as the outcome of incompatible cultural values, the confrontation between a displaced but ineluctable Asian-ness/Muslim-ness and a modern, coherent White English/Britishness, in which the inevitabilities of racial-cultural difference are played out – Huntington's (1996) 'clash of civilisations' writ small.

The representation of the 'riots' as irrational, 'wanton' acts of self-destruction, outlined above, is reinforced through the equation of the violence with simple criminality – as deviant and anti-social behaviour rather than legitimate protest (Riches 1986). The Burnley Task Force Summary Report described the events as:

> Disturbances [which] were caused originally by *criminal acts* involving both Asian and White *criminal gangs*, which were followed by deliberate attempts to turn the *violent acts* into racial confrontation. (Cited in Farrar 2002, my emphasis)[5]

In Bradford, the construction of the 'rioters' as criminals was vividly illustrated by the issuing of nine 'Wanted' posters picturing 212 young Asian men implicated in the violence. As Christopher Allen has noted (2003) 'Operation Wheel' became Britain's largest criminal investigation, and a showcase for Labour's pledge to be tough on crime (though in this case, apparently, *not* on the causes of crime). Immediately after the events, Labour MP for Bradford North, Terry Rooney, demanded that the 'troublemakers' be dealt with swiftly and harshly, 'we've got to *root them out*, get them banged up and show people that justice will apply to anybody that engages in this *mindless thuggery*' (ibid.: 24, my emphasis).

Since the disturbances in Bradford, 270 people have been arrested, over 90 per cent of whom are Asian-Muslim young men. Some 145 of these have been charged with 'riot' (Allen 2003) with 134 receiving sentences between 18 months and five years. Derek McGhee (2003) notes that the rarely used charge of 'riot' carries a heavier maximum sentence of up to ten years, compared with the lesser and more usual charges brought under the 1986 Public Order Act, and which were used to prosecute offenders in Burnley and Oldham.[6] In August 2002, Amjid Rashid was given an unprecedented eight years for his involvement in the violence, while other young men were sentenced to between four and six and a half years for throwing stones at the police (*The Guardian*, 31 October 2003).[7] In defending the sentences, Judge Stephen Gullick described the incidents as acts of 'wanton, vicious and prolonged violence' (*The Guardian*, 6 September 2002).

The implementation of Gullick's 'scorched-earth' sentencing (McGhee 2003) on the Bradford 'rioters' can be read as a broader demonisation and penalisation of the Muslim community in its entirety. In sentencing the first defendant to be convicted, Shazad Ashraf, Gullick noted that, like the Home Secretary, he was 'not concerned with [the disturbances'] origins' (Allen 2003: 47) but with setting an example to others in the community.[8] Thus he stated:

> It must be made equally clear, both to those who are apprehended and to those who might be tempted to behave this way in the future … it is a message which I trust will deter others from engaging in this type of behaviour in the future. (Ibid.: 47)[9]

All Asian-Muslim young men in Bradford, and elsewhere, are thus presumed guilty and implicated in the sentencing of each defendant. At the same time, each defendant is held to represent the community as a whole and the punishment of one is the symbolic punishment of all – what Allen refers to as 'community sentencing' (ibid.: 46). At a later trial, Gullick claimed:

> That charge [of community responsibility] I have sought to stress every time that I have passed sentence … includes not only the actions of the individual defendants such as yourselves, but also the unlawful conduct of all those around you as well. (Ibid.: 46)

Whilst the harshness of the sentences has been criticised – for example, by Sir Herman Ouseley, who described them as 'undeniably unfair and possibly racist' (*The Guardian*, 31 August 2002) – the message from the Home Office has been unambiguous:

> *Maniacs* who were engaging in [the disturbances] are now whining about sentences they have been given ... at last the courts are handing out sentences that are *a genuine reprisal but also a message to the community*. (David Blunkett quoted in The Guardian, 6 September 2002, my emphasis)

The linkage between individual punishment and the wider Muslim community is stark. Similarly, the presentation of the events as acts of fanaticism and the notion of the sentences as revenge, in a post-9/11 scenario, are startlingly clear. As Imran Khan has argued:

> The Asian community has been criminalised with the paint of one brush. To add to that, since September 11, the community is looked upon with great suspicion. Their dignity and respect has been removed and they have been made a scapegoat. (Cited in Allen 2003: 38)

The sentencing in Bradford must be placed, then, against the larger backdrop of fears around potential Muslim violence, particularly in the wake of the September 11th attacks, and the subsequent moves to control unruly or potentially dangerous elements within Britain and globally.[10] As mentioned earlier, this is centred on a racialised perception of who constitutes such a threat, and this is read off from physical and cultural markers – skin, hair, language, religion.[11] These ethnoracial markers are filtered through additional symbols of gender and age: the focus of concern is on Muslim *young men*, who are seen to embody a triple threat, as Muslims, as youth and as men – all categories associated with disorder and potential violence (Alexander 2000b). However, as the sentencing makes clear, the individual is also seen as a corollary of the 'community', and Muslim young men thus stand as the embodiment of a broader concern around alien cultural encampments at the heart of the British nation.

The 'riots' were understood, then, as at once the actions of criminal individuals and 'maniacs' and as the inevitable consequence of a broader cultural breakdown – the failure of a premodern/immigrant community to adjust to the demands of modern/Western life. It is interesting to note that compared to the understanding of the unrest of the 1980s, which paid at least some recognition to racism and social disadvantage as causal factors (Keith 1993), marginalisation of the northern Muslim communities was laid explicitly at the feet of Culture.[12] Consequently, rather than implement a dual response of social reform and social control (Solomos 1986) to the 2001 disturbances, the emphasis has been on a dual level of control – of the young men involved in the violence and of the cultures which produced them. This is most clearly signalled in the move away from 'celebrating difference', which lay at the heart of the cultural pluralist arguments of the Parekh Report (2000) towards the exigencies of 'managing diversity'.

This strategy is laid out in the Denham Report, which provides the template for the Home Office's new strategy for improving race relations – 'community cohesion'. In the introduction, Lord Denham writes:

> We recognise that in many areas affected by disorder or community tensions, there is little interchange between members of racial, cultural and religious communities and that *proactive measures will have to be taken* to promote dialogue and understanding. We also take on board the need to generate a widespread and open debate about identity, *shared values and common citizenship* as part of the process of building cohesive communities. (2002, my emphasis)

Although apparently about dialogue and exchange, the notion of 'community cohesion' reflects the Home Secretary's demands that ethnic minorities adopt British social values and 'norms of acceptability' (*The Guardian*, 11 December 2001), symbolised in the suggested oath of loyalty to the British nation. The movement integral to building cohesive communities is, then, strictly one-way, from 'immigrant' margin to 'host' centre, through a process of cultural eradication and legislation. As Arun Kundnani has argued, 'community cohesion' signals *The Death of Multiculturalism* (2002) and a return to an earlier 'race-relations' model with a strong focus on integration to an imagined cultural mainstream, or what Blunkett refers to as 'core [British] values'. As Tufyal Choudhury has argued, 'debate on Muslims and the integration of Muslims, has always focused on what Muslims must do' (cited in Allen 2003: 29).

Uncivilised bodies and the management of culture: masculinity, violence and control

'Community cohesion' carries within in it a dual notion of 'community', one which opposes 'bad' versions of culturally bounded and segregated collectivities with 'good' locally based sensibilities fully integrated into the mainstream of national culture – what Gary Armstrong refers to as the pursuit of 'purified community' (1998: 136).[13] As mentioned earlier, the blame for 'bad communities' lies in their possession of traditional

'Culture', which seemingly prevents their participation in wider society. The remedy is to break down these traditions and values and replace them with the appropriate 'core values', which can be seen to underpin the attainment of 'citizenship'. What community cohesion entails, then, is the management of 'Culture', which in turn is held to be the property of ethnic minority groups (Alleyne 2002). Of course, some communities are seen to have more 'culture' than others (Benson 1996) and pose different challenges for assimilation – or, in the case of Muslim communities particularly, are seen as unassimilable.

There is, however, a crucial inconsistency in the move to 'managing diversity' centred on this reification of 'Culture', and which has its roots in the management of colonial communities. Arjun Appadurai (1996) has thus argued that this anthropological perspective views culture as a possession or property of 'ethnic' groups, rather than as part of a social field of interaction – a category of absolute difference rather than of relationality. It imbues cultural identity with physical or spiritual essence which places culture as part of 'the discursive space of race' (ibid.: 12), so that ethnicity constitutes what Paul Gilroy (1992) has described as 'race without the biology' or what Tariq Modood (1992) calls 'the mode of being'. This forms part of a 'colonial sociology of rule' (Appadurai 1996: 98), which first creates and then fixes social categories and communal identities, facilitating the bureaucratic management of that culture – what Barnor Hesse (1997) has termed 'white governmentality'.[14] This serves to obscure and naturalise processes of power through which each ascribed culture is unequally positioned and attributed 'differential prestige' (Appadurai 1996: 12).

The Denham Report and the pursuit of 'community cohesion' clearly exemplify the exercise of bureaucratic power as part of the classification and control of ethnic identities on a communal basis. In so doing, they use 'culture' as a mechanism both for explanation and for the allocation of blame (Keith 1993) – laying causality and guilt squarely at the door of 'the Muslim community', conveniently and clearly predefined. The expressed government remedy, 'Building Cohesive Communities' carries within it a clear pedagogic message, which works both to render Asian-Muslim cultures separate and unequal and to inscribe a version of hegemonic English/British culture and identity as the culture of choice – or, indeed, of necessity.[15] It can thus be understood as a form of indirect educative control which is a counterpart to the more explicitly coercive power of the state embodied in the police and criminal justice system. Community cohesion as discourse and practice becomes part of a process of cultural recolonisation and regulation.

Of course, and here's the twist, the concept of culture as 'mode of being' which underpins the 'parallel lives' motif means that it cannot easily be traded for the pleasures of citizenship, even if this were desired or desirable. The notion that ethnicity constitutes what Gilroy terms 'a pseudo-biological property of communal life' (1993: 24) thus becomes a self-fulfilling and self-sustaining condition of irrevocable difference beyond the possibilities of education and acculturation. On reflection, then, the notion of 'community cohesion' is necessarily a culturally exclusive one – more a blueprint for the demarcation of those who belong and those 'others', the barbarians at the gate (Benson 1996), who must be kept out and controlled.

This control works both at the general level of community and the more particular level of the individual, who, as discussed above, stands as the embodiment of the community. The management of cultural communities is also inescapably the management of cultural bodies – this can be clearly seen in the forms of legislation that surround and intersect the bodies of ethnic minorities in a range of contexts, from the state control of movement through immigration, the increasingly inter-ventionist strategies around language, dress and sexuality (especially marriage practices), the institutions of civil society (from the education system to welfare, housing and employment) (Modood et al. 1997), and ultimately to the altogether more visceral realities of racist violence. Following Foucault (1979), Appadurai argues that ethnicised/cultural bodies form the locus for the inscription of disciplines of self- and group control, often reflecting the interests of the state (1996: 148).[16] Along with other axes of differentiation, such as gender, age and class, racialised/ ethnicised bodies become the bearers of moral worth and social difference, which mark them out as inferior and dangerous (Stallybrass & White 1986).

Appadurai notes that this notion of cultural identity underscores an incipient sense of danger through its evocation of irrationality and primordiality – cultural bodies are then inescapably uncivilised or 'grotesque' (Stallybrass & White 1986) bodies. As Elias has argued (1982), a key marker of 'the civilising process' is held to be the increased control over the use and forms of violence, with the means of violence being concentrated in the instruments of the state – the army or the police. The 'civilised' individual is one who can suppress the urge for spontaneous acts of violence, and who recognises the network of social consequences of any failure of self-control. By the same token, any threat to this monopoly of violence is seen as a threat to civilisation (Appadurai 1986: 140), signifying the absence of control and self-control and precipitating the descent into terror. These discursive symbols are each clearly apparent in the reactions to the 'riots' of 2001 – the 'rioters' become the epitome of incivility; the bearers of inferior and hostile cultures, incapable of self-control, irrational and 'wanton' in their actions, threatening the fabric of the social order. The actions of the instruments of state violence, the police and the criminal justice system, in turn, become the reinscription of social order and authority at a corporeal level.[17] The arrest and sentencing of the Bradford 'rioters' can then be understood as the public performance of state-sanctioned violence, which acts in concert with the attempted symbolic violence of the management of minority communities, to define and regulate unwanted cultures and uncivilised bodies.

There is, of course, a gendered dimension to this clash of 'Culture', on the one hand, and of 'civilisation', on the other. If the focus on the management of culture has been placed primarily on the traditionally female institutions of civil society – family and education – the confrontation between the state and the boundaries of community has been between men, as 'defenders of the nation'. The Denham Report thus notes of the 'riots', 'the participants were overwhelmingly young men' (2001: 8), while the actions of the police can also be understood as the performance of masculine state power (Westwood 1995). In intersection with the marker of racialised difference, the violence can, then, be partially framed as the encounter between a hegemonic White (state) masculinity and a subordinated (Asian) masculinity (Connell 1995).[18] The 'riots' themselves were presented as the performance of a pathologised masculine identity, rooted in a failing patriarchal culture. Marie Macey, for example, has linked the 'riots' in Bradford in 1995 to the growth of organised criminal 'gangs' and drug culture, and bases both in 'a religious and cultural tradition which militate against the progress of the Muslim community' (2002: 41) in which *'young men* have mobilized a particular Islamic code as a power resource *against both women and the white establishment'* (1999: 857, my emphasis). The commonsense links between culture, crime and gender are clearly made, and fused with the inevitabilities of violence – an evocation of fears around a racialised hypermasculinity that has come to redefine Asian-Muslim masculinities in Britain since the *Satanic Verses* affair in 1989 (Alexander 2000a, 2000b).

The sentencing of the Bradford 'rioters' can, then be placed as part of the inscription of a racialised and gendered hegemonic power – what James Messerschmidt has termed 'Doing White-Supremacist Masculinity' (1997: 140). Messerschmidt has argued that the violence of lynching in the United States has to be understood as the performance of White masculine hegemony in the face of the changing social relationships between black and white men in the period after slavery. This violence allows for the reinforcement of traditional power relationships *on the bodies* of black men, using eroticised fears around black violence and sexuality as a rationale (Davis 1983).[19] Mrinalini Sinha (1995) has similarly argued that opposed constructions of racialised masculinities were used in colonial India both to constitute notions of Western superiority, to regulate forms of interaction and to legitimate forms of domination and subordination in a colonial setting.[20] In the same way, I would argue that the state violence aimed at the containment of *the bodies* of Asian-Muslim young men in the wake of the 'riots' can also be seen as part of an attempt to revalidate White British masculine identities, and invalidate Asian-Muslim masculine identities, in the face of the local and global traumas of the summer of 2001. This serves to legitimate and reinforce traditional relationships of inequality and subordination and to, literally and figuratively, *embody* the reach for control.

The gendering of the 'riots', along with the foundational myth of primordial ethnic/cultural conflict, serves to doubly naturalise the violence, and to place it outside the realm of social analysis. John Solomos (1986) has argued that 'rioting' is popularly understood as an aberrant and abnormal phenomenon, a temporary and irrational disruption in the prevailing social order (Keith 1993; Jeganathan 2000). While there is an alternative perspective, which reifies and celebrates urban violence as political resistance – what Kundnani refers to as 'the violence of the violated' (2001) – both work to simplify and homogenise a very complex, disparate and often highly localised phenomenon. Both the 'violence-as-culture' and the 'violence-as-political-protest' versions retreat to essentialised notions of race, class, culture, gender and so on as the inevitable basis for conflict. This ignores two very important aspects: firstly, both underplay the pervasiveness of everyday violence in the lives of communities and individuals (Armstrong 1998), and secondly, it ignores the multiple and shifting meanings attached to the performance of violence by the actors concerned. Thus, the normalcy and the internal (rather than the attributed collective) rationality of events is ignored or dismissed, substituting polemic and politics for understanding. It is worth observing that amidst the clamour of expert opinions, policy makers and ethnic/political opportunists seeking to voice their interpretations of the 2001 'riots', it is the young men themselves who remain silent and invisible.

Michael Keith argues that a distinction needs to be made between the 'public' and 'private' lives of a 'riot' (1993: 92), or between the *processes* that underpin urban violence and its *meaning* to the parties involved. In his work on football hooligans, Armstrong notes that violence needs to be viewed as a 'social drama', and quotes Victor Turner's exhortation that:

> To analyse satisfactorily even a single social drama it is necessary to place it firmly in what may be called its field context, to give a preliminary account, whenever possible, of the history of the field context, of how the kinds of groups came to be where they are and

what accounted for their present mode of relationship. (Turner 1957, cited in Armstrong 1998: 20)

The remainder of this chapter will explore the private life of a 'riot' which took place in 1996 during my own fieldwork with Bangladeshi young men in London. The research was an ethnographic study of Asian youth identities, which took place over five years, and was based in a youth project for Bangladeshi young men – the Stoneleigh Asian Youth Project (SAYO). The research was not focused specifically on violence, though incidents of violence, large and small, were a ubiquitous feature of the fieldwork. These are explored in detail in *The Asian Gang* (Alexander 2000a), but what follows is an analysis of one particular set of incidents that were publicly portrayed and understood as a mini-'riot'. The account that follows is necessarily brief and decontextualised, but hopes to give a small insight into some of the lived complexities of this set of encounters.

Unexamined lives:[21] anatomy of a 'riot'

The mini-'riot' reported in the local press in the summer of 1996 represented the culmination of a series of smaller, sporadic clashes between the Bengali young men of the SAYO project and a group of black (African and African-Caribbean) youths, who were all in Year 10 of the nearby Thomas More secondary school. The initial impetus for the conflict was a small incident, several weeks earlier, in which two black young men had tripped up two of the Bengali young men, Ifti and Malik, during some lunchtime revelry. This had resulted in angry words and a minor scuffle when blows were exchanged. The following day, Ifti's older brother, Humzah, came into the school looking for the attackers and a fight broke out in the library. The police were called and Ifti was suspended for three days. Several other fights in school followed, leading to an unprovoked attack on Hanif in the school canteen, in which he suffered head injuries and a black eye. As news of this incident spread, a number of the older Bengali young men, including Hanif's older brothers, gathered outside the school and again the police intervened, arresting one for possession of an offensive weapon (a chair leg). The following afternoon, a number of the Bengali youths, supported by a group of friends from East London, spotted the main attacker, Hansel, chased him into a garden and beat him with belts and sticks. Hansel escaped with a fractured arms and bruises to his legs. A number of the Bengali young men were picked up and questioned by the police, but none were charged. The next day, Hansel and some friends from nearby Clifton returned to the school and attacked two other Bengali boys, giving one a severe head gash with a belt buckle. A few days later, a large number of black youths from Clifton arrived at the school looking for the Bengali group, and a tense stand-off ensued. Rumours spread that the same Clifton group was due to return in large numbers to the Stoneleigh Estate, which led to the flurry of preparations reported in the local press and the increase in police activity. The confrontation never took place.

Of course, in many ways, this 'riot-that-wasn't' is very different in its events, scale and motivations from the events of 2001 discussed above. However, there are some interesting parallels that can be drawn, both in its external representation and its internal mechanisms, which throw light on the construction of violence and alternative routes to understanding.

Firstly, there is the way in which the violence was framed in terms of a racial/cultural divide – in this case, marked by the signifiers 'Asian' versus 'Black'. As with the 2001 'riots' this serves to naturalise the conflict as an inevitable result of racial/cultural difference, and to ignore its more complex local, historical and interpersonal context. Secondly, there is the intervention of particular institutions to contain the violence through the control of uncivilised bodies: this is clearly seen in the intervention of the Territorial Support Group (TSG) on the estate and the series of arrests that followed. It is also apparent in the actions of the school throughout this period, which failed to address the underlying causes of the conflict but responded with a rash of knee-jerk suspensions and exclusions – employing, as with the TSG, a very literal, physical interpretation of containment and control. Thirdly, it is important to recognise the raced, gendered and generational locus of the concern – the focus for control was primarily the Bengali young men on the estate, who had long been seen as a 'problem group'. The repeated racialised labelling used in the media article clearly highlights this aspect, and uses a very similar script of irrational violence and threat – these are youths 'roaming the estate', threatening the 'eruption' of violent conflict, armed and dangerous. They are also portrayed as out of control ('taking the law into their own hands'), destructive and self-destructive ('damaging the quality of life for everyone where they live') and as criminal. The Bengali young men particularly were viewed by media, the police and the school as 'a gang', with all its intimations of deviance and danger, a perception which preceded and subsequently structured the responses to the violence. This worked in concert with the notion of racial/ethnic hostility to attribute to the conflict a level of homogeneity, organisation and a clear locus for collective/'community' guilt and blame.

As with the 2001 'riots', however, the rush for easy culturalist explanations denies the more complex contours of violence, substituting instead a meta-rationale that obscures more than it reveals. The conflicts of 1996 need, then, to be placed within a specific local and historical context, and within the altogether more personal dynamics of a small group of young men in this time and place. In this case, the conflict between the Bengali young men and the black young men from Clifton can be seen to partially arise from the local history of the Stoneleigh Estate, which is positioned in a predominantly White borough of London, and which has a history of racist violence against the Bengali community since their arrival in the 1970s. The young men of the SAYO project have, then, been brought up in an environment where their families were the targets of racist violence and abuse and they themselves had only recently started to strike back in defence of their community (see Back, Chapter 1, this volume). Before and during my fieldwork, the Stoneleigh Estate was the site for a number of community-defence-based confrontations, which were sometimes exclusively Bengali-focused, but on other occasions were based around a broadly inclusive, territorial notion of community. In this case, the notion of territorial pride and collective defence was reinforced by a more recent history of conflict between some of the Bengali and Black young men within the Thomas More school, which had begun two years previously with some of the older youths (now left school) and had been inherited by their younger brothers.[22]

This particular dynamic was very specific in terms of age and gender, but also in terms of the individuals involved. Thus, while it was a conflict between young men, it was also very much a personality-led issue. Although the sides involved were characterised as 'Asian' and 'Black', the events of 1996, and previously, were centred on only a small subsection of the Bengali young men at the school, and an even smaller proportion of the 80 per cent Black, 80 per cent male school population. This was true even of the year groups involved, since the violence mainly centred on a small core group of Bengali boys in Year 10. The contours of this conflict are, then, drawn across the boundaries of a specific friendship group, although these boundaries were themselves very fluid, and could be expanded to include Chinese class mates, other Bengali friends from other local schools, nearby estates, or even other areas (such as the young men from East London who took part in the attack on Hansel).

At the same time, the events were shaped by culturally inflected notions of family and masculinity, particularly formed through ideas of age and family status. This meant that the young men of Year 10 both saw themselves as having responsibility for a broader collective sense of honour and safety within their 'community'. An attack on these young men was, then, on the one hand read as an attack on the community as a whole, although it is likely that this 'community' was imagined in highly gendered and spatial terms, centred on the physical, embodied performance of masculine strength, control and protection within a territorial framework of 'the Estate' (Alexander 1998). On the other hand, this more abstracted sense of 'community' was filtered through strong familial ties and obligations, both on the part of the biological brothers, and their friends, who stood in the position of 'fictive' kin, or '*bhayas*' (older brothers). As argued elsewhere (Alexander 2000a, 2000b) the role of *bhaya* carries with it duties of protection, which are integrally bound up with obligations of 'respect'. This served to mediate the peer group/friendship ties of the immediate protagonists and to constrain the autonomy of the younger group in responding to future violence. It is significant, however, that in shifting the focus of the conflict away from interpersonal hostility to a 'community'/territorial playing field, the stakes were also raised and expanded. Several weeks after the first grand no-show, a group of young men from Clifton returned to the Stoneleigh Estate and attacked a young white boy and an older Bengali young man, Khalid (Hanif's brother, who had not been involved in the first round of events). The conflict was then reframed as a territorial one, irrespective of ethnicity, peer group, age or personal involvement. In response, over 60 young men of diverse racial/ethnic backgrounds, ages, peer and friendship groups massed in the youth club building in preparation for the next rumoured incursion. Although again nothing happened, the response was an astonishing, and even moving, demonstration of mutual support and collective strength which muted other antagonisms and divisions in defence of an inclusive, if temporary, version of 'community' and 'belonging'.

Although much of the texture and complexity of these events are lost in this narration, there are three significant points. Firstly, although the conflict was represented in very stark ways as about race/culture, the events themselves require recognition of the more nuanced social, historical and local contexts through which ideas of difference and hostility are imagined. Secondly, the notion of the violence as illegitimate and irrational, as the actions of young men out of control, is contested when the internal logics and the rules of its performance are explored. This needs to take into account the intersection of racialised identities with gender, age, location, class and so on, but is also important in placing 'culture' not as a primordial possession or sensibility but as a mode or field of interaction. Thirdly, although this has not formed part of the present discussion, there is the more intimate level of personality and emotionality in the consideration of conflict: the individual motivations of the actors, the sense of excitement or pleasure, anger, distaste or pain, that is evoked, and the moral codes at work – around loyalty and trust, and even sympathy with your enemy.[23] Ifti, for example, told me that he had eventually stopped the attack on Hansel because he 'felt sorry for him' (interview 28 September 1996).

Concluding comments: public discourses and private lives – placing violence in context

The stress on history, context and performance moves away from the naturalisation of violence in either straightforwardly racial/ethnic or gendered terms, towards the recognition of the role of agency, strategy and rationality on the part of the actors concerned (Riches 1986; Elwert, Feuchtwang & Neubert 1999). It also allows for the enactments of codes of conduct and the internal logics and constraints of seemingly random acts. My own work on 'the Asian Gang' (2000a, 2000b) suggests that even seemingly simple and everyday acts of violence are underpinned by a complex and shifting web of motivations, rationales and alliances. However, a recognition of complexity and multiplicity is not to assume disorder or randomness within violent encounters; rather it is to place violence as a *social* phenomenon with roots and 'channels' (Elwert et al. 1999) which can be unearthed and contours which can be mapped and engaged.

Rather than viewing violence as a disturbance in an otherwise stable state of social order, then, violence can be understood as a set of practices that reinscribe or contest social norms and boundaries. More than this, however, it is these very norms and boundaries which create the conditions and the 'space for violence' (Jeganathan 2000: 61). This space is formed in the intersection of wider structural processes with the lives of individuals and groups, and in the encounter between the external search for control and the internal reach for agency (Bourgois 1995). It is important, then, to place violence *in context*, to recognise the classification of 'violence' as itself a product of wider systems of meaning and power, and to acknowledge at once the rationality and indeterminacy of its performance. Although classified as abnormal, irrational or even 'bestial' behaviour (Riches 1986), it is the very normality and banality – not to mention the humanity – of violence that begs to be understood and explained. This is not to seek to excuse, trivialise or even celebrate acts of violence, but it is to insist on their validity as objects of analysis and to thereby accept the possibility of, and responsibility for, change.

Understanding both the space for and performance of violence necessitates a more up-close-and-personal approach than is usual, or indeed comfortable, for social analysis (Bourgois 1995; Armstrong

1998; Nandy 2002). However, it is at this more 'private', intimate level that violence is lived through, as social drama and as experience, and can unsettle its more public claims to easy 'Truths' and 'parallel lives'.

Notes

1. All identifying names and markers have been changed in this article to maintain anonymity.
2. Labour MP for Bradford West, Marsha Singh, thus stated that the riots had 'nothing to do with deprivation, this was sheer criminality' (Allen 2003: 24).
3. The Burnley Task Force Report led by Lord Tony Clarke, the Oldham Review headed by David Ritchie, and the influential Cantle Report on Community Cohesion, all came out in late 2001. These three reports then formed the basis for the Denham Report (2002) on *Building Cohesive Communities* which is the government blueprint for the future of multiethnic Britain (to borrow a phrase from the Parekh Report, 2000).
4. The report also quotes Herman Ouseley's earlier (2001) report on Bradford, which states that, 'different ethnic groups are increasingly *segregating themselves* from each other and retreating into "*comfort zones*" *made up of people like themselves*' (ibid.: 12, my emphasis).
5. The Cantle Report stated: 'One activity which sadly seems to be present with all the communities we visited was drug dealing. There was even some suggestion that in Burnley some of the rioting ... was in fact the result of a "turf war" between drug gangs' (2001: 16). The later Denham Report (2002) stated that there was little to substantiate these claims.
6. These latter offenders, according to McGhee, received maximum sentences of two to three years, compared to an average of five years for those charged in Bradford. Chris Allen (2003) similarly notes that youths on the predominantly white Ravenscliffe Estate in Bradford, who took part in violent disturbances the day after those in Manningham, received sentences averaging not more than two years.
7. Allen notes that many of these young men were community- or self-volunteered and were first-time offenders, with no history of criminal activity. Some 38 of those sentenced were refused individual leave to appeal (Allen 2003). The sentences were largely upheld on appeal (*The Guardian*, 31 January 2003).
8. The belief in 'exemplary sentencing' (Hall et al. 1978) is a recurrent tactic in controlling black youth, such as 'muggers' in the 1970s.
9. Ashraf, who was a first-time offender, was imprisoned for five years for throwing 'two missiles' and 'waving your arms' to encourage others (Allen 2003: 39).
10. In the United States, almost 1,200 Muslims were arrested and detained, while in Britain, the government rushed through anti-terrorism legislation that allowed them to detain indefinitely non-UK nationals as 'suspected international terrorists' – a power that was aimed specifically at Arab,

South Asian or Muslim men and was later ruled to be discriminatory (Amnesty International 2002; Sheill 2003).

11. Akram and Johnson (2002) thus note the increased public acceptance of racial profiling of potential 'terrorists' after September 11th and the centrality of visible, embodied difference in the targeting of Muslim/Asian/Middle Eastern men in both the US and UK as part of increased security measures (in Sheill 2003).

12. Bradford MP Anne Cryer, for example, was quoted as saying that social exclusion amongst Muslim minorities could be traced to the practice of marrying women from the Indian subcontinent, who did not speak English and perpetuated foreign cultures within the home – 'importing poverty' (*The Guardian*, 12 July 2001).

13. The term is Richard Sennett's (Sennett & Cobb 1977). Armstrong notes that 'purified community' is the pursuit of order in 'the city' leading to 'an intolerance of difference, a fear of change and a society afraid of difference, which is "willing to be dull and sterile in order not to be confused or overwhelmed" ' (1998: 136).

14. Hesse defines 'white governmentality' as the representation and regulation of non-whites in the West, which uses racial/ethnic characterisations as a basis of creating and sustaining hierarchies and practices of exclusion.

15. Bhikhu Parekh has thus written of the 'moral covenant' of citizenship, in which he asserts of ethnic minority cultures, 'Some of their values and practices might be unacceptable and then they need to be changed, by consensus when possible and *by law if necessary*' (in Modood et al. 1997: x, my emphasis).

16. Foucault thus points to the significance of 'biopolitics' in which the body 'is directly involved in a political field; power relations have an immediate hold on it; they invest it, mark it, train it, torture it, force it to carry out tasks, to perform ceremonies, to emit signs' (1979: 25).

17. David Riches (1986) notes that the designation of 'violence' carries with it the connotation of illegitimate or unacceptable behaviour. He also cites Radcliffe-Brown's telling observation that 'the physical force employed by the state is … *government … not violence*' (ibid.: 3, my emphasis).

18. This encounter can be read against a global shift in Western fears around 'martial men' and Islamic militancy since the 1970s and of course in the wake of September 11th (Said 1978; Akram & Johnson 2002, Mamdani 2002, Waseem 2002). I am grateful to Kate Sheill (2003) for her insights into this global dimension.

19. It is interesting that one of the primary expressed rationales for the legislation of Britain's Muslim communities and the 'War on Terror' is the protection of Asian-Muslim women from the barbarisms of their menfolk (Abu-Lughod 2002). This is a key feature of Macey's (1999, 2002) account of Bradford described above, in which violence against women and protests against racial inequality are seen as part of the same culturally dysfunctional process. Significantly, it is Asian-Muslim women who have spearheaded the 'Fair Justice for All' campaign against the Bradford sentences (Allen 2003).

20. Sinha (1995) points to the distinction made between the 'martial' Sikh and Muslim masculinities (including Bengali Muslims) and the perceived effeminacy of Bengali Hindus. She also explores the colonial intervention in Indian gendered practices and sexuality (around age of consent, for example) which has significant echoes in the community cohesion debates.
21. The phrase is from Nandy (2002: 13).
22. Cf. *The Asian Gang* (Alexander 2000a), Chapters 2 and 3 for greater detail.
23. Cf. *The Asian Gang* (2000a), Chapter 4 for a discussion of these issues.

Afterwards

DAVID THEO GOLDBERG

Race matters, we now know, even as its matter and reach are ignored, denied, repressed, erased.

In matters racial there have been a series of old historical saws, increasingly replaced (at least overtly) by a set of contemporary critical conventions. The older historical views regarding race often enacted acute social conditions, the troubling legacies of which continue to linger institutionally and ideationally, even under the gathering weight of their denial. The more recent critical conventions, while having made a considerable contribution to loosening the grip of exclusionary racisms on social arrangements in various sites worldwide, nevertheless have sometimes tended also to reify critical responses to racist social arrangements.

Historically, race was overwhelmingly linked to biology, phenotype, blood, epidermal shades. In this scheme of things race was deemed naturally ordered, as such unavoidable and for the most part unchangeable. A leopard, it has been said too often, cannot change its spots. There is of course now a voluminous body of literature revealing the large and small, all-too-common dire effects of this scheme.

We have witnessed more recently the recognition that race figures a complex set of political relations, historically fashioned and culturally conceived. That it is molded and remolded on the anvil of politics and culture, history and relations of power. These insights have led to powerful insights about the machinations of race and the destructiveness of racisms. And they have underpinned a vigorous and oftentimes quite effective range of interventions to address, and occasionally redress, the social debilities to which racial arrangement and insistence have contributed.

The scope of these critical ideas, however, signals distinctive limits. For one, the now-imperative critical confession that race is a 'social construction' quite regularly ends with silence about what sort of social construction it is, how its constructedness might differ across time and place, what the material implications are. The taken-for-grantedness of anti-essentialist jibes repeatedly leaves us guessing about how to read race, and reduces to silence critical analysis of racisms, their range and restrictions. The easy resort to the language of 'racialization' is a primary case in point. The social world is racialized in various ways, we are told, though often not exactly how and in what ways. Does it mean, simply descriptively, that racial meanings, value, and significance are markers of some or other social formation? Does it entail that social members are possibly, likely, inevitably going to act in their name, on their terms? And if so, to what conceivable or actual ends, to whose benefit and whose disvalue? Does the circulation of racial ideas in a society – of its racialization – inevitably entail racist denigrations and exclusions, manifestation in short of individual or institutional racisms? What, I am insisting on querying, is the relation between a society's purported racialization and racist institutionalization? It is one thing *to assume* an analytic, political, or ethical connection; another thing entirely, if connectedly, to offer a compelling set of arguments.[1]

Moreover, there has been a strong tendency to focus on a single state formation, or at best to compare discrete, supposedly self-contained state experiences regarding race with each other. The most common comparisons concerning historical and contemporary racial formations have concerned the US, Brazil, and South Africa, and occasionally Britain. This has privileged the racial history of the US as the generalized comparison point, the yardstick of racial experience historically understood. But it has likewise tended to limit the comprehension of race in Latin America to the Brazilian case, to occlude European understandings of racial sociologies by thinking largely, if not exclusively, in terms of the British experience, and perhaps most understandably to think of racial histories in Africa overwhelmingly in light of apartheid rather than in terms of colonialisms throughout Africa more broadly and relatedly. These leanings have recently begun to be righted in current writing on race, most vigorously in the case of Latin America, a little less so regarding Europe, and almost not at all in respect of Africa. This prevailing conceptual bubble has tended to place Asia and its colonial histories outside of racial reference, a bubble contemporary scholarship has begun to prick in productive ways also.

This suggests another absence, even more glaring, at work too in race-inflected scholarship. Scholars have overwhelmingly thought of experiences and social formations regarding race and its histories of constitution independently of migration and refugee experiences, as though these conditions and their histories of formation have had no relation, constitutively or experientially, to each other. There are of course, some notable recent exceptions, though they prove the rule. I think here of Stephen Castles' work, for instance, some of Robert Miles' earlier writing, or even more presciently recent work of Philomena Essed's.[2]

It is useful to think of Claire Alexander's and Caroline Knowles's volume in light of the challenges I note here to prevailing trajectories on critical scholarship regarding race and racisms. *Making Race*

Matter: Bodies, Space, and Identity is concerned with the contemporary matter(s) of race, with whether and how race has matter(ed) and is made to matter, again and again, and what historical and contemporary political weight it has been made to bear. Materially and critically. As social ordering and as redressive intervention. How are we moved to think differently about race when we alter the terms of reference, temporally and spatially, conceptually and empirically, ethnographically and politically?

Race is made to matter – it is substantiated, materialized – through the material conditions of space and bodies. Race is embodied and spatialized, is sourced and sensed through the interactive play and performance of space(s) and bodies. Space and bodies enfold and materialize meanings, enact exclusions, articulate challenges, signal dangers, project anxieties and insecurities (as Denise Noble tracks in relation to the nation-state). Race, in short, relationally embodies meaning and materiality, significance and social structure.

The book's location is largely Britain and its global extensions. Britain through its global reach historically, imperialistically, and in its global shrinkage, redounding back upon the location of contemporary Britain itself, as place and concept, people and culture. We can think of this as the pulse of race, through expansion and contraction. The racial heartbeat of that nation, once thought strong, pulsating, producing adrenaline rushes, now is stricken by murmurs, shadows, arrhythmic flutterings, giving rise to shortness of breath, self-doubt, but also to lifestyle reconfigurations, new appreciations to those willing to pay notice, new social relations and conceivably novel coalitions and new social transactions, if not movements. The dynamics, for all the determination in the details, might be applied more generally. Britain can be taken as exemplifying the prevailing principles at work. A national formation as constituted historically and reconstituted contemporarily through global circulations racially refracted – of people, power, capital, and commerce. The broad racially inflected and invested themes – identity formation, social tensions and dissonance, impacts of moving Islams, disabilities, gendered and sexed lives, clothing and cultural style – are those we can see marking many a late-modern national formation, if not precisely in the same ways, on similarly particular terms. That play of the general(izable) and specific is the virtue of ethnographic research and paying attention to the micro-details of the particular.

There are, accordingly, some important general lessons to glean from reading race, explicitly or implicitly, as this volume does, in relation to the twin frames of postcoloniality and the global. First, as I have hinted thus far, race cannot be understood outside of the framework of relationalities, in particular, of relations of power. Race oozes out of the cauldron of power, both the effects and affects of relations of assertion and imposition, of domination and subjugation. Second, the postcolonial can be understood in a variety of complex ways. We can think of – use the notion of – *the postcolonial* as descriptive marker of interactions between space and time, as sociospatial embodiments of histories, of lived conditions. But we can think of it too as movement, as migrations or circuits at once internal to a society and globally transient. Third, though, the global and the movements for which it has stood and effected cannot be fully comprehended without understanding it as racially configured. Mapping race can only be completed as a cartography of global relations, of embodiments of social structures and configurations of power; and global mappings can only be constituted in the final analysis through cartographies of racial orderings, their effects and eventualities.

In locating itself in its particularities, the contributions to *Making Race Matter* begin to reveal some of the threads of a theory, an accounting, of racial globality and global racialities. Les Back indicates how racially marked subjects inhabit space – making it 'ours' and not 'theirs', rendering it lived, embodied, habituated, and the challenges, the racially prompted and pronounced dangers, that mark many moments of everyday experience in trying to make it so. The shifting codes of keeping in and keeping out order lives and choices from one moment to another, displacing possibilities as they seek to contain and constrain the already transformed. At the same time Parminder Bhachu reveals the ways in which local fashion is unsettled as race is refabricated through a re*new*ed embodiment, where styles from the old country are recut in conversation with a resituated set of localities, embodying a different experience, new significance, refashioned lives now as much local as global.

The dangers and anxieties faced in being made strange, again, in a strange land play out differently for the postcolonizing whose legacies extend from the traditions of colonizing invasion than for those whose histories have been the conditions of colonized imposition. Patrolling is differently experienced in and across different racially inscribed neighborhoods: as security and as invasiveness, as order and restriction, as protecting the homeland or neighborhood, even from itself, and as unwanted, unnecessary, and unjustified intrusion. This is as much the case, though differently inflected, in metropoles left (behind) as metropoles claimed (anew), in the likes of Los Angeles and London, or Hanoi and Hong Kong, as Miri Song, Caroline Knowles, and Claire Alexander variously reveal.

Ossie Stuart meditates painfully, ironically, at times even humorously on the magnification produced by intersecting modes of self-estrangement. Complexly embodied lives spotlight the lived weights buckling backs, physically and spiritually, but also the possibility of changed meanings and transformed social conditions. Relatedly, Constantinos Phellas reveals the constraints of family and the painful, restricting but also sometimes attracting familiarity of ethnoracially cohering community life.

As my remarks suggest, a strong undercurrent in this book concerns the jolt of racial violence marking dislocation and relocation, displacement and re-placement in the late modern everyday of racially driven lives. This is not to say violence exhausts or even comes close to marking all of everyday experience. But its irrefutable presence haunts the lives of those marked in late-modern societies as racially distinct, clinging to the skin like a sore that never heals. The attraction of better social conditions and improved lives, of liberal liberties and 'Western' rights, barely hides from view the racial exclusions and delimitations but also the ironies and contradictions, themselves often shifting, that are made again and again to come with the new turf. I want to end with some thoughts in this regard.

Every war transforms a nation-state, as much from without as from within. The shifts are not just in spirit but in kind, not just in the marks death leaves on the mind but in the flows of people that inevitably follow in its wake, the children born of its violence at once denied and claimed, the flights from and to. And given that wars, invasions, empires are so often, if not constitutively, made up of those marked as different, ethnoracially, quintessentially between those who are us and those deemed not, between those recognized and those we denied, the aftermath is more than likely the transformation of the commonplace, not just for the invaded but for the invading society. And again not just for those shipped off to foreign lands but at 'home', in the fabric of what counts as home and who counts *in* 'the homeland'. The *afterwards* of war is not only distantiation but connection, oddly organic even as persistently perverse.

Violence, accordingly, is threatened or experienced in or as the everyday in societies the multicultural character of which has been produced out of postcolonial politics. It is not the exception for and by those rendered marginal, for those not invariably rendered the embodiment of social enmity in societies as much of their own making as of their collective inheritance. There is the violence faced by those regarded as (more) recently arrived in 'modern' societies from those societies presumed less modern, even when they might have inhabited the dominant society for generations, contributing substantively to its welfare, in war and peace. Often such contributions are more direct and substantial than those whose personal biographies, while drawing them to far-flung places of national empire, are taken ideologically, conceptually, to be more natural members of the national stock, as Hazel Carby puts it in her

Foreword to this volume. This violence is ascribed too often not to the alienating, discriminatory, excluding, estranging, debilitating, and disenfranchising conditions to which they are subjected but to the claim of the subjugated's own deficiencies, as Claire Alexander shows. The violence is discounted to the poverty of the heritage culture of and from the displaced, the product accordingly of presumptively anti-social and uncivilized behavior. At the same time, a prevailing metropolitan response to perceived postimperial population deluge and its attendant challenges, material and representational, has been to fashion – really to embroider – an already existing culture of control, of policing, containment, repression, denial. These cultures of control have been represented or rationalized in the name, at best, of the power of tolerance, at worst of explicitly racist infantilization and aggression.

Claire Alexander closes the volume by calling for more personalized, contextualized, located accounts in the analysis of violence, merging structural analysis with the agential. The result would be a more complex, nuanced, and subtle explanation or portrayal of particular expressions of violence rather than a reduction to the facile and politically questionable generalization of cultural poverty. As such, social violence is to be seen not as exceptional to stable social order but a pushing back, a questioning of prevailing social values and limits, the latter prompting the social rending that we understand as violence to begin with.

To imagine a different afterwards, then, one for and from which the constitutive violence of ethnoracial distinction has retreated, for and from which it has been made alien, would quite literally amount to imagining a new world. And perhaps to a different sort of historical possibility. *Making Race Matter* moves us assuredly in that direction.

Notes

1. Some recent work is just beginning to address these sorts of issues in the racialization literature. See, for example, Solomos and Murji (2005).
2. Miles (1982); Castles (2003); Essed et al. (2004).

Bibliography

Abbas, A. (1997) 'Hong Kong: other histories, other politics', *Public Culture*, vol. 9: 293–313.

Abbas, A. (1998) 'Building, dwelling, drifting: migrancy and the limits of architecture. Building Hong Kong: from migrancy to disappearance', *Postcolonial Studies*, vol. 1, no. 2: 185–99.

Abu-Lughod, L. (2002) 'Do Muslim women really need saving?', *American Anthropologist*, vol. 104, no. 3: 783–90.

Adler, P. A. and Adler, P. (1991) *Backboards and Blackboards: College Athletes and Role Engulfment*, New York: Columbia University Press.

Ager, A., Malcolm, M., Sadollah, S. and O'May, F. (2002) 'Community contact and mental health amongst socially isolated refugees in Edinburgh', *Journal of Refugee Studies*, vol. 15: 71–80.

Ahmed, S. (1997) ' "It's a sun-tan isn't it?": autobiography as identificatory practice', in Mirza (1997).

Ahmed, S. (1999) 'She'll wake up one of these days and find she's turned into a nigger: passing through hybridity', in Bell (1999).

Ahmed, S. (2000) *Strange Encounters: Embodied Others in Postcoloniality*, London: Routledge.

Akram, S. and Johnson, K. (2002) 'Race, civil rights and immigration law after September 11, 2001: the targeting of Arabs and Muslims', *NYU Annual Survey of American Law*, vol. 58: 295–355.

Alexander, C. (1996) *The Art of Being Black*, Oxford: Oxford University Press.

Alexander, C. (1998) 'Re-imagining the Muslim community', *Innovation*, vol. 11, no. 4: 439–50.

Alexander, C. (2000a) *The Asian Gang: Ethnicity, Identity, Masculinity*, Oxford: Berg.

Alexander, C. (2000b) '(Dis)Entangling the "Asian Gang": ethnicity, identity, masculinity', in Hesse (2000).

Alexander, C. and Alleyne, B. (2002) 'Introduction: framing difference: racial and ethnic studies in twenty-first-century Britain', *Ethnic and Racial Studies*, vol. 25, no. 4: 541–51.

Alexander, C., Edwards, R. and Temple, B. (2004) *Access to Services with Interpreters: User Views*, York: The Joseph Rowntree Foundation.

Ali, S. (2003) *Mixed-Race, Post-race: Gender, New Ethnicities and Cultural Practices*, Oxford: Berg.

Ali, S. (2004) 'Reading racialised bodies: learning to see difference', in H. Thomas, and J. Ahmed (eds) *Cultural Bodies: Theory and Ethnography*, Oxford: Blackwell.

Alland, A. (2002) *Race in Mind: Race, IQ, and Other Racisms*, Basingstoke: Palgrave Macmillan.

Allen, C. (2003) *Fair Justice: the Bradford Disturbances, the Sentencing and the Impact*, London: Forum against Islamophobia and Racism.

Allen, S. (1994) 'Race, ethnicity and nationality: some questions of identity', in H. Afshar and M. Maynard (eds) *The Dynamics of 'Race' and Gender*, London: Tavistock.

Alleyne, B. (2002) 'An idea of community and its discontents: towards a more reflexive sense of belonging in multicultural Britain', *Ethnic and Racial Studies*, vol. 4, no. 25: 607–27.

Alloula, M. (1998) 'From *The Colonial Harem*', in Mirzoeff (1998).

Alridge, J. (2004) 'Forget black, forget white: the future is generation E.A.', *The Observer*, 4 January 2004.

Amin, A. (2002) *Ethnicity and the Multicultural City*, London: Report for the Department of Transport, Local Government and the Regions.

Amnesty International (2002) 'United Kingdom: detaining non-UK nationals indefinitely is discriminatory', *AI Index*, EUR 45/014/2002, 30 July 2002, London: Amnesty International.

Amos, V. and Parmar, P. (1997) 'Challenging imperial feminism', in Mirza (1997).

Ang, I. (1994) 'On not speaking Chinese', *New Formations*, vol. 24, November: 1–18.

Anionwu, E. and Atkin, K. (2001) *The Politics of Sickle Cell and Thalassaemia*, Buckingham: Open University Press.

Anthias, F. (1998) 'Evaluating diaspora: beyond ethnicity?', *Sociology*, vol. 32, no. 3: 557–80.

Antze, P. and Lambek, M. (eds) (1996) *Tense Past: Cultural Essays in Trauma and Memory*, London/New York: Routledge.

Anwar, M. (1979) *The Myth of Return*, Oxford: Oxford University Press.

Appadurai, A. (1990) 'Disjuncture and difference in the global cultural economy', in Featherstone (1990).

Appadurai, A. (1996) *Modernity at Large: Cultural Dimensions of Globalisation*, Minneapolis, MN: University of Minnesota Press.

Appiah, K. A. (1997) 'Europe upside down: fallacies of the new Afrocentrism, perspectives in Africa', in R. R. Grinker and C. B. Steiner (eds) *A Reader in Culture, History, and Representation*, Oxford: Blackwell.

Armstrong, G. (1998) *Football Hooligans: Knowing the Score*, Oxford: Berg.

Asante, M. K. (1990) *Afrocentricity and Knowledge*, Trenton, NJ: Africa World Press.

Asante, M. K. (2001) 'Locating the Eurocentric assumptions about African history', in M. K. Asante and A. Mazama (eds) *Egypt vs Greece and the American Academy: the Debate over the Birth of Civilization*, Chicago: African Images.

Asylum Aid (2002) 'Refugee women's resource project', www.asylumaid.org.uk/ RWRP/RWRP.htm.

Back, L. and Keith, M. (1999) ' "Rights and wrongs": youth, community and narratives of racial violence', in P. Cohen (ed.) *New Ethnicities, Old Racisms* London and New York: Zed Books.

Back, L. and Solomos, J. (2000) *Theories of Race and Racism: a Reader*, London: Routledge.

Banks, I. (2000) *Hair Matters: Beauty, Power and Black Women's Consciousness*, New York: New York University Press.

Banton, M. (1998) *Racial Theories*, second edition, Cambridge: Cambridge University Press.

Barker, M. (1981) *The New Racism*, London: Junction Books.

Barkley, C. (1996) 'Introduction', in B. Joravsky, *Hoop Dreams: a True Story of Hardship and Triumph*, New York: Harper Perennial.

Barnes, C. (1991) *Disabled People in Britain and Discrimination*, London: Hurst in association with BCODP.

Barnes, C. and Mercer, G. (eds) (2004) *Implementing the Social Model of Disability: Theory and Research*, Leeds: University of Leeds.

Barnes, C., Mercer, G. and Shakespeare, T. (eds) (1999) *Exploring Disability: a Sociological Introduction*, Cambridge: Polity Press.

Barnhart, E. (1975) 'Friends and lovers in a lesbian counterculture community', in N. Glazer-Malbin (ed.) *Old Family/New Family*, New York: van Nostrand.

Barthes, F. (1969) *Ethnic Groups and Boundaries*, Oslo: Oslo University Press.

Begum, N., Hill, M. and Stevens, A. (1994) *Reflections: Voices of Black Disabled People on their Lives and Community Care*, London: Central Council on the Education of Social Workers.

Bell, D. A. (1998) 'Hong Kong's transition to capitalism', *Dissent*, Winter: 15–23.

Bell, V. (ed.) (1999) *Performativity and Belonging*, London: Sage.

Benjamin, W. (1999) 'The work of art in the age of mechanical reproduction', in *Illuminations* (H. Zorn trans.), London: Pimlico.

Benson, S. (1996) 'Asians have culture, West Indians have problems: discourses of race and ethnicity in and out of anthropology', in T. Ranger, Y. Samad and O. Stuart (eds) *Culture, Identity and Politics*, Aldershot: Avebury.

Berger, J. (1991) *And Our Faces, My Heart, Brief as Photos*, New York: Vintage.

Berger, R. M. (1982) 'What is a homosexual? A definitional model', *Social Work*, vol. 28: 132–5.

Bernal, M. (1987) *Black Athena: the Afroasiatic Roots of Classical Civilization, Vol. 1*, New York: Free Association Press.

Bhabha, H. (1994) *The Location of Culture*, London/New York: Routledge.

Bhabha, H. (ed.) (1990) *Nation and Narration*, London/New York: Routledge.

Bhachu, P. (1985) *Twice Migrants*, London: Tavistock.

Bhachu, P. (1991) 'Culture, ethnicity and class among Punjabi Sikh women in 1990s Britain', *New Community*, vol. 17, no. 3: 401–12.

Bhachu, P. (1996) 'The multiple landscapes of transnational Asian women in the Diaspora', in V. Amit-Talai and C. Knowles (eds) *Resituating Identities: the Politics of Race, Ethnicity and Culture*, Peterborough: Broadview Press.

Bhachu, P. (2004) *Dangerous Designs: Asian Women Fashion the Diaspora Economies*, London/New York: Routledge.

Bhattacharyya, G. (2002) *Sexuality and Society*, London: Routledge.

Bloch, A. (2000) 'A new era or more of the same? Asylum policy in the UK', *Journal of Refugee Studies*, vol. 13: 29–42.

Boli, J. and Thomas, G. (1999) *Constructing World Culture*, Stanford, CA: Stanford University Press.

Bourdieu, P. (1990) 'Programme for a sociology of sport', in *In Other Words: Essays Towards a Reflexive Sociology*, Cambridge: Polity Press.

Bourdieu, P. (1992) 'How can one be a sports fan?', in S. During (ed.) *The Cultural Studies Reader*, London: Routledge.

Bourgois, P. (1995) *In Search of Respect: Selling Crack in El Barrio*, Cambridge: Cambridge University Press.

Brah, A. (1996) *Cartographies of Diaspora*, London: Routledge.

Brah, A., Hickman, M. and Mac an Ghaill, M. (eds) (1999) *Global Futures: Migration, Environment and Globalization*, London: Macmillan (now Palgrave Macmillan).

Breakwell, G. (1986) 'Sexual activities and preferences in A United Kingdom sample of 16 to 20 year-olds', *Archives of Sexual Behaviour*, vol. 21: 271–93.

Breytenbach, B. (1991) 'The long march from hearth to home', *Social Research*, vol. 58, no. 1: 69–87.

Brohm, J.-M. (1978) *Sport, a Prison of Measured Time: Essays*, London: Ink Links.

Browne, D. (1997) *Black People and Sectioning: the Black Experience of Detention under the Civil Sections of the Mental Health Act*, Little Rock, AR: Little Rock Publishing.

Budge, A. E. W. (trans.) (1895/1967) *The Egyptian Book of The Dead*, New York: Dover.

Bulmer, M. and Solomos, J. (eds) (1999) *Ethnic and Racial Studies Today*, London: Routledge.

Burfoot, A. (1999) 'African speed, African endurance' in R. R. Sands (ed.) *Anthropology, Sport, and Culture*, Westport, CT: Bergin and Garvey.

Burgess, Ernest (1925/1967) 'The growth of the city: an introduction to a research project', in R. E. Park, M. Burgess and R. D. McKenzie (eds) *The City*, Chicago: University of Chicago Press.

Burkitt, R. (1999) *Bodies of Thought: Embodiment, Identity and Modernity*, London: Sage.

Bush, B. (1990) *Slave Women in Caribbean Society, 1650–1838*, Bloomington, IN: Indiana University Press.

Butler, J. (1993) *Bodies that Matter: On the Discursive Limits of 'Sex'*, London/New York: Routledge.

Calhoun, C. (ed.) (1994) *Social Theory and the Politics of Identity*, Oxford: Blackwell.

Calvino, I. (1997) *Invisible Cities*, London: Vintage.

Cambridge, A. X. and Feuchtwang, S. (1992) *Where You Belong*, Aldershot: Avebury.

Campbell, J. K. (1964) *Honour, Family and Patronage: a Study of Institutions and Moral Values in a Greek Mountain Community*, Oxford: Clarendon Press.

Cantle, T. (2001) *Community Cohesion*, London: HMSO.

Caplan, P. (1989) *The Cultural Construction of Sexuality*, London: Routledge.

Carby, H. (1982) 'White woman listen! Black feminism and the boundaries of sisterhood', in CCCS Collective, *The Empire Strikes Back: Race and Racism in 70s Britain*, London: Hutchinson.

Carrier, J. M. (1985) 'Mexican male bisexuality', in F. Klein and T. Wolf (eds) *Bisexualities: Theory and Research*, New York: Haworth.

Carrington, B. and McDonald, I. (eds) (2001) *'Race', Sport and British Society*, London: Routledge.

Cartwright, L. (1998) 'Science and the cinema', in Mirzoeff (1998).

Cashmore, E. (1982) *Black Sportsmen*, London: Routledge and Kegan Paul.

Castles, S. (2000) 'Migration', in T. Goldberg and J. Solomos (eds) *A Companion to Racial and Ethnic Studies*, Oxford: Blackwell.

Castles, S. (2003) *The Age of Migration*, second edition, Basingstoke: Palgrave Macmillan.

Ceneda, S. (2003) 'Women asylum seekers in the UK', *Feminist Review*, vol. 73: 126–8.

Chamberlain, M. (1994) 'Family and identity: Barbadian migrants to Britain', in R. Benmayor and A. Scotness (eds) *Migration and Identity*. Oxford: Oxford University Press.

Chan, C. S. (1992) 'Cultural considerations in counseling Asian American lesbians and gay men', in S. Dworkin and F. Gutierrez (eds) *Counseling Gay Men and Lesbians: Journey to the End of the Rainbow*, exandria, VA: American Association for Counselling and Development.

Chauncey, G. (1989) 'Christian brotherhood or sexual perversion? Homosexual identities and the construction of sexual bouindaries in the World War I era', in M. Duberman, M. Vicinus and G. Chauncey (eds) *Hidden from History: Reclaiming the Gay and Lesbian Past*, New York: Meridian.

Cheng, L. and Yang, P. (1996) 'Asian Americans: the model minority deconstructed', in R. Waldinger and M. Bozorgmehr (eds) *Ethnic Los Angeles*, New York: Russell Sage Foundation.

Chun, A. (2000) 'Colonial "govern-mentality" in transition: Hong Kong as imperial object and subject', *Cultural Studies*, vol. 14, no. 3/4: 430–61.

Clifford, J. (1994) 'Diasporas', *Cultural Anthropology*, vol. 9, no. 3: 302–38.

Clifford, J. and Marcus, G. (eds) (1986) *Writing Culture: The Poetics and Politics of Ethnography*, Berkeley, CA: University of California Press.

Coakley, J. J. (1998) *Sport in Society: Issues and Controversies*, Boston, MA: Irwin McGraw-Hill.

Cochrane, R. and Sashidharan, S. P. (1996) 'The mental health needs of ethnic minorities', in W. Ahmad and T. A. Sheldon (eds) *The Health Needs of Ethnic Minorities*, York: York University Press.

Cohen, A. (1994) 'Boundaries of consciousness and consciousness of boundaries', in H. Vermeulen and C. Govers (eds) *The Anthropology of Ethnicity: Beyond Ethnic Groups and Boundaries*, Amsterdam: Het Spinhuis.

Cohen, P. (1996) 'All white on the night? Narratives of nativism on the Isle of Dogs', in T. Butler and M. Rustin (eds) *Rising in the East*, London: Lawrence and Wishart.

Cohen, P. (1998) *The Last Island*, London: Centre for New Ethnicities Research.

Cohen, P. (1972) 'Subcultural conflict and working class community', *Working Papers in Cultural Studies*, Centre for Contemporary Cultural Studies, University of Birmingham.

Cohen, P. (1997) 'Labouring under Whiteness', in R. Frankenberg (ed.) *Displacing Whiteness*, Durham, NC: Duke University Press.

Cohen, S. (1972) *Folk Devils and Moral Panics: The Creation of the Mods and Rockers* London: MacGibbon and Kee.

Colley, L. (1992) *Britons: Forging the Nation 1707–1837*, New Haven, CT: Yale University Press.

Connell, R. W. (1995) *Masculinities*, London: Polity Press.

Crary, J. (1990) *Techniques of the Observer: Vision and Modernity in the Nineteenth Century*, Cambridge, MA: MIT Press.

Crawley, H. (2001) *Refugees and Gender: Law and Process*, Bristol: Jordan.

Crossley, N. (1995) 'Merleau-Ponty, the elusive body and carnal sociology', *Body and Society*, vol. 1, no. 1: 43–63.

Cuthbert, A. R. and McKinnell, K. (1997) 'Ambiguous space, ambiguous rights – corporate power and social control in Hong Kong', *Cities*, vol. 14, no. 5: 295–311.

D'Augelli, A. R., and Garnets, L. D. (1995) 'Lesbian, gay, and bisexual communities', in A. R. Augelli and C. J. Patterson (eds) *Lesbian, Gay, and Bisexual Identities over the Lifespan*, New York: Oxford University Press.

Dahya, B. (1974) 'The nature of Pakistani ethnicity in industrial cities in Britain' in A. Cohen (ed.) *Urban Ethnicity*, London: Tavistock.

Darwin, C. (1866) *On The Origin Of The Species By Means Of Natural Selection, or The Preservation of Favoured Races in The Struggle For Life*, fourth edition, London: John Murray.

Darwin, C. (1901) *The Descent of Man and Selection in Relation to Sex*, new edition, London: John Murray.

Davis, A. (1983) *Women, Race and Class*, New York: Women's Press.

Davis, A. (1990) *Women, Culture and Politics*, London: Women's Press.

Davis, L. R. and Harris, O. (1998) 'Race and ethnicity in US sports media', in L. A. Wenner (ed.) *MediaSport*, London: Routledge.

de Beauvoir, S. (1953) *The Second Sex*, London: Jonathan Cape.

de Marco, J. (1983) 'Gay racism', in M. J. Smith (ed.) *Black Men/White Men: a Gay Anthology*, San Francisco, CA: Gay Sunshine Press.

Denham, Lord (2002) *Building Cohesive Communities*, London: HMSO.

Deptford City Challenge Evaluation Project (1997) *City Challenge in Deptford*, London: CUCR.

Desai, P. (1999) *Spaces of Identity, Cultures of Conflict: The Development of New British Asian Masculinities*, PhD thesis, Goldsmiths College, University of London.

Descartes, R. (1998a) 'Discourse on the Method', in *Descartes: Selected Philosophical Writings*, (trans. J. Cottingham, R. Stoothoff and D. Murdoch), Cambridge: Cambridge University Press.

Descartes, R. (1998b) 'Passions of the Soul', in *Descartes: Selected Philosophical Writings*, (trans. J. Cottingham, R. Stoothoff and D. Murdoch), Cambridge: Cambridge University Press.

Diop, C. A. (1974) *The African Origin Of Civilization: Myth Or Reality?* Westport, CT: Lawrence Hill.

Diop, C. A. (1989, original in French 1963) *The Cultural Unity of Black Africa*, London: Karnak House.

Donald, J. and Rattansi, A. (eds) *Race, Culture, Difference*, London: Sage.

Doy, G. (1996) *Black Visual Culture: Modernity and Postmodernity*, London/New York: Routledge.

Du Bois, W. E. B. (1903/1969) *The Souls of Black Folk*, New York: New American Library.

Du Bois, W. E. B. (1995) *The Souls of Black Folk*, New York: Signet Books.

Duster, T. (2003) *Backdoor to Eugenics*, New York/London: Sage.

Dyer, R. (1997) *White*, London: Routledge.

Dyne, L. (1980) 'Is D.C. becoming the gay capital of America?', *Washingtonian*, September: 96–101, 133–41.

Eitzen, D. S. (1999) *Fair and Foul: Beyond the Myths and Paradoxes of Sport*, Lanham, MD: Rowman and Littlefield.

Elias, N. (1982) *The Civilising Process*, Oxford: Basil Blackwell.

Elias, N. (1986) 'An essay on sport and violence', in Elias and Eric Dunning, *Quest for Excitement: Sport and Leisure in the Civilizing Process*, Oxford: Basil Blackwell.

Elwert, G., Feuchtwang, S. and Neubert, D. (eds) (1999) *Dynamics of Violence: Processes of Escalation and De-escalation in Violent Group Conflicts*, Berlin: Duncker and Humblot.

Entine, J. (2000) *Taboo: Why Black Athletes Dominate Sports and Why We're Afraid to Talk about It*, New York: Public Affairs.

Espin, O. M. (1984) 'Cultural and historical influences on sexuality in Hispanic/Latin women: implications for psychotherapy', in C. Vance (ed.) *Pleasure and Danger: Exploring Female Sexuality*, London: Routledge and Kegan Paul.

Espin, O. M. (1987) 'Issues of identity in the psychology of Latina lesbians', in Boston Lesbian Psychologies Collective (ed.) *Lesbian Psychologies: Explorations and Challenges*, Chicago: University of Illinois Press.

Espiritu, Y. (1992) *Asian-American Panethnicity*, Philadelphia, PA: Temple University Press.

Essed, P., Frerks, G. and Schrijfers, J. (2004) *Refugees and the Transformation of Societies*, Oxford: Berghahn.

Evans, A. S. (1997) 'Blacks as key functionaries: a study of racial stratification in professional sport', *Journal of Black Studies*, vol. 28, no. 1: 43–59.

Eze, E. C. (2001) *Achieving Our Humanity: the Idea of the Postracial Future*, London: Routledge.

Eze, E. C. (ed.) (1997) *Post-colonial African Philosophy: a Critical Reader*, Oxford: Blackwell.

Fanon, F. (1967/1986) *Black Skin, White Mask*, London: Pluto.

Farrar, M. (1997) 'Migrant spaces and settlers' time', in S. Westwood and J. Williams (eds) *Imagining Cities*, London: Routledge.

Farrar, M. (2002) 'The Northern "race riots" of the summer of 2001 – were they riots, were they racial?', presentation to 'Parallel Lives and Polarisation' workshop, BSA 'Race' Forum, City University, London.

Feagin, J. (2000) *Racist America*, New York: Routledge.

Featherstone, M. (1996) 'Localism, globalism, and cultural identity', in R. Wilson and D. Wilmal (eds) *Global/Local*, Durham, NC: Duke University Press.

Featherstone, M. (ed.) (1990) *Global Culture*, London: Sage.

Featherstone, M. and Lash, S. (eds) (1995) *Global Modernities*, London: Routledge.

Featherstone, M., Lash, S. and Robertson, R. (1995) *Global Modernities*, London: Sage.

Ferguson, N. (2003) *Empire: How Britain Made the Modern World*, London/New York: Allen Lane.

Feuchtwang, S. (1992) 'Policing the streets', in Cambridge and Feuchtwang (1992).

Fleming, S. (2001) 'Racial science and South Asian and Black physicality', in B. Carrington and I. McDonald (eds) *'Race', Sport and British Society*, London: Routledge.

Flowerdew, J. (1998) *The Final Years of British Hong Kong: the Discourse of Colonial Withdrawal*, Basingstoke: Macmillan (now Palgrave Macmillan).

Foucault, M. (1978/1990) *The History of Sexuality, Volume 1*, New York: Vintage.

Foucault, M. (1982) 'Afterword: the subject and power', in H. L. Dreyfus and P. Rabinow (eds) *Michel Foucault: Beyond Structuralism and Hermeneutics*, Chicago: University of Chicago Press.

Foucault, M. (1970) *The Order of Things: an Archaeology of the Human Sciences*, London: Routledge.

Foucault, M. (1972) *Archaeology of Knowledge*, London: Tavistock.

Foucault, M. (1975) *The Birth of the Clinic: an Archaeology of Medical Perception*, New York: Vintage Books.

Foucault, M. (1979) *Discipline and Punish: the Birth of the Prison*, Harmondsworth: Penguin.

Foucault, M. (1984) 'Part II – practices and knowledge', in P. Rabinow (ed.) *The Foucault Reader*, Harmondsworth: Penguin.

Foucault, M. (1994) 'Technologies of the self', in P. Rabinow (ed.) *Michel Foucault: Ethics. The Essential Works of Foucault 1954–1984*, Harmondsworth: Penguin.

Franklin, V. P. (2002) 'Introduction: cultural capital and African American education', *The Journal of African American History*, vol. 87, Spring: 175–81.

Fygetakis, L. M. (1994) 'Greek American lesbians', in B. Greene (ed.) *Psychological Perspectives on Lesbian and Gay Issues, Volume 3: Ethnic and Cultural Diversity among Lesbians and Gay Men*, Thousand Oaks, CA: Sage.

Gadalla, M. (2003) *Egyptian Cosmology: the Animated Universe*, USD eBook www.Egypt-tehuti.org/books.Egyptian-cosmology-pg.html (visited 20 February 2003).

Gans, H. (1999) 'The possibility of a new racial hierarchy in the twenty-first century United States', in M. Lamont (ed.) *The Cultural Territories of Race*, Chicago: University of Chicago Press.

Gardiner, P. (1979) 'Freedom as an aesthetic ideal', in A. Ryan (ed.) *The Idea of Freedom: Essays in Honour of Isaiah Berlin*, Oxford: Oxford University Press.

Gardner, K. and Shukur, A. (1994) 'I'm Bengali, I'm Asian, and I'm living here', in R. Ballard (ed.) *Desh Pardesh*, London: Hurst.

Garnets, L. and Kimmel, D. (1991) 'Lesbian and gay male dimensions in the psychological study of human diversity', in J. Goodchilds (ed.) *Psychological Perspectives on Human Diversity in America*, Washington, DC: American Psychological Association.

Gates, H. L. (1992) *Loose Canons: Notes on the Culture Wars*, New York: Oxford University Press.

Georgiou, G. J. and Veresies, K. (1991) *The Knowledge, Attitudes, Beliefs and Practices Survey of 15–18 year old Cypriot Schoolchildren Regarding AIDS*, Geneva: World Health Organisation.

Giddens, A. (1990) *The Consequences of Modernity*, Cambridge: Polity Press.

Giddens, A. (1991) *Modernity and Self-Identity*, Cambridge: Polity Press.

Giddens, A. (1998) *The Third Way: the Renewal of Social Democracy* Cambridge: Polity Press.

Gilman, S. (1985) *Pathology and Difference*, Ithaca, CA: Cornell University Press.

Gilman, S. (1992) 'Black bodies, white bodies', in Donald and Rattansi (1992).

Gilroy, P. (1992) 'The end of antiracism', in J. Donald and A. Rattansi (eds) *'Race', Culture and Difference*, London: Sage.

Gilroy, P. (1993) *The Black Atlantic*, London: Verso.

Gilroy, P. (1994) 'After the Love Has Gone: bio-politics and ethno-poetics in the black public sphere', *Public Culture*, vol. 7, no. 1: 49–76.

Gilroy, P. (2000) *Between Camps: Nations, Cultures and the Allure of Race*, London: Allen Lane/The Penguin Press.

Glick-Schiller, N. (1999) 'Transmigrants and nation-states', in C. Hirschman, P. Kasinitz and J. DeWind (eds) *Handbook of International Migration: the American Experience*, New York: Russell Sage Foundation.

Gold, S. (2000) 'Transnational communities: examining migration in a globally integrated world', in P. Aulakh and M. Schechter (eds) *Rethinking Globalization(s)*, New York: St Martin's Press.

Goldberg, D. T. (1993) *Racist Culture*, Oxford: Blackwell.

Goldberg, D. T. (ed.) (1990) *Anatomy of Racism*, Minneapolis, MN/London: University of Minnesota Press.

Goldberg, D. T. and Quayson, A. (eds) (2002) *Relocating Postcolonialism*, Oxford: Blackwell.

Greene, B. (1994) 'Ethnic minority lesbians and gay men: mental health and treatment issues', *Journal of Consulting and Clinical Psychology*, vol. 7: 49–66.

Gruneau. R. (1983) *Class, Sports and Social Development*, Amherst, MA: University of Massachusetts Press.

Guardian, The (2001) 'MP urges review of immigration law' (Staff and agencies), 12 July.

Guardian, The (2001) 'Race riots reports urge immigrant "loyalty" ' (Staff and agencies), 11 December.

Guardian, The (2002) '8 years for petrol bomber' (Martin Wainwright), 31 August.

Guardian, The (2002) 'Anger at Blunkett's "whining maniacs" attack' (Alan Travis), 6 September 2002.

Guardian, The (2003) 'Anger as court's stance on riot upheld' (Vikram Dodd), 31 January 2003.

Gutierrez, F. and Dworkin, S. (1992) 'Gay, lesbian, and African-American: managing the integration of identities', in S. Dworkin and F. Gutierrez (eds) *Counselling Gay Men and Lesbians: Journey to the End of the Rainbow*, Alexandria, VA: American Association of Counselling and Development.

Guttmann, A. (1978) *From Ritual to Record: the Nature of Modern Sports*, New York: Columbia University Press.

Hacker, A. (1997) 'Introduction', in R. Delgado (ed.) *The Coming Race War*, Philadelphia, PA: Temple University Press.

Hall, C. (1992) *White, Male and Middle Class: Explorations in Feminism and History*, London: Polity Press.

Hall, S. (1991) 'Old and new identities, old and new ethnicities', in A. King (ed.) *Culture, Globalization and the World-System*, Basingstoke: Macmillan (now Palgrave Macmillan).

Hall, S. (1992) 'New ethnicities', in Donald and Rattansi (1992).

Hall, S. (1996) 'New ethnicities', in D. Morley and C. Kuan-Hsing (eds) *Stuart Hall – Critical Dialogues in Cultural Studies*, London: Routledge.

Hall, S. (1997) 'The spectacle of the Other', in Hall (ed.) *Representation: Cultural Representation and Signifying Practices*, London: Sage.

Hall, S. (1999) 'Introduction to Part II', in J. Evans and Hall (eds) *Visual Culture: the Reader*, London/New York: Sage.

Hall, S., Critcher, C., Jefferson, T., Clarke, J. and Roberts, B. (1978) *Policing the Crisis*, London: Hutchinson.

Hall, S., Held, D. and McGrew, A. (eds) (1992) *Modernity and its Futures*, Milton Keynes: Open University Press.

Hallam, E. and Street, B. V. (eds) (2000) *Cultural Encounters: Representing 'Otherness'*, London/New York: Routledge.

Hannerz, U. (1990) 'Cosmopolitans and locals in world culture', in Featherstone (1990).

Haraway, D. (1997) *Modest_Witness@Second_Millenium. FemaleMan©Meets OncoMouse™: Feminism and Technoscience*, London/New York: Routledge.

Harvey, David (1989) *The Condition of Postmodernity*, Oxford: Blackwell.

Hassan, L. (2000) 'Deterrence measures and the preservation of asylum in the United Kingdom and United States', *Journal of Refugee Studies*, vol. 13: 184–204.

Hayes, S. and Sugden, J. (1999) 'Winning through "naturally" still? An analysis of the perceptions held by physical education teachers towards the performance of black pupils in school sport and in the classroom', *Race, Ethnicity and Education*, vol. 2, no. 1: 93–107.

Hegel, G. W. F. (1975) *Lectures on the Philosophy of World History: Introduction, Reason in History*, Cambridge: Cambridge University Press.

Hein, J. (1994) 'From migrant to minority: Hmong refugees and the social construction of identity in the United States', *Sociological Inquiry*, vol. 64, no. 3: 281–306.

Herdt, G. (1981) *Guardians of the Flutes: Idioms of Masculinity*, New York: McGraw-Hill.

Hesse, B. (1997) 'White governmentality: urbanism, nationalism, racism', in S. Westwood and J. Williams (eds) *Imagining Cities*, London: Routledge.

Hesse, B. (1999) 'Reviewing the Western spectacle: reflexive globalization through the Black diaspora', in Brah, Hickman and Mac an Ghaill (1999).

Hesse, B. (ed.) (2000) *Un/Settled Multiculturalisms*, London: Zed Press.

Hewitt, R. (1997) *Routes of Racism*, London: Trentham.

Hidalgo, H. (1984) 'The Puerto-Rican lesbian in the United States', in T. Darty and S. Potter (eds) *Women Identified Women*, Palo Alto, CA: Mayfield.

Hill, M. (1994) 'They are not our brothers; the disability movement and the black disability movement', in Begum et al. (1994).

Hill-Collins, P. (1990/1993) *Black Feminist Thought: Knowledge, Consciousness and the Politics of Empowerment*, London: Harper Collins.

Hill-Collins, P. (2004) *Black Sexual Politics: African-Americans, Gender and the New Racism*, New York/London: Routledge.

Hoberman, J. (1997) *Darwin's Athletes: How Sport Has Damaged Black America and Preserved the Myth of Race*, New York: Houghton Mifflin.

hooks, b. (1982) *Ain't I a Woman? Black Women and Feminism*, London: Pluto Press.

hooks, b. (1990) *Yearning: Race, Gender and Cultural Politics*, Boston, MA: South End Press.

hooks, b. (1992) 'Selling hot pussy: representations of Black female sexuality in the cultural marketplace', in *Black Looks: Race and Representation*, Boston, MA: South End Press.

Howe, S. (1998) *Afrocentrism: Mythical Pasts and Imagined Homes*, London: Verso.

Hume, D. (1987) 'Of national characters', in E. F. Miller (ed.) *Essays: Moral, Political and Literary*, Indianapolis, IN: Liberty Classics.

Humphries, L. and Miller, B. (1980) 'Identities in the emerging gay culture', in J. Marmor (ed.) *Homosexual Behaviour: a Modern Reappraisal*, New York: Basic Books.

Huntington, S. (1996) *The Clash of Civilisations and the Remaking of the World Order*, New York: Simon and Schuster.

Husbands, C. T. (1983) *Racial Exclusion and the City: the Urban Support for the National Front*, London: Allen and Unwin.

Ifwekunigwe, J. (2000) *Scattered Be-longings: Cultural Paradoxes of 'Race', Nation, and Gender*, London: Routledge.

India.Org (2003) www.tourismofindia.com/newsletter/globalbeauty.htm.

Inglis, D. and Hughson, J. (2000) 'The beautiful game and the proto-aesthetics of the everyday', *Cultural Values*, vol. 4, no. 3: 279–97.

Jefferson, T. (1988) 'Race, crime and policing', *International Journal of the Sociology of Law*, vol. 16, no. 4: 521–39.

Jeganathan, P. (2000) 'A space for violence: anthropology, politics and the location of a Sinhala practice of masculinity', in P. Chatterjee and P. Jeganathan (eds) *Community, Gender and Violence*, London: Hurst.

Jolly, M. (1997) 'From Point Venus to Bali Ha'i: eroticism and exoticism in representations of the Pacific', in L. Manderson and M. Jolly (eds) *Sites of Desire, Economies of Pleasure: Sexualities in Asia and the Pacific*, Chicago: University of Chicago Press.

Jones, L. (1995) *Bullet Proof Diva*, London/New York: Doubleday.

Kant, I. (1997) 'On the different races of man', in E. C. Eze (ed.) *Race and the Enlightenment: a Reader*, Oxford: Blackwell.

Karenga, M. (1989) *An Introduction to Black Studies*, Los Angeles: University of Sankor Press.

Karenga, M. (trans.) (1984) *Selections from the Husia: Sacred Wisdom of Ancient Egypt*, Los Angeles: University of Sankor Press.

Karpf, A. (2002) 'We've been here before', *The Guardian*, 8 June.

Kasinitz, P., Waters, M., Mollenkopf, J. and Merih, A. (2002) 'Transnationalism and the children of immigrants in contemporary New York', in P. Levitt and M. Waters (eds) *The Changing Face of Home*, New York: Russell Sage Foundation.

Kay, D. and Miles, R. (1992) *Refugees or Migrant Workers?* London: Routledge.

Keith, M. (1993) *Race, Riots and Policing: Lore and Disorder in a Multi-racist Society*, London: UCL Press.

Keith, M. (1995) 'Making the street visible: placing racial violence in context', *New Community*, vol. 21, no. 4: 551–65.

Keith, M. (2003) 'Postcolonial London and the allure of the cosmopolitan city', *AA files – London: Postcolonial City*, vol. 49: 57–67.

Kent, R. A. (1981) *A History of British Empirical Sociology*, Aldershot: Gower.

Kettle, M. and Hodges, L. (1982) *Uprising: the Police, the People and the Riots in Britain's Cities*, London: Pan.

Kim, C. J. (2004a) 'Imagining race and nation in multiculturalist America', *Ethnic and Racial Studies*, vol. 27, no. 6: 987–1005.

Kim, C. J. (2004b) 'They are more like us: the salience of ethnicity in the global workplace of Korean transnational corporations', *Ethnic and Racial Studies*, vol. 27, no. 1: 69–94.

Knowles, C. (2003) *Race and Social Analysis*, London: Sage.

Knowles, C. and Mercer, S. (1993) 'Feminism and antiracism: an exploration of the political possibilities', in Donald and Rattansi (1992).

Knox, R. (1996) 'The races of men', in H. F. Augstein (ed.) *Race: the Origins of an Idea*, Bristol: Thoemmes Press.

Kohn, M. (1996) *The Race Gallery – the Return Of Racial Science*, London: Vintage.

Koser, K. and Lutz, H. (eds) (1998) *The New Migration in Europe*, Basingstoke: Macmillan (now Palgrave Macmillan).

Krieger, S. (1982) 'Lesbian identity and community: recent social science literature', *Signs*, vol. 8: 91–108.

Kundnani, A (2001) 'From Oldham to Bradford: the violence of the violated', *Race and Class*, vol. 43, no. 2: 105–10.

Kundnani, A. (2002) *The Death of Multiculturalism*, Institute of Race Relations (online resources), www.irr.org.uk/cantle/index.htm (visited 24 April 2002).

Kushner, T. (2003) 'Meaning nothing but good: ethics, history and asylum seeker phobia in Britain', *Patterns of Prejudice*, vol. 37, no. 3: 257–76.

Lam, J. T. M. (1997) 'Sino-British relations over Hong Kong during the final phase of political transition', *International Studies*, vol. 34, no. 4: 425–44.

Latouche, Serge (1996) *Westernization of the World*, Cambridge: Polity Press.

Lazarides, G. (1994) 'Sexuality and its cultural construction in rural Greece', paper presented to British Sociological Association conference 'Sexualities in Social Context', University of Central Lancashire, 28–31 March.

Leach, N. (2003) 'Belonging', *AA files – London: Postcolonial City*, vol. 49: 76–82.

Lefebvre, H. (1996), *The Production of Space*, Oxford: Blackwell.

Lefkowitz, M. (1996) *Not Out of Africa: How Afrocentrism Became an Excuse to Teach Myth as History*, New York: Basic Books.

Lemelle, S. (1997) 'Black Underclass and culture', in N. BaNikongo (ed.) *Leading Issues in African-American Studies*, Durham, NC: Carolina Academic Press.

Levine, R., Locke, C., Searles, D. and Weinberger D. (2001) *The Cluetrain Manifesto: the End of Business as Usual*, Cambridge, MA: Perseus.

Levitt, P. and Waters, M. (eds) (2002) *The Changing Face of Home: the Transnational Lives of the Second Generation*, New York: Russell Sage Foundation.

Lewis, G. (1985) 'From Deepest Kilburn', in L. Heron (ed.) *Truth, Dare or Promise: Girls Growing Up in the Fifties*, London: Virago.

Lewis, O. (1966) *La Vida: A Puerto-Rican Family in the Culture of Poverty*, New York: Random House.

Lewis, R. (1995) *Gendering Orientalism: Race, Femininity, and Representation*, London/New York: Routledge.

Li, F. L. N., Findlay, A. M. and Jones, H. (1998) 'A cultural economy perspective on service sector migration in the global city: the case of Hong Kong', *International Migration*, vol. 36, no. 2: 131–57.

Lloyd, K and Moodley, P. (1992) 'Psychotropic medication and ethnicity: an in-patient survey', *Social Psychiatry and Psychiatric Epidemiology*, vol. 27: 95–101.

Locke, J. (1960) *Two Treatises of Government*, Cambridge: Cambridge University Press.

Loicano, D. (1989) 'Gay identity issues among Black americans: racism, homophobia, and the need for validation', *Journal of Counselling and Development*, vol. 68: 21–5.

Loizos, P. and Papataxiarchis, E. (1991) 'Gender, sexuality and the person in Greek culture', in Loizos and Papataxiarchis (eds) *Contested Identities: Gender and Kinship in Modern Greece*, Princeton, NJ: Princeton University Press.

Lopez, D. and Espiritu, Y. (1990) 'Panethnicity in the United States', *Ethnic and Racial Studies*, vol. 13, no. 2: 198–224.

Lorde, A. (1984) 'Uses of the erotic: the erotic as power', in *Sister Outsider: Essays and Speeches*, Freedom, CA: The Crossing Press.

Lorde, A. (1974/1994) 'Who said it was simple?', in M. Schneir (ed.) *Feminism in Our Time*, New York: Vintage.

Louie, A. (2002) 'Creating histories for the present: second-generation (re)definitions of Chinese American culture', in P. Levitt and M. Waters (eds) *The Changing Face of Home*, New York: Russell Sage Foundation.

Lury, C. (2002) 'The United Colours of Diversity: essential and inessential culture', in S. Franklin, C. Lury and J. Stacey (eds) *Global Nature/Global Culture*, London: Sage.

MacCabe, C. and Kureishi, H. (2003) 'Hanif Kureishi and London', *AA files – London: Postcolonial City*, vol. 49: 40–50.

Macey, M. (1999) 'Gender, class and religious influences on changing patterns of Pakistani Muslim male violence in Bradford', *Ethnic and Racial Studies*, vol. 22, no. 5: 845–66.

Macey, M. (2002) 'Interpreting Islam: young Muslim men's involvement in criminal activity in Bradford', in B. Spalek (ed.) *Islam, Crime and Criminal Justice*, Cullompton: Willan Publishing.

Macpherson Report (1999) *The Stephen Lawrence Inquiry: Report of an Inquiry by Sir William Macpherson Of Cluny*, London: The Stationery Office.

Mamdani, M. (2002) 'Good Muslim, Bad Muslim: a political perspective on culture and terrorism', *American Anthropologist*, vol. 104, no. 3: 766–75.

Man, S. W. and Wai, C. Y. (2000) 'Postcolonial law in the global economy: the case of Hong Kong', *International Journal of the Sociology of Law*, vol. 28: 291–306.

Mandell, R. D. (1998) *The Nazi Olympics*, Urbana, IL: University of Illinois Press.

Marcus, G. (1994) 'After the critique of ethnography', in R. Borofsky (ed.) *Assessing Cultural Anthropology*, New York: McGraw-Hill.

Mason, D. (1994) 'On the dangers of disconnecting race and racism', *Sociology*, vol. 28, no. 4: 845–58.

Mason, D. (1995) *Race and Ethnicity in Modern Britain*, Oxford: Oxford University Press.

Mason, D. (2000) *Race and Ethnicity in Modern Britain*, second edition, Oxford: Oxford University Press.

Massey, D. (1994) *Place, Space and Gender*, Cambridge: Polity.

Massey, D. (1999) 'Imagining globalization: power geometries of time-space', in Brah et al. (1999).

Mays, V. and Cochran, S. (1988) 'The Black Women's Relationship Project: a national survey of Black lesbians', in M. Shernoff and W. Scott (eds) *The Sourcebook on Lesbian/Gay Health Care*, Washington, DC: National Lesbian and Gay Health Foundation.

McClintock, A. (1995) *Imperial Leather: Race, Gender and Sexuality in the Colonial Context*, London/New York: Routledge.

McFee, G. and Tomlinson, A. (1999) 'Riefenstahl's Olympia: ideology and aesthetics on the shaping of the Aryan athletic body', in J. A. Mangan (ed.) *Shaping the Superman: Fascist Body as Political Icon: Aryan Fascism*, London: Frank Cass.

McGhee, D. (2003) 'Moving to "our" common ground – a critical examination of community cohesion discourse in 21st century Britain', *Sociological Review*, vol. 51, no. 3: 383–411.

McIntosh, M. (1968) 'The homosexual role', *Social Problems*, vol. 16: 182–92.

McNay, L. (1992) *Foucault and Feminism: Power, Gender and the Self*, Cambridge: Cambridge University Press.

Mercer, K. (1994) 'Black hair/style politics', in *Welcome to the Jungle: New Positions in Black Cultural Studies*, London/New York: Routledge.

Mercer, K. (1994) *Welcome to the Jungle*, London: Routledge.

Messerschmidt, J. W. (1997) 'Men victimizing men: the case of lynching 1985–1900', in L. Bowker (ed.) *Masculinities and Violence*, London: Sage.

Miles, R. (1982) *Racism and Migrant Labour*, London: Routledge and Kegan Paul.

Miles, R. (1989) *Racism*, London: Routledge.

Miles, R. and Torres, R. (1996) 'Does "race" matter? Transatlantic perspectives on racism after race relations', in V. Amita-Talai and C. Knowles (eds) *Resituating Identities: the Politics of Race, Ethnicity and Culture*, Peterborough: Broadview Press.

Mills, C. W. (1997) *The Racial Contract*, Ithaca, NY: Cornell University Press.

Min, P. G. (1998) *Changes and Conflicts: Korean Immigrant Families in New York*, Boston, MA: Allyn and Bacon.

Min, P. G. (1999) 'A comparison of post-1965 and turn of the century immigrants', *Journal of American Ethnic History*, vol. 18, no. 3: 65–94.

Mirza, H. S. (ed.) (1997) *Black British Feminism: a Reader*, London: Routledge.

Mirzoeff, N. (ed.) (1998) *The Visual Culture Reader*, London/New York: Routledge.

Mirzoeff, N. (ed.) *The Visual Culture Reader*, London and New York: Routledge.

Mitchell, T. (1998) 'Orientalism and the exhibitionary order', in N. Mirzoeff (ed.) *The Visual Culture Reader*, London/New York: Routledge.

Modood, T. (1992) *Not Easy Being British*, Stoke-on-Trent: Trentham.

Modood, T. et al. (1997) *Ethnic Minorities in Britain: Diversity and Disadvantage*, London: PSI.

Mohanram, R. (1999) *Black Body: Women, Colonialism, Space*, Minneapolis, MN: University of Minnesota Press.

Morales, E. (1983) 'Third world gays and lesbians: a process of multiple identities', paper presented at the 91st National Convention of the American Psychological Association, Anaheim, CA.

Morales, E. (1989) 'Ethnic minority families and minority gays and lesbians', *Marriage and Family Review*, vol. 14: 217–39.

Morales, E. (1990) 'Ethnic minority families and minority gays and lesbians', in F. Bozett and M. Sussman (eds) *Homosexuality and Family Relations*, New York: Haworth.

Moretti, F. (1998) *Atlas of the European Novel 1800–1900*, London: Verso.

Morgan, W. J. (1994) *Leftist Theories of Sport: a Critique and Reconstruction*, Urbana, IL: University of Illinois Press.

Morley, D. and Robins, K. (1995) *Spaces of Identity: Global Media, Electronic Landscapes and Cultural Boundaries*, London: Routledge.

Motherland (2003) London: BBC Productions.

Murray, S. O. (1992) 'Components of gay community in San Francisco', in G. Herdt (ed.) *Gay Culture in America*, Boston, MA: Beacon.

Nagel, J. (2003) *Race, Ethnicity and Sexuality: Intimate Intersections, Forbidden Frontiers*, Oxford: Oxford University Press.

Nandy, A. (2002) 'Telling the story of communal conflicts in South Asia', *Ethnic and Racial Studies*, vol. 25, no. 1: 1–19.

National Statistics Online (2004) 'Migration', Immigration, Research and Statistics Service, Home Office www.statistics.gov.uk/cci/nugget.asp?id=261 (visted December 2004).

Nazroo, J. (2003) 'Patterns of and explanations for ethnic inequalities in health', in D. Mason (ed.) *Explaining Ethnic Differences: Changing Patterns of Disadvantage in Britain*, Bristol: Policy Press.

Neal, S. (2002) 'Rural landscapes, representations and racism: examining multicultural citizenship and policy-making in the English countryside', *Ethnic and Racial Studies*, vol. 25, no. 3: 442–61.

Nicolaus, R. A. (2003) 'The nature of animal Blacks (the chemical enigma solved: perspectives in biology)', www.tightrope.it/nicolaus/metadoc10.htm (visited 7 May 2003).

Noble, D. (2000) *Ragga Music: Dis/Respecting Black Women and Dis/reputable Sexualities*, in Hesse (2000).

Oliver, M. (1990) *The Politics of Disablement*, Basingstoke: Macmillan (now Palgrave Macmillan).

Omi, M. and Winant, H. (1994) *Racial Formation in the United States*, New York: Routledge.

Ong, A. (1999) *Flexible Citizenship*, Durham, NC: Duke University Press.

Ongley, P. (1995) 'Post-1945 international migration: New Zealand, Australia and Canada compared', *International Migration Review*, vol. xxix, no. 3: 765–93.

Ouseley, H. (2001) *Community Pride not Prejudice*, Bradford: Bradford Vision.

Parekh, B. (2000) *The Future of Multi-Ethnic Britain*, London: Profile Books.

Park, R. E. (1925/1967) 'The city: suggestions for the investigation of human behaviour in an urban environment', in Park et al. (1967).

Park, R. E., Burgess, M. and McKenzie, R. D. (eds) (1967) *The City*, Chicago: University of Chicago Press.

Parker, D. and Song, M. (eds) (2001) *Rethinking 'Mixed Race'*, London: Pluto Press.

Parker, D. (1995) *Through Different Eyes: the Cultural Identities of Young Chinese People in Britain*, Aldershot: Avebury.

Parker, D. (1998) 'Rethinking British Chinese identities', in T. Skelton and G. Valentine (eds) *Cool Places*, London: Routledge.

Paul, K. (1997) *Whitewashing Britain: Race and Citizenship in the Postwar Era*, Ithaca, NY: Cornell University Press.

Phellas, C. N. (2002) *The Construction of Sexual and Cultural Identities: Greek-Cypriot Men in Britain*, Aldershot: Ashgate.

Phoenix, A. (1998) ' "Multicultures", "Multiracisms" and Young People', *Soundings*, vol. 10, Autumn: 86–96.

Pieterse, J. N. (1994) 'Globalisation as hybridisation', *International Sociology*, vol. 9, no. 2: 11–84.

Pilkington, A. (2003) *Racial Disadvantage and Ethnic Diversity in Britain*, Basingstoke: Palgrave Macmillan.

Pirouet, L. (2001) *Whatever Happened to Asylum in Britain? A Tale of Two Walls*, Oxford: Berghahn.

Plummer, K. (1975) *Sexual Stigma*, London: Routledge and Kegan Paul.

Porter, K. and Weeks, J. (1990) *Between the Acts*, London: Routledge.

Portes, A., Guarnizo, L. and Landholt, P. (1999) 'Introduction: Special Issue on Transnational Communities', *Ethnic and Racial Studies*, vol. 22, no. 2: 217–37.

Prashad, V. (2000) *The Karma of Brown Folk*, Minneapolis, MN: University of Minnesota Press.

Putler, D. S. and Wolfe, R. A. (1999) 'Perceptions of intercollegiate athletic programs: priorities and tradeoffs', *Sociology of Sport Journal*, vol. 16, no. 4: 301–25.

Puwar, N. (2000) 'Making space for South Asian women: what has changed since issue 17', *Feminist Review*, vol. 66.

Queen Afua (2000) *Sacred Woman: a Guide to Healing the Feminine Body, Mind and Spirit*, New York: One World/Ballantine.

Queen Afua, interview with Angie La Mar on *The Women's Room*, Choice FM 107.1, London 2000. Transcript: www.blacknet.co.uk/sacredwoman/ladiesroom.htm (visited 20 July 2002).

Rainone, F. L. (1987) 'Beyond community: politics and spirituality', in Boston Lesbian Psychologies Collective (ed.) *Lesbian Psychologies: Explorations and Challenges*, Chicago: University of Illinois Press.

Ramazanoglu, C. (ed.) (1993) *Up Against Foucault: Explorations of Some Tensions Between Foucault and Feminism*, London/New York: Routledge.

Ray, L. and Reed, K. (2005) 'Community, mobility and racism in a semi-rural area: comparing minority experience in East Kent', *Ethnic and Racial Studies*, vol. 28, no. 2: 212–34.

Reed, K. (2000) 'Dealing with difference: researching health beliefs and behaviours of British Asian mothers', *Sociological Research Online*, vol. 4, no. 4 www.socresonline.org.uk/4/4/reed.html (visited December 2004).

Reed, K. (2003) 'Gendering asylum: the importance of diversity and context', *Feminist Review*, vol. 73: 114–18.

Reich, R. (1991) *The Work of Nations*, New York: Knopf.

Reiss, A. (1961) 'The social integration of queers and peers', *Social Problems*, vol. 9: 102–19.

Rex, J. (1981) 'Urban segregation and inner city policy in Great Britain', in C. Peach, V. Robinson and S. Smith (eds) *Ethnic Segregation in Cities*, London: Croom Helm.

Rex, J. and Moore, R. (1967) *Race, Community and Conflict: a Study of Sparkbrook*, London: Oxford University Press.

Riches, D. (ed.) (1986) *The Anthropology of Violence*, Oxford: Basil Blackwell.

Richmond, A. (1992) 'Immigration and structural change: The Canadian experience', *International Migration Review*, vol. xxiv, no. 4: 1200–21.

Ritzer, G. (1996) *The McDonaldization of Society*, Thousand Oaks, CA: Pine Forge.

Robertson, R. (1992) *Globalization*, London: Sage.

Robinson, V. and Segrott, J. (2002) *Understanding the Decision Making of Asylum Seekers*, London: Home Office Research, Development and Statistics Directorate, July.

Robson, G. (2000) *'No One Likes Us We Don't Care': the Myth and Reality of Millwall Fandom*, Oxford: Berg.

Roediger, D. (1992) *The Wages of Whiteness: Race and the Making of the American Working Class*, London: Verso.

Roediger, D. (1994) *Towards the Abolition of Whiteness*, London: Verso.

Roosens, E. (1989) *Creating Ethnicity*, Newbury Park, CA: Sage.

Rose, G. (1993) *Feminism and Geography*, London: Polity Press.

Ross, L. (1993) 'African-American women and abortion: 1800–1970', in S. L. James and A. Busia (eds) *Theorizing Black Feminisms*, London/New York: Routledge.

Rutherford, J. (1997) *Forever England: Reflections on Masculinity and Empire*, London: Lawrence and Wishart.

Said, E. (1978) *Orientalism: Western Conceptions of the Orient*, London: Penguin.

Samuel, T. J. (1988) 'Family class immigrants to Canada 1981–1984', *International Migration*, vol. xxvi, no. 2: 171–299.

Sarason, S. B. (1974) *The Psychological Sense of Community: Prospects for a Community Psychology*, San Francisco, CA: Jossey-Bass.

Sartre, J.-P. (1962) *Sketch for a Theory of the Emotions*, London: Methuen.

Sassen, S. (1990) 'U.S. Immigration policy towards Mexico in a global economy', *Journal of International Affairs*, vol. 43, no. 2: 369–83.

Schama, S. (1995) *Landscape and Memory*, New York: Alfred A. Knopf.

Schuster, L. and Solomos, J. (2002) 'Rights and wrongs across European borders: migrants, minorities and citizenship', *Citizenship Studies*, vol. 6, no. 1: 37–54.

Schuster, L. and Solomos, J. (2004) 'Race, immigration and asylum: New Labour's agenda and its consequences', *Ethnicities*, vol. 4, no. 2: 267–300.

Segal, L. (1990) *Slow Motion: Changing Masculinities, Changing Men*, London: Virago.

Seidman, S. (1995) 'Deconstructing queer theory or the under-theorizing of the social and the ethical', in L. Nicholson and S. Seidman (eds) *Social Postmodernism*, Cambridge: Cambridge University Press.

Senior, O. (1991) *Working Miracles: Women of the English-speaking Caribbean*, London: Currey.

Sennett, R. and Cobb, J. (1977) *The Hidden Injuries of Class*, Cambridge: Cambridge University Press.

Sharma, A., Hutnyk, J. and Sharma, S. (eds) (1996) *DisOrienting Rhythms: the Politics of the New Asian Dance Music*, London: Zed Press.

Sheill, K. (2003) 'What does a terrorist look like?', unpublished MSc essay, South Bank University.

Sheller, M. (2003) *Consuming the Caribbean: from Arawaks to Zombies*, London/New York: Routledge.

Shilling, C. (1993) *The Body and Social Theory*, London: Sage.

Shilling, C. (1997) 'The Body and Difference' in K. Woodward (ed.) *Identity and Difference*, London: Sage.

Silverman, M. and Yuval-Davis, N. (1998) 'Jews, Arabs and the theorization of racism in Britain and France', in A. Brah, M. Hickman and Mac an Ghaill, M. (eds) *Thinking Identities: Ethnicity, Racism and Culture*, Basingstoke: Macmillan (now Palgrave Macmillan).

Simon, W. and Gagnon, J. H. (1967) 'Homosexuality: the formulation of a sociological perspective', *Journal of Health and Social Behaviour*, vol. 8: 177–85.

Sinha, M. (1995) *Colonial Masculinity*, Manchester: Manchester University Press.

Sivanandan, A. (2001) 'Poverty is the new black', *Race and Class*, vol. 43, no. 2: 1–5.

Skeggs, B. (1997) *Formations of Class and Gender*, London: TCS Sage.

Skeldon, R. (1997) 'Hong Kong: colonial city to global city to provincial city', *Cities*, vol. 14, no. 5: 265–71.

Skelton, T. and Valentine, G. (eds) (1998) *Cool Places*, London: Routledge.

Smith, A. (1990) 'Towards a global culture?', in Featherstone (1990).

Smith, S. J. (1993), 'Residential segregation and the politics of racialization', in M. Cross and M. Keith (eds) *Racism, the City and the State*, London: Routledge.

Snyder, P. L. (1996) 'Comparative levels of expressed academic motivation among Anglo and African American University student-athletes', *Journal of Black Studies*, vol. 26, no. 6: 651–67.

Soja, E. (1989) *Postmodern Geographies: the Reassertion of Space in Critical Social Policy*, London: Verso.

Solomos, J. (1986) *Riots, Urban Protest and Social Policy: the Interplay of Reform and Social Control*, Warwick University: Centre for Research in Ethnic Relations.

Solomos, J. (1988) *Black Youth, Racism and the State*, Cambridge: Cambridge University Press.

Solomos, J. and Back, L. (1996) *Racism and Society*, Basingstoke: Macmillan (now Palgrave Macmillan).

Solomos, J. and Murji, K. (eds) (2005) *Racialization*, Oxford: Oxford University Press.

Song, M. (1999) *Helping Out: Children's Labor in Ethnic Businesses*, Philadelphia, PA: Temple University Press.

Song, M. (2001) 'Comparing minorities' ethnic options: do Asian Americans possess "more" ethnic options than African Americans?', *Ethnicities*, vol. 1, no. 1: 57–82.

Song, M. (2003) *Choosing Ethnic Identity*, Cambridge: Polity Press.

Sontag, S. (1980) 'Fascinating Fascism', in *Under the Sign of Saturn*, New York: Farrar, Strauss and Giroux.

Spivak, G. (1990) *The Post-colonial Critic: Interviews, Strategies, Dialogue*, New York/London: Routledge.

St Louis, B. (2000) 'Readings within a diasporic boundary: transatlantic black performance and the poetic imperative in sport', in Hesse (2000).

St Louis, B. (2004) 'Sport and commonsense racial science', *Leisure Studies*, vol. 23, no. 1: 31–46.

Stallybrass, P. and White, A. (1986) *The Politics and Poetics of Transgression*, Ithaca, NY: Cornell University Press.

Stoler, A. L. (1995) *Race and the Education of Desire: Foucault's History of Sexuality and the Colonial Order of Things*, Durham, NC: Duke University Press.

Stuart, O. (1992) 'Race and disability: just a double oppression?', *Disability, Handicap and Society*, vol. 7, no.2: 177–88.

Sturken, M. and Cartwright, L. (eds) (2001) *Practices of Looking: an Introduction to Visual Culture*, Oxford: Oxford University Press.

Takenaka, A. (1999) 'Transnational community and its ethnic consequences', *American Behavioral Scientist*, vol. 42, no. 9: 1459–74.

Tambling, J. (1997) 'The History Man: the last Governor of Hong Kong', *Public Culture*, vol. 9: 355–75.

Tapinct, H. (1992) ' Masculinity, femininity, and Turkish male homosexualty', in K. Plummer (ed.) *Modern Homosexualities: Fragments of Lesbian and Gay Experience*, London/New York: Routledge.

Tate, S. (2003) 'What's shade got to do with it? Anti-racist aesthetics and black beauty', unpublished paper presented at LSE 'Feminism and Postcolonialism: Knowledge/Politics' workshop.

Thrift, N. (1996) *Spatial Formations*, London: Sage.

Thurow, L. (1999) *Building Wealth: the New Rules for Individuals, Companies and Nations in a Knowledge-based Economy*, New York: HarperCollins.

Trenchard, L. and Warren, H. (1984) *Something to Tell You ... the Experiences and Needs of Young Lesbians and Gay Men in London*, London: London Gay Teenage Group.

Trumbach, R. (1977) 'London's sodomites: homosexual behaviour in the eighteenth century', *Journal of Social History*, vol. 11: 1–33.

Tuan, M. (1998) *Forever Foreigners or Honorary Whites?* New Brunswick, NJ: Rutgers University Press.

Turner, B. S. (1996) *The Body and Society*, London: Sage.

Twine, F. W. (1998) *Racism in a Racial Democracy: the Maintenance of White Supremacy in Brazil*, New Brunswick, NJ: Rutgers University Press.

van Binsbergen, W. M. J. (1999) 'With Black Athena into the third millennium CE?', in R. E. Docter and E. M. Moormann (eds) *Proceedings of the XVth International Congress of Classical Archaeology, Amsterdam, 12–17 July,*

1998: Classical Archaeology towards the Third Millennium: Reflections and Perspectives: [Volume I] Text, Amsterdam: Allard Pierson Museum, Allard Pierson Series, vol. 12: 425–7. A longer version of this is available at www.geocities.com/warriorvase/with.htm.

Vanzant, I. (1993) *Act of Faith: Daily Meditations for People of Colour*, New York: Simon and Schuster.

Vanzant, I. (1998) *In the Meantime: Finding Yourself and the Love You Want*, New York: Simon and Schuster.

Vanzant, I. (1999) *Faith in The Valley: Lessons for Women on the Journey to Peace*, New York: Simon and Schuster.

Vanzant, I. (2001) *Living Through the Meantime – Learning to Break the Patterns of the Past and Begin the Healing Process*, London: Simon and Schuster.

Verdery, K. (1994) 'Ethnicity, nationalism and state-making', in Vermeulen and Govers (1994): 33–58.

Vermeulen, H. and Govers, C. (eds) (1994), *The Anthropology of Ethnicity: Beyond Ethnic Groups and Boundaries*, Amsterdam: Het Spinhuis.

Vertovec, S. (1997) 'Three meanings of diaspora exemplified among South Asian religions', *Diaspora*, vol. 6, no. 3: 277–99.

Ware, V. and Back, L. (2002) *Out of Whiteness: Color, Politics, and Culture*, Chicago/London: University of Chicago Press.

Ware, V. (1992) *Beyond the Pale: White Women, Racism and History*, London: Verso.

Waseem, M. (2002) 'Observations on the terrorist attacks in New York and Washington', *Ethnicities*, vol. 2, no. 2: 139–41.

Waters, M. (1995) *Globalization*, London: Routledge.

Webster, C. (2002) 'Race, space and fear: imagined geographies of racism, crime, violence and disorder in Northern England', *Capital and Class*, vol. 80: 95–122.

Weekes, D. (1997) 'Shades of blackness: young female constructions of beauty', in Mirza (1997).

Weeks, J. (1986) *Sexuality*, London: Tavistock.

West, C. (1994) *Race Matters*, New York: Vintage Books.

Westwood, S. (1995) 'Gendering diaspora: space, politics and South Asian masculinities in Britain', in P. van Der Veer (ed.) *Nation and Migration: Politics of Space in the South Asian Diaspora*, Philadelphia, PA: University of Pennsylvania Press.

Whitehead, H. and Ortner, S. (1981) *Sexual Meanings: the Cultural Construction of Gender and Sexuality*, Cambridge: Cambridge University Press.

Wildeblood, P. (1957) *Against the Law*, London: Penguin.

Williams, W. L. (1986) *The Spirit and the Flesh: Sexual Diversity in American Indian Culture*, Boston, MA: Beacon Press.

Winant, H. (1994) 'Racial formation and hegemony: global and local developments', in A. Rattansi and S. Westwood (eds) *Racism, Modernity and Identity*, London: Polity Press.

Wolf, D. G. (1979) *The Lesbian Community*, Berkeley, CA: University of California Press.

Wooden, W. S., Kawasaki, H. and Mayeda, R. (1983) 'Lifestyles and identity maintenance among gay Japanese-American males', *Alternative Lifestyles*, vol. 5: 236–43.

Yelvington, K. (1993) *Trinidad Ethnicity*, London: Macmillan (now Palgrave Macmillan).

Yeung, Y. M. (1997) 'Planning for the Pearl City: Hong Kong's future, 1997 and beyond', *Cities*, vol. 14, no. 5: 249–56.

Young, A. (1996) 'Bodily memory and traumatic memory', in P. Antze and M. Lambek (eds) *Tense Past: Cultural Essays in Trauma and Memory*, New York: Routledge.

Young, I. M. (2002) 'The ideal of community and the politics of difference', in G. Bridge and S. Watson (eds) *The Blackwell City Reader*, Oxford: Blackwell.

Young, M. and Wilmott, P. (1957) *Family and Kinship in East London*, London: Penguin.

Young, R. (1995) *Colonial Desire: Hybridity in Theory, Culture, Race*, London/New York: Routledge.

Zinn, D. L. (1994) 'The Senegalese immigrants in Bari: what happens when Africa peers back', in R. Benmayor and A. Scotness, *Migration and Identity*, Oxford: Oxford University Press.

Zlotnik, H. (1999) 'Trends in international migration since 1965: what existing data reveal', *International Migration*, vol. 37, no. 1: 21–61.

Index